Ann and Myron Sutton

CRATER LAKE
NATIONAL PARK

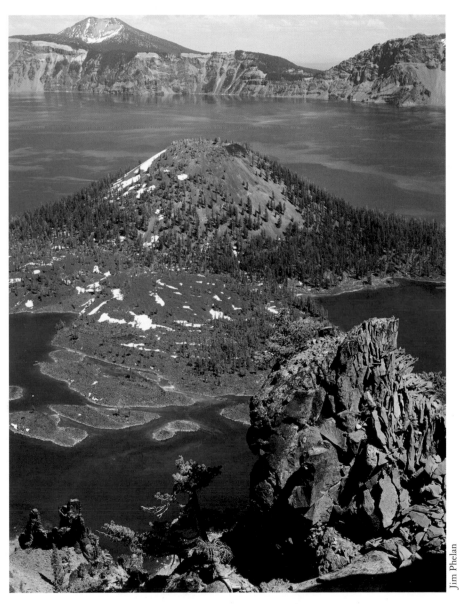

Jim Phelan

A Global Treasure

SILVER RIVER BOOKS
MEDFORD, OREGON

Crater Lake

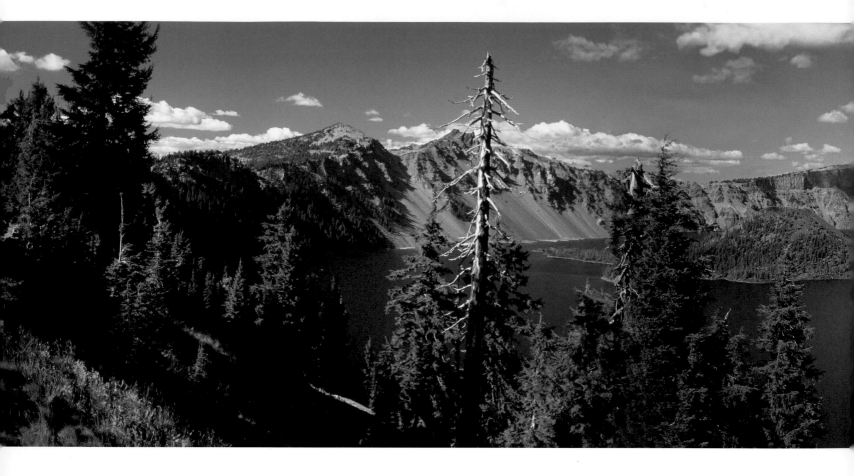

Ann and Myron Sutton

National Park

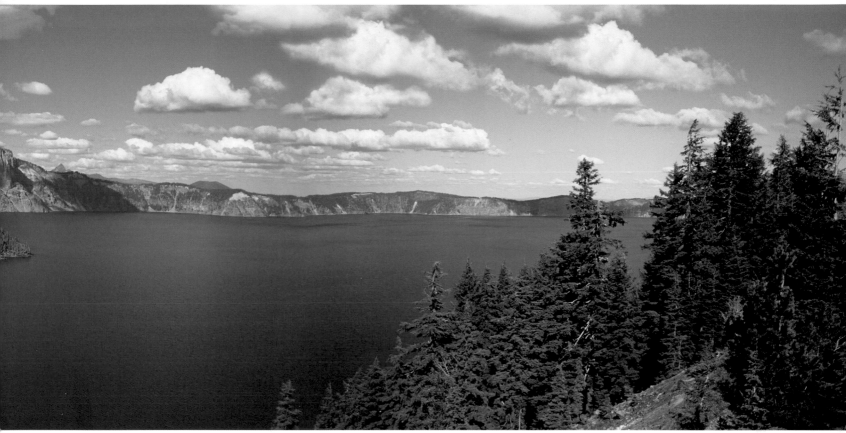

A Global Treasure

Art Direction, Design and Production, Dan Schiffer

Crater Lake National Park: A Global Treasure

First Edition May 2002

© Copyright 2002 by Ann and Myron Sutton

For information address:
Silver River, Inc., 1606 Meadowview Drive, Medford, Oregon 97504, USA.
E-mail: silverriv@aol.com. Web site: www.silverriver.com.

Library of Congress Card Number: 00-193510
Cloth ISBN: 0-9662817-8-0
Paper ISBN: 0-9662817-9-9
PRINTED IN CHINA by C&C OFFSET PRINTING CO. LTD.

10 9 8 7 6 5 4 3 2 1

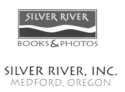

SILVER RIVER, INC.
MEDFORD, OREGON

TABLE OF CONTENTS

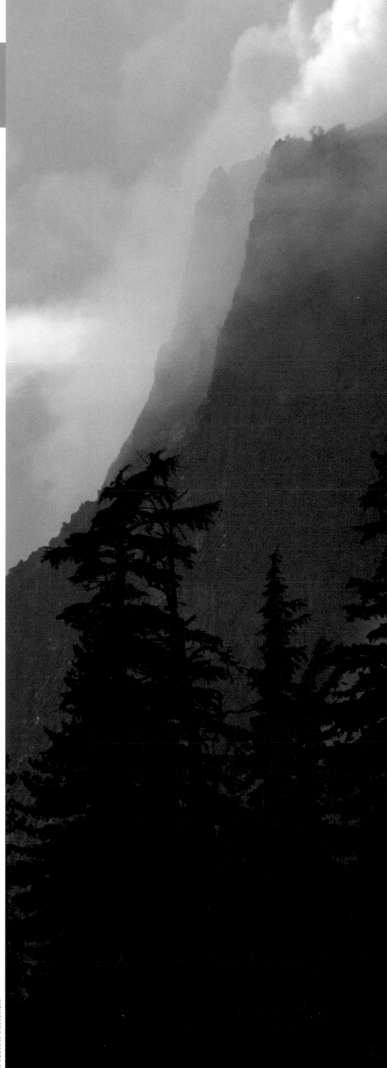

Preston Mitchell

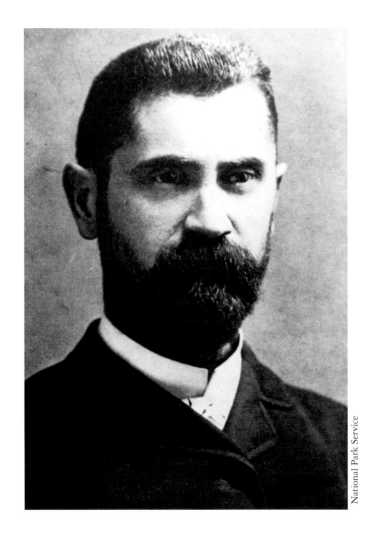

This book is dedicated to the memory of

WILLIAM GLADSTONE STEEL

who, with the support of many others, led the
seventeen-year crusade to establish
Crater Lake National Park,
which was signed into law by
President Theodore Roosevelt
on May 22, 1902.

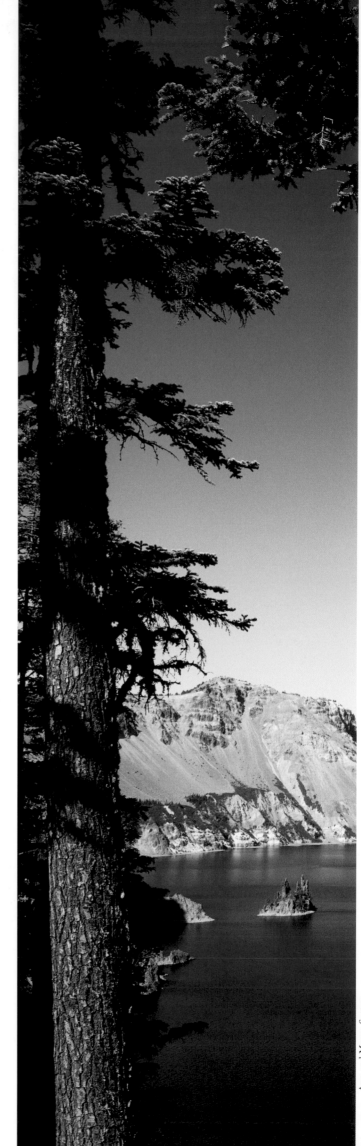

8

INTRODUCTION

In 1942, the eminent geologist, Howel Williams, wrote a detailed geology of Crater Lake National Park, which was published by the Carnegie Institution of Washington. He also produced a small book for the general reader on the origin of Crater Lake, published by the University of California Press. In writing these, Williams made clear that you cannot tell the story of Mount Mazama, in whose remains Crater Lake lies today, without drawing on references far beyond the lake, and far beyond Oregon. He referred to hundreds of areas around the world, and even included a dramatic photo of the 1902 eruption of Mont Pelée, on the Caribbean island of Martinique. To him, the closeness of such parallels helped modern readers understand what happened at Mount Mazama thousands of years ago.

We honor his all-seeing approach by casting the present centennial volume in a global perspective related not to geology or ecology alone but to national parks and other protected areas.

This book is a sampling of Crater Lake's geology and first century as a national park, organized and written for the general reader, who is neither geologist nor historian. We focus on the *legacy* of that park, an untold story of which all Americans can be proud. Certainly this park is a fitting "crown jewel" of Oregon. But it is also an American wonder and a wonder of the entire world.

As Crater Lake National Park begins its second century, we live in a world of global business, global communications, and global transport, as well as a global system of protected areas.

We start with an introduction to how the lake, and the caldera in which it lies, were formed, followed by a brief history of the crusade to establish the park, insights on how the park has been managed over the years, and details about the rangers and others who have worked hard to make it what it is today. We tell about the weather at the lake, and the first venture out on the lake during one of those rare times when the surface froze. There is a great deal of adventure in the history of Crater Lake, and we include the descent to the bottom in a submersible, all in the words of the people who did it.

And all the time there was another story, little noticed and seldom told, one that quietly became the biggest story on national parks and other protected areas in the twentieth century.

For more than a hundred years since the preservation of Yellowstone in 1872, rangers and others have been grappling with the difficulties of trying to manage the growing number of American national parks in a more or less pristine condition. They committed grievous errors and achieved lasting triumphs.

All the time, they may have been too busy to notice, but the eyes of others around the world watched them closely. Their errors and triumphs in pioneering parks like Crater Lake became, in a sense, a classic textbook and a world role model for saving outstanding sites on the entire planet.

Lest that seem an unsustainable sweeping statement, consider the United Nations List of World Protected Areas. In 1902, when Crater Lake National Park was established, there were scarcely a dozen protected areas of any size. Today the number is 30,000. Yellowstone was the largest national park in the world for many years. Not any more. The record today is a national park *four times the size of Oregon*. That the American system of parks was a guide and inspiration to other countries in achieving this has been established again and again.

Crater Lake itself has appeared on television screens world wide. U.S. park rangers have toured the globe, at the behest of the U.S. Departments of Commerce and State, to promote American parks as remarkable travel destinations. These programs, glorifying Crater Lake as one of the most beautiful lakes in the world, were broadcast to millions via television. A U.S. ranger once appeared in uniform on the extremely popular Dave Allen show in Australia, with an estimated audience of twelve million viewers. Two rangers in uniform toured Europe for 29 days in 1961, lecturing in English and French, showing high-powered audiences in seven countries what the USA had accomplished. A typical session where they presented Crater Lake was a rapt audience of business and government professionals in the Georges V Hotel in Paris. Similar programs were shown in Canada, Japan, New Zealand, Fiji, and Malaysia.

By the 1970s most countries around the world had established a system of national parks. What they clamored for was instruction on how to establish, protect, manage and use a park system. They sought help from the USA because that was where they could get an accumulation of more than 50 years of experience. Some countries, of course, such as Japan, New Zealand, and Australia, sent their own park officials to examine the American and Canadian systems. Other countries wanted experts sent to help them devise master plans. Still others, like Mexico, established a system, then built roads and modest picnic grounds until they could afford more developments.

American advice centered on setting up a diversity of areas: historic and prehistoric sites, deserts, swamps, mountains, canyons, caves, seashores, islands, and lakes. The last item was where Crater Lake shone as a prime example of what should be done. The next step was a diversity of uses: recreation, education, research. Hundreds of officials from abroad came to training courses offered by North American government agencies.

U.S. park specialists were invited to dozens of countries to help establish parks and develop master plans for protection and public use. Thus, not only did Crater Lake gain fame as a major tourist destination, but as one of America's role models for saving prime sites around the world.

All this was in direct contradiction to "The Ugly American." These people left a trail of good will among grateful governments with their own lakes, volcanoes and mountains yet to be saved.

Case in point: After discussions of planning during a visit by a U.S. park ranger in 1964, the Commissioner of Crown Lands in New Zealand ordered all the country's national parks master planned in the shortest possible time.

Then came honors to America. On the eastern shore of Argentina is a wildlife reserve where colonies of sea lions gather. Just back from the rim of the cliff that borders the sea is a small visitor center containing exhibits on coastal marine life such as sea lions and Magellanic penguins. Nothing unusual about this—until you come to the name over the entrance to the building: *Centro de Interpretación Yellowstone*. In that way, the Argentines pay tribute to an American idea that has traveled the world for more than a century.

If Patagonia seems a far-off place to pay homage to American ingenuity, welcome to the international community of national parks and other protected reserves—including Crater Lake.

As we pondered how to honor Crater Lake National Park on its first centennial, we were urged to write a "coffee-table book," which a friend defined as "a book scanned briefly and put back on the coffee table."

We did not wish to produce a paean of self-inflating lyrical prose. Or a mishmash of daily cuts from newspapers. This book is a tribute to a park celebrating its hundredth year. As such, we felt, a centennial book should not be a potpourri of events and people, or a textbook crammed with esoteric data. Such books about Crater Lake can be found elsewhere.

In a hundred years, Crater Lake National Park has grown immensely in international stature, right along with the other national parks of America. When the Director of National Parks of Venezuela saw the lake for the first time, he said simply: "Increíble!" ("Unbelievable!")

When the Director of National Parks of Colombia observed a program on American national parks, he shook his head and said: "When I come to the American parks, I need more than two eyes!"

And in case you are wondering, the Chinese, always adept with gracious and respectful phrases, call Crater Lake 裏海 *Li Hai*, Inland Sea.

The 2002 Centennial thus seems an appropriate time to give Crater Lake National Park a new and different world view by comparing it with other volcanic parks, and answering a lot of "what ifs?"

What if Crater Lake had overflowed and the waters eroded a deep notch down its side? The lake would have drained away, and we thought you might like to see a national park in Spain where exactly that has happened.

With the help of professional physicists, we explain why Crater Lake is so richly blue. But what if a crater lake isn't blue? We show you another "crown jewel" that is green, and another that is brown, both in the same national park.

What if Mazama erupted again and threw out the lake? We'll take you to another park where that happens regularly.

And was this the largest of eruptions? Far from it. Mount Mazama was huge because it ejected more than 50 cubic kilometers of debris. Another volcano on this planet once ejected more than 2,000 cubic kilometers.

And then there is the story of how Crater Lake was "connected" to the establishment of Sagarmatha (Mount Everest) National Park, in Nepal.

The proliferation of protected areas worldwide shows few signs of stopping. Omitting Crater Lake as one of the pioneering role models in all this would be an empty tribute to an incredible century.

Today, the world—with more than thirteen million square kilometers under protection—is a better place in which to live. The first hundred years at Crater Lake is both a testimonial to that and a reason for it, a perspective told here for the first time.

There's a special pride in all this. If you go to the Centro de Interpretación Yellowstone in Argentina, you'll know the meaning. If you could see the glow of pride in the eyes of Latin rangers, and Canadian, Turkish, Thai, European, Australian, New Zealand, African and others, you could rest assured that the prime lands on this planet are in capable and dedicated hands.

And you could just be a little more proud of this park, of America, and of what the pioneers did during the first rugged century of Oregon's Crown Jewel.

Ann and Myron Sutton

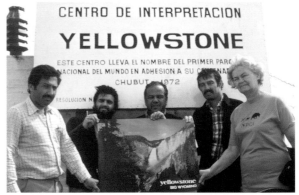
Ann and Myron Sutton

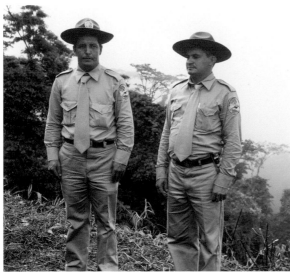
Park rangers, Venezuela.   Ann and Myron Sutton

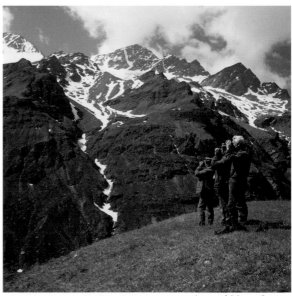
Park rangers, Italian Alps.   Ann and Myron Sutton

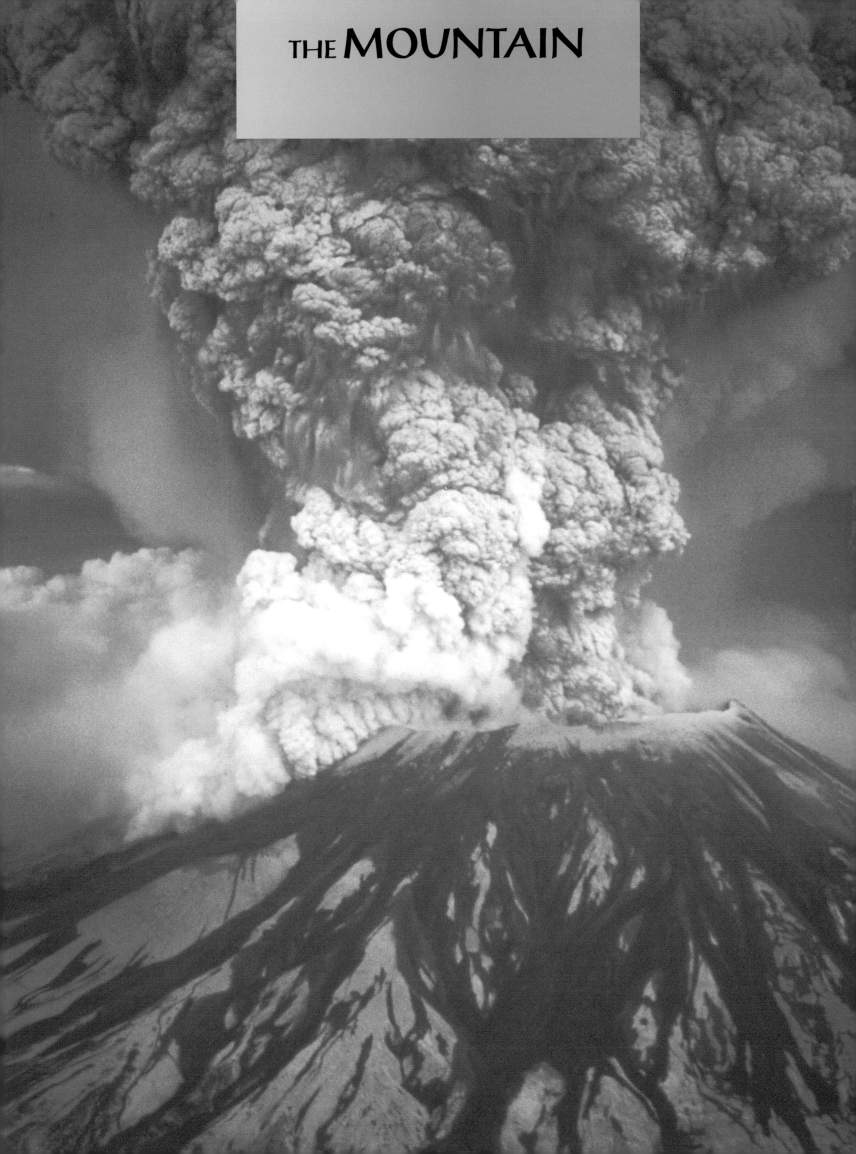

THE **MOUNTAIN**

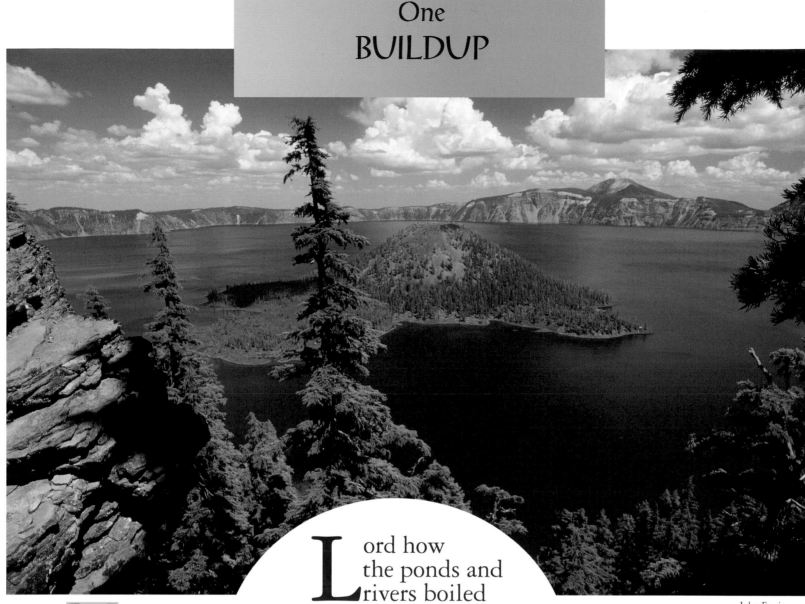

Lord how the ponds and rivers boiled

John Erwin

Holmes wrote those lines about a hurricane, but well they could apply to the roaring cloud from a volcano, a hurricane of fire, brimstone, and ballistic missile if there ever was one.

As we look out over this gigantic, peaceful lake of topaz blue, set in a wide volcanic caldera, and breathe the aromatic gifts from forests of pine and hemlock around, we cannot relate very easily to a hurricane of wind or one of fire.

When the universe presents us with such a masterpiece of breathless beauty and almost silent repose, four hundred

And how the shingles rattled
And oaks were scattered on the ground
As if the Titans battled.
And all above was in a howl
And all below a clatter,—
The earth was like a frying pan
Or some such hissing matter.

Oliver Wendell Holmes

thousand years in the making, where lilies bloom and thrushes sing, we often have a giant leap of faith to realize that all before us was forged in fire and blinding heat, and could be once again.

That all the stately trees, flying jays and scurrying squirrels exist where every living thing was once incinerated.

Nor was there, at the end, when this volcano had erupted and collapsed, much more than sulphur fumes in a charred and steaming basin—fallen crags, sizzling landslides, and suffocating, settling dust. Time has forgotten those events so long ago. The gaping hole has filled with water from rain and melting snow, five trillion gallons of it, producing a silent lake two thousand feet deep, resting in a giant chalice of the gods.

Cascade Eruptions During The Past 4,000 Years

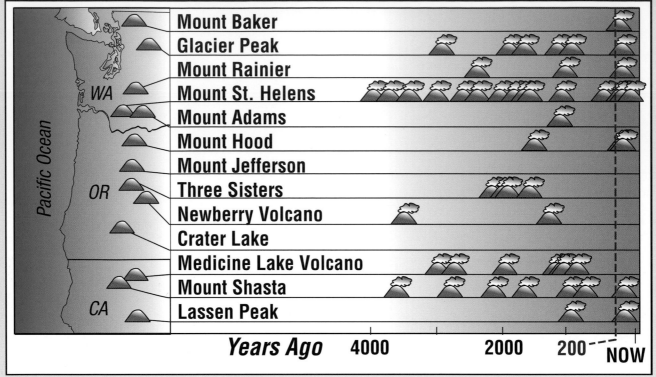

Cascades Volcano Observatory, United States Geological Survey

Everywhere around that lake today is a land of giants, a region where violence and beauty are the norm, where nature sets the stage for chaos and intensity. Across a thousand miles between Lassen Peak in California and Mount Garibaldi in British Columbia lie the Cascades, composed of the massive peaks of Baker, Glacier Peak, Rainier, Adams, St. Helens, Hood, Jefferson, The Three Sisters, Shasta, and what is left of Mount Mazama, in which Crater Lake is located. Every one of these volcanoes lies within 130 miles of the restless Pacific Coast, and nearly all of them have erupted at least once within the last eight thousand years.

Prevailing winds bring masses of moisture overland and as a result, every peak has deep, dense forests on its lower slopes—or, as in the case of Mount St. Helens, did until recently. The volcanoes of the Cascades have erupted frequently down through history. Seventy-seven hundred years ago, Mazama, near the southern border of what is now Oregon, erupted with great force and ejected many times the volume of material thrown from Mount St. Helens in 1980.

Eviscerating itself, Mazama discharged fifty cubic kilometers of debris at more than a thousand degrees temperature, mowing down dense forests and obliterating surface life for miles around. Then the summit and walls collapsed. When Mazama had finished, all that remained was a gaping, gutted hole six miles across and three thousand feet deep.

Gem of the Earth

The end of the eruption marked the beginning of an amazing event in the history of human beings and planet Earth. The eruption of Mount Mazama left one of the deepest volcanic basins in North America. Notably symmetrical in form, devoid of major outlets, sealed at the bottom, the basin was not yet exhausted of further explosive power. Wizard Island, Merriam Cone and a central platform (the latter two features now beneath the surface) were built up in later eruptions. In due course, the lake

One – Buildup

filled with water to within 600 feet of the rim. Why the water level didn't rise to the rim and spill over remains a question. In any case, there has to be an outflow somewhere down there.

Thus was born one of the scenic, topographic, and geologic crown jewels of the American landscape.

Few volcanic lakes on earth compare with it. Few other are so richly blue, so deep and tranquil.

After Mazama erupted, precipitation in the Cascades, one of the rainiest, snowiest regions in North America, required three hundred years, according to the estimates of scientists, to fill Mazama's maw to its present level.

And there it remained for millenniums, a volcanic basin filled with tranquil blue waters, known only to wildlife and early settlers in the forests below.

So do the tranquil waters, pine-scented breezes and singing thrushes mean that Mazama is extinct?

For many years people have asked that question about this remarkable mountain. Other Cascade volcanoes have erupted repeatedly. Why not Mazama? The answer is now available.

In 1853, gold seekers from California discovered the lake by accident. They and those who followed gave it a number of names, until eventually one alone caught on: Crater Lake.

Since then, millions of visitors have discovered and rediscovered this jewel of the Oregon landscape, many pronouncing it the most beautiful and breathtaking lake on earth.

For more than a hundred years, federal, state and university scientists have studied this terrain intently and pronounced on every aspect, including whether Mazama will erupt again.

What they have discovered is almost beyond conception by human senses.

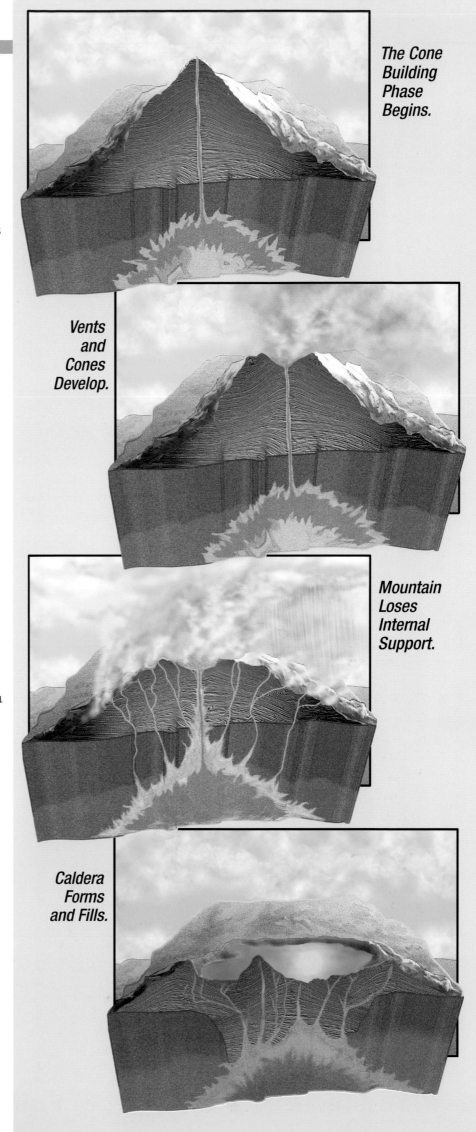

The Cone Building Phase Begins.

Vents and Cones Develop.

Mountain Loses Internal Support.

Caldera Forms and Fills.

It is possible to experience nature's violence and survive. You can endure a hurricane by being within it and emerge more or less unscathed. You can be barely missed by a tornado, and live to tell the tale. Far less is the chance of surviving a volcanic eruption by being inside it or even miles away.

The total destruction wrought by these infernos can cover hundreds of square miles. A fragile human being cannot even be near it and survive because the ejected steam, gases, and rocks emerge at high speed and blistering temperatures. Some eruptions are so powerful and hot, ash clouds so fast moving, that under certain circumstances, you could not even outrun it if you lived up to forty miles away.

One silver lining, however: some volcanic explosions can be predicted. With new technologies and the eruption of Mount St. Helens, scientists have enlarged human understanding of what used to be called, amusingly, terra firma. Nevertheless, says Willard Scott of the Cascades Volcano Observatory, in Vancouver, Washington, "there is a lot about volcanic systems that we do not understand. In fact, volcanic crises are times of great uncertainty as to the timing and scale of impending eruptions."

Gathering Storm

Mazama took a long time to build. For 400,000 years, gas, ashes, dust, and fragments of the volcano poured out periodically or erupted in explosive columns. The ejected materials built up a volcanic peak which glacial ice sculpted into valleys and ridges. The summit reached an estimated 12,000 feet above sea level. At that height, Mazama may have borne some resemblance to modern Mount Rainier.

Pressure continued to build as gases were released from the rising magma. Now and then Mazama erupted in relatively small outbursts. Geologists infer from known measurements at other volcanoes in modern times that the temperature of all that gas, steam and magma within Mazama must have reached 2,000 degrees Fahrenheit.

For a modest sample of such heat, walk up to a barbecue pit in Timanfaya National Park, on the island of Lanzarote in Spain's Canary Islands, off the western coast of Africa. Look down into the pit. It gives way to darkness far below. The air coming out of the pit is 600 degrees Fahrenheit. A hand held over that grill is withdrawn immediately. One can imagine what happens when a steak is placed above 600 degrees for several minutes.

If it was anything like more recent eruptions, the steam, ash, and pumice started out at high speed. To quote the U.S. Geological Survey regarding Mount St. Helens: "The moving front of the ash cloud may have surpassed 730 mph as it rolled onward 19 miles north of the crater." At that speed, the destructive force of a cloud full of rocks and ash becomes very believable.

Alas, no videotape recorders captured the events at Mount Mazama. There were no computers, no television

Barbecue pit, Timanfaya National Park, Canary Islands, Spain.

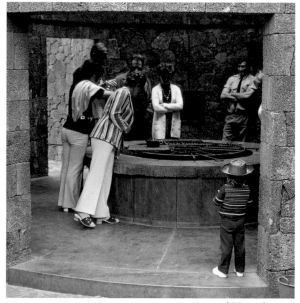

Ann and Myron Sutton

reporters, no roads, no autos, not even a United States of America.

Socrates and Plato had not been born. Nor Confucius. There was no Great Wall of China, and wouldn't be for another four thousand years. No Ramses II. No Egyptian dynasties at all. It would be two thousand years before the giant pyramids of Giza would be built.

Some of the earliest human species, the Cro-Magnons, had run their course in Europe, and human evolution had reached the Bronze Age. Early peoples had begun populating the Americas.

Massive glaciers of the Ice Age in the northern hemisphere had mostly gone. Whatever ice may have been left on Mazama must have melted very fast.

All of which leads to a burning question. Did any human being see Mazama explode?

The answer: yes, very probably. When we find in a cave a primitive atlatl (spear thrower) dusted by ash from the explosion, we can safely say that someone had been there before the eruption. So, then, there were witnesses, if they dared to look back while fleeing. Which leads to the crucial question: what did they see? And to the modern visitors' question: What happened?

While we have no way of going back over seven thousand years and reconstructing those calamitous days from eyewitness reports, we can come pretty close in several ways. Volcanologists often study other volcanic eruptions for parallels. You could run through the tapes of the eruption at Mount St. Helens, read about what happened between 1914 and 1917 at Lassen Peak, California. Or Parícutin, in Mexico, from 1943 to 1952, or Novarupta in Alaska in 1912, the largest eruption in the twentieth century.

The Fire of Pelée

There have been a number of eruptions in the West Indies, none more devastating to human life than that of Mont Pelée, on the island of Martinique, which erupted on May 8th, 1902, two weeks before Crater Lake became a national park.

Perhaps it is too great a leap of fantasy to bring up Pelée when we are talking about Mazama. But Geologist Howel Williams did so in his 1941 books on the geology of Crater Lake. That is a valid method of geologic learning, especially when we are trying to imagine how human beings and other animal life might have reacted during the eruption of Mount Mazama.

The two were different volcanoes, of course, but at Pelée we have remarkable descriptions by human beings who survived.

Pelée had at its base St. Pierre, a city of 30,000 people. Lafcadio Hearn called it "the quaintest, queerest, and the prettiest withal, among West Indian cities; all stone-built and stone-flagged, with very narrow streets, wooden or zinc awnings, and peaked roofs of red tile, pierced by gable dormers."

From the eyes and pens of St. Pierre's inhabitants, history has obtained a rare dramatic glimpse of what happens when this kind of a volcano goes up and people stay too close too long. For once, at least, we can use human terms instead of scientific.

Let us insert, parenthetically, what kind of volcanic explosion we are talking about at Mazama and at Pelée. These were not the towering orange fountains of lava as seen in Hawaii. These were pyroclastic explosions, essentially dry debris hurled out at high temperature. With a tall cloud reaching high into the atmosphere, like Mount St. Helens. And incandescent clouds roaring along the ground.

In St. Pierre, the rumblings of Mont Pelée should have been a warning to depart. "The rain of ashes never ceases," said the town newspaper *Les Colonies*. Palms and hibiscus disappeared under a mantle of white. Birds fell from the sky. Horses refused to work. Cattle were asphyxiated.

Ash could well have fallen at Mazama, too, coating the woods and valleys with white dust for miles around. Birds may have flown into clouds of ash and died, but others could have flown out of the way.

"The smell of sulphur is so strong," wrote the wife of the American Consul in a letter from Martinique, "that horses in the street stop and snort, and some of them drop in their harness and die from suffocation."

In the Pacific Northwest, this scenario could have meant death to animals such as bears and deer. They would probably have been confused, unable to figure out what was going on. If they fled such a rain of death, they escaped. If they were disoriented, they may have run wildly toward the mountain instead of away from it.

As the rumbling sounds from Pelée grew louder, according to eyewitnesses, lightning flashed in the black cloud above the mountain. Thunder mingled with the hollow bellowing of the crater. Enormous columns of ash and cinders rose from the summit. Forests burned. Tree branches broke under the weight of ashes.

Any prehistoric people around Mount Mazama very likely fled the vicinity, frightened with superstitious fear at this wrath of the gods. Perhaps some braver individuals stopped at a distance to watch. What they saw could well have been more petrifying than the scene at Mont Pelée.

Mont Pelée, Martinique, French West Indies, in 1976.

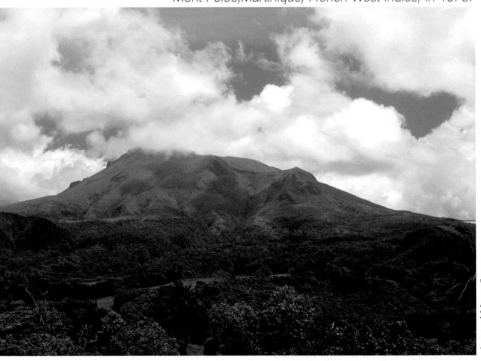

Ann and Myron Sutton

"Since four o'clock in the morning," wrote the vicar-general of Martinique, "when I was awakened in my room at the Séminaire-Collège by loud detonations, I have been watching the most extraordinary pyrotechnic display—at one moment a fiery crescent gliding over the surface of the crater, at the next long perpendicular gashes of flame piercing the column of smoke, and then a fringe of fire, encircling the dense clouds rolling above the furnace of furnaces…

"I distinguished clearly four kinds of noises; first, the claps of thunder, which followed the lightning at intervals of twenty seconds; then the mighty muffled detonations of the volcano, like the roaring of many cannon fired simultaneously; third, the continuous rumbling of the crater, which the inhabitants designated the 'roaring of the lion,' and then last, as though furnishing the bass for this gloomy music, the deep noise of the swelling waters…rising of thirty streams at once."

This should have been enough to frighten the wits out of everyone in the city below. Some people did leave in fright. Others, believe it or not, came from around the island to see what was going on. Eighteen sailing ships lay in the harbor, their decks gray with ash.

If Mazama had erupted in modern America, everybody would have known it well in advance and the government organized an orderly evacuation plan.

On the morning Pelée erupted, a Monsieur Arnoux, on Mont Parnasse, watched in stunned surprise. "I noted a small cloud pass out, followed two seconds afterwards by a considerable cloud, whose flight to the Pointe du Carbet *occupied less than three seconds…* thus showing that it developed almost as rapidly in height as in length. Innumerable electric scintillations played through the chaos of vapors, at the same time the ears were deafened by a frightful fracas…

"As the monster seemed to near us, my people, panic-stricken, ran to a neighboring hill that dominated the house, begging me to do the same. At this moment a terrible aspiring wind arose, tearing the leaves from the trees and breaking the small branches, at the same time offering strong resistance to us in our flight. Hardly had we arrived at the summit of the hillock when the sun was suddenly veiled, and in its place came an almost complete blackness. Then only did we receive a fall of stones, the largest of which were about two centimetres of average diameter…"

The heat of such stones at Mazama very likely killed everything within contact, and any powerful clouds that rolled down the mountainside would have killed every living tree, incinerating the forest as though it were made of match sticks.

Captain Freeman, on the *Roddam*, afloat in the bay at St. Pierre, witnessed the spectacle and, above the roaring of the volcano, heard the terrifying cries of agony and despair from the thirty thousand people perishing in St. Pierre. Against the flames of the city he saw a few people running wildly about the beach when the overwhelming cloud caught them in their tracks and he saw no more.

Ships were struck and capsized by the incandescent cloud. One after another, and in the twinkling of an eye, they burst into flames and sank. Thousands of casks of rum stored in St. Pierre exploded and flowed like a burning river down the streets and out onto the surface of the sea, surrounding the ships and setting them afire.

In three minutes, all was over in St. Pierre…30,000 people were dead.

Geologists say that the radius of that kind of total destruction from Mazama was something like twenty miles.

The ruins of St. Pierre, in the words of the vicar-general, "stretch before us, wrapped in their shroud of smoke and ashes, gloomy and silent, a city of the dead. Our eyes seek out the inhabitants fleeing distracted, or returning to look for the dead. Nothing to be seen. No living soul appears in this desert of desolation encompassed by appalling silence."

Among the Bombs

Pelée kept on erupting, and foreign reporters arrived to cover the story. A science writer named Angelo Heilprin actually *hiked up to the summit.* Anyone who goes to the summit of an exploding volcano is putting himself into potentially extreme danger.

With some of his colleagues he crawled up, immersed in clouds of steam and mist and rain and falling cinders. Volcanic bombs—chunks of hardened lava—flew past, unseen, and thudded into the desolate earth around them. They heard explosions in the air, and the ominous crunching of rocks striking the ground.

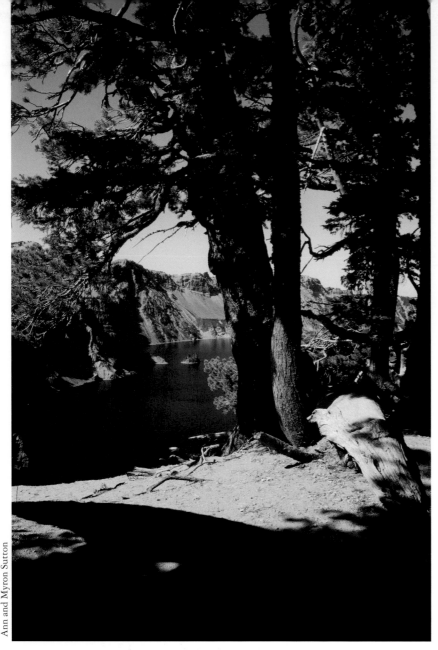

Ann and Myron Sutton

"The fusillade of bombs," he wrote, "became overpoweringly strong, and we were obliged to retreat. We were in battle. The clouds had become lighter, and we could at times see the bombs and boulders coursing through the air in parabolic curves and straight lines, driven and shot out as if from a giant catapult. They whistled past us on both sides, and our position became decidedly uncomfortable... They flew by us at close range... Descending perhaps one hundred feet lower on the slope, we took shelter...and waited for a possible cessation of the fusillade."

Later, as he descended, he described the eruption: "For the first time...we were permitted to see...that furious, swirling mass ahead of us, towering miles above the summit, and sweeping up in curls and festoons of white, yellow and almost black. It boiled with ash.

The majestic cauliflower clouds rose on all sides, joining with the central column, and it was evident that the entire crater was working, bottom as well as summit... Higher and higher they mount, until the whole is lost in the great leaden umbrella which seemed to overspread the whole earth. I estimated the diameter of the column as it left the crest of the mountain to be not less than fifteen hundred feet, and its rate of ascent from one and a half to two miles a minute, and considerably greater at the initial moment of every new eruption."

That is probably as close as our imagination will ever take us to what really went on at Mount Mazama. Pelée and Mazama, of course, were two different eruptions, one in the Caribbean a century ago, the other in what is now Oregon more than seven thousand years ago. But the similarities of these and other pyroclastic eruptions (St. Helens included) are inescapable.

The Restless Crust

We know that the solid mantle of the Earth's crust is locally and partially molten. Usually, we are well insulated from those regions. But the earth's surface is broken into rocky plates that float on the magma, gnashing against each other. These tectonic plates, as they are called, have enough energy to rile up the molten rock below and bring it out through openings in the surface. A lot of this goes on along the edges of continents, where giant plates beneath the sea clash with continental plates.

That is basically what happened to Mazama.

With molten magma boiling up from below, it is amazing that the rocks of the mountain held together as long as they did. Forty thousand years is a very long time for any rock to be confined at high pressure and baked in gases and steam at 2000 degrees. Rocks can melt at high temperatures. Smaller eruptions every hundred or thousand years may have released the pressure temporarily.

But that only delayed the big day.

Two
ERUPTION

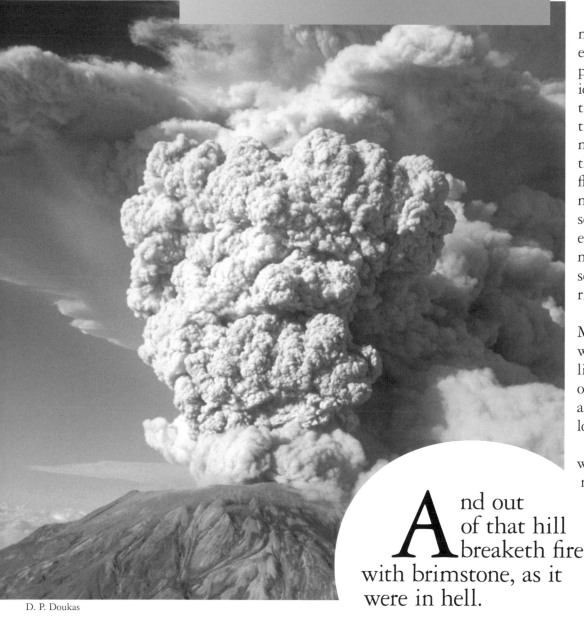

D. P. Doukas

After 400,000 years, the mountain had become the equivalent of a gigantic powder keg, a snow-capped, ice-covered massive peak that rose to ten or twelve thousand feet, seething and melting within. This was the result of repeated lava flows down through the millenniums, stacking up so steadily that Mazama eventually became not one mountain but a cluster of several, overlapping, a peak rivaling Shasta and Rainier.

The history of Mount Mazama is written in the walls of Crater Lake, in the lines, colors and contortions of the rocks. Take a hike or a boat trip for a close-up look.

The cliffs are patterned with gray, brown and red rocks, some welded together, and, more cogently, rock layers containing different chemical components. Those are the vital clues. They may seem like complete disorder

And out of that hill breaketh fire with brimstone, as it were in hell.

Bartholomaeus

The above photograph shows Mount St. Helens as it erupted in July, 1980. The whole mass continues to explode as it comes up out of the crater, and curtains of dust form. We don't know whether Mount Mazama looked this way when it erupted, but it probably did. With two key differences: Mazama's eruption was a lot larger and went on for a lot longer.

If the Vicar of Martinique, a veteran volcano watcher, had been around when Mazama threatened to erupt, he would have moved back, far back.

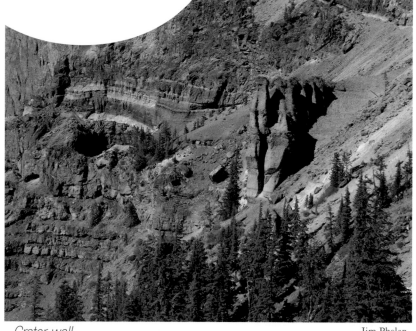

Crater wall.

Jim Phelan

to most observers, warped by time, defaced by erosion, unfathomable.

"Not so," the geologist might say. "Everything I see along that cliff is a clue to what went on."

Pause now to get the exact words of Charles Bacon, a specialist on the geology of Crater Lake National Park. This is not the kind of writing you get in everyday reading, but anyone curious about how geologists converse in their own language, hear this:

Some 15,000 to 40,000 years were apparently needed for development of the climactic magma chamber, which had begun to leak rhyodacitic magma by 7015 +/- 45 years B.P. [before the present]. Four rhyodacitic lava flows and associated tephras were emplaced from an arcuate array of vents north of the summit of Mount Mazama, during a period of approximately 200 years before the climactic eruption.

The climactic eruption began 6845 +/- 50 years B.P., with voluminous airfall deposition from a high column, perhaps because ejection of approximately 4-12 cubic kilometers of magma to form the lava flows and tephras depressurized the top of the system to the point where vesiculation at depth could sustain a Plinian column. Ejecta of this phase issued from a single vent north of the main Mazama edifice but within the area in which the caldera later formed. The Wineglass Welded Tuff of Williams (1942) is the proximal featheredge of thicker ash-flow deposits downslope to the north, northeast, and east of Mount Mazama and was deposited during the single-vent phase, after collapse of the high column, by ash flows that followed topographic depressions.

Approximately 30 cubic kilometers of rhyodacitic magma were expelled before collapse of the roof of the magma chamber and inception of caldera formation ended the single-vent phase. Ash flows of the ensuing ring-vent phase erupted from multiple vents as the caldera collapsed. These ash flows surmounted virtually all topographic barriers, caused significant erosion, and produced voluminous deposits zoned from rhyodacite to mafic andesite. The entire climactic eruption and caldera formation were over before the youngest rhyodacitic lava flow had cooled completely, because all the climactic deposits are cut by fumaroles that originated within the underlying lava, and part of the flow oozed down the caldera wall.

A total of approximately 51-59 cubic kilometers of magma was ejected in the precursory and climactic eruptions, and approximately 40-52 cubic kilometers of Mount Mazama was lost by caldera formation.

The spectacular compositional zonation shown by the climactic ejecta -- rhyodacite followed by subordinate andesite and mafic andesite -- reflects partial emptying of a zoned system, halted when the crystal-rich magma became too viscous for explosive fragmentation. This zonation was probably brought about by convective separation of low-density, evolved magma from underlying mafic magma. Confinement of postclimactic eruptive activity to the caldera attests to continuing existence of the Mazama magmatic system.

That is an example of the richly detailed writings of a geologist on an extremely dramatic event.

Mazama history is also written in the soils of eight western states and three Canadian provinces. And along the Rogue River can be seen the trunks of ponderosa pine trees buried in the ash fall.

Geologists are so good these days at identifying clues that they can recognize the Mazama debris, no matter where they find it. Eruptive material distributed across the landscape often has special "signatures" in the way of chemical content, tiny embedded crystals and type of rock. That makes it unique.

The mountain deposited its contents far and wide, and they remain in place as clues awaiting discovery by specially-trained geologic detectives. The lightweight frothy pumice is rhyodacitic in composition. Silicon dioxide is present, not as quartz but as the major component of the dominant glass in pumice and ash.

No matter where it flew on the primitive winds, or where it settled in layers across the landscape, it constitutes what geologists call a "stratigraphic marker." Mazama ash marks a specific time (=eruption). Its chemical composition is distinctive, allowing it to be identified on the basis of trace elements and other contents. Find it in Saskatchewan, 745 miles away, and they know it came from Mazama. Find it in northern Washington, and they see Mazama written all over it. These deposits, and where they lie reveal a lot of other things about that climactic eruption, including wind direction, distribution of contents, and duration of eruption.

Warnings

Since Pelèe caught the citizens of St. Pierre by surprise because they did not move away at the first warnings, and were caught by an incandescent cloud, we can assume that something of the same types of warnings took place at Mazama. Any human beings or wildlife staying too long in the vicinity of Mazama were also very likely incinerated within seconds. For 40,000 years before the big blast, Mazama erupted repeatedly. After it had achieved its maximum size, and even after it had been crowned with glaciers during the last Ice Age, the powerful buildup of magma and steam produced some early eruptions.

Those preliminary eruptions of Mazama were pretty big, but they didn't compare with the climactic blowout.

From multiple eruptive vents, Mazama blew out cubic miles of debris before the final event. Scattered it across the landscape. Left some behind. Piled up distinctive layers. Left abundant clues such as small cinder cones on its flanks.

To get a taste of that today, and try to imagine the events at Mazama, one needs only go to Kagoshima, Japan, seven kilometers from the summit of Sakura-jima, one of the most active volcanoes on earth. So active that it seems almost constantly in eruption. The ground trembles repeatedly. In an annual report for 1997, authorities stated that Sakura-jima was relatively quiet throughout the year, only 4,466 earthquakes and 60 eruptions.

The debris ejected from Sakura-jima reaches an average of six million tons a month, emerging as incandescent dust accompanied by volcanic lightning. A swarm of earthquakes there can last as long as seven hours, and in a busy period there can be 80 eruptions a *month*. We can only ask: will the volcano ever be exhausted? Which is a little like asking, will the earth ever be exhausted?

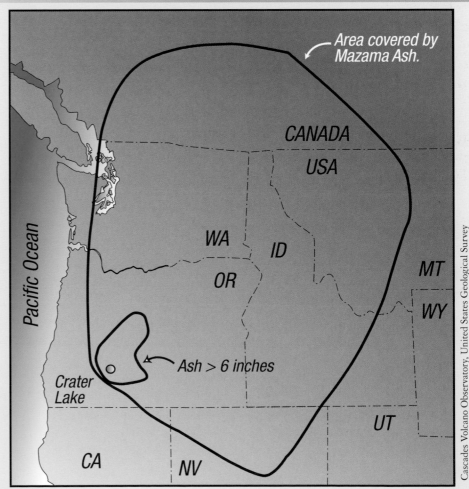

ASH AND DEBRIS DISTRIBUTION FROM MOUNT MAZAMA ERUPTION

Area covered by Mazama Ash.

Pacific Ocean

CANADA
USA

WA
ID
OR
MT
WY

Ash > 6 inches

Crater Lake

UT

CA
NV

Cascades Volcano Observatory, United States Geological Survey

HOW HOT, HOW FAST?

For details on the eruption of volcanoes, here are excerpts direct from the Cascades Volcano Observatory.

High-speed avalanches of hot ash, rock fragments, and gas move down the sides of a volcano during explosive eruptions or when the steep edge of a dome breaks apart and collapses. These pyroclastic flows, which can reach 1,500 degrees Fahrenheit (815 degrees Celsius), and move 100-150 miles an hour, are capable of knocking down and burning everything in their paths.

Temperatures in the pyroclastic-flow deposits at Mount St. Helens were 780 degrees Fahrenheit (415 degrees Celsius) two weeks after the May 18, 1980, eruption.

Destructive mudflows and debris flows began within minutes of the onset of the May 18, 1980 eruption as the hot pyroclastic materials in the debris avalanche, lateral blast, and ash falls melted snow and glacial ice on the slopes of Mount St. Helens. On the upper steep slopes of the volcano, the mudflows traveled as fast as 90 miles an hour...

This is not to say that Mazama was as active as Sakura-jima. What we do see is that the earth can be very active for a very long time. And there is a lot of molten material waiting to be blown out.

There had to be a gigantic pool of molten magma under Mazama to keep supplying those ancient eruptions for so long a time and with such volume.

But wait. There are seething magmatic pools elsewhere. Why Mazama? If there were similar molten pools beneath other volcanoes between here and Canada, was it just random choice? Why didn't they go off, too?

Answer: Some did.

And, to put it bluntly, some day in the future, others will. Mazama was just the biggest.

So far.

It is difficult to assemble every detail about underground plumbing beneath volcanic regions of the earth. Even if that were possible, conditions change. The earth's crust is fragile, mobile, and sometimes shifts with sudden violence. For the most part, however, earth movements are slow-moving, on the order of perhaps half an inch a year. And with new computer and imaging technology, earth scientists are keeping up with a great many of these changes and movements.

From eyewitnesses on Martinique, and from images exposed at Mount St. Helens, we have seen that a volcano can erupt and send out its debris at high speed. The Vicar saw the volcanic cloud at Pelèe descend the mountain at an estimated 150 miles an hour and wipe out the city of St. Pierre in three seconds.

Viewed from a distance, the upward progress of a volcanic column may not seem to be so fast. That is only

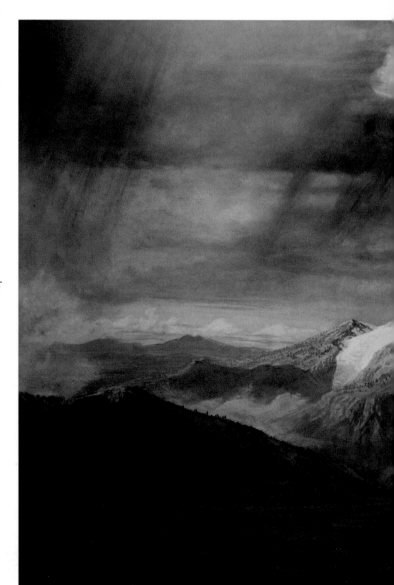

Two – Eruption

a matter of scale. Look closely, and you will see clouds exploding within clouds. Mazama's column apparently shot straight up in what has come to be called a Plinian column, something like the one at Mount Vesuvius, in Italy, where Pliny the Younger described the towering cloud in the eruption of 79 A.D. This churning cloud of ash, dust, rock, gases and steam, could have been, as at Pelèe, accompanied by brilliant lightning flashes and deafening thunder.

Lightweight pumice and ash went high into the atmosphere, drifted away on prevailing winds, and settled back to earth. Where the debris at very high

In the 1930's artist Paul Rockwood was commissioned to create a series of classic oil paintings of the national parks, many of which hang in the Interior Building in Washington, D.C.. A copy of one, his version of the eruption of Mount Mazama, is stored in the park collections.

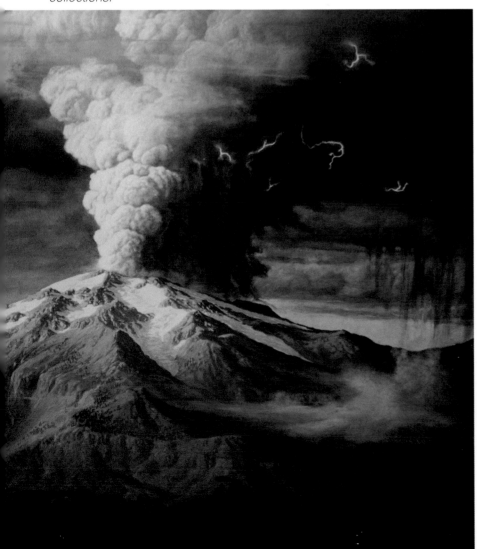

temperatures fell, it set forests afire and killed everything in sight. Days later, the fallen pumice was probably still too hot to touch. No bird could alight on it. No animal, if any were left, could have walked across it.

The result, where much of this tephra flowed, was severe devastation. Total sterilization at the surface.

Changing Winds

At this point, geologists in modern times have made a remarkable discovery. They can tell from the spread of debris that the eruption of Mazama apparently went on for *days*.

Airborne fragments of pumice, lightweight frothy rock full of holes, were carried by the winds considerable distances. Ash particles, derived from the same magma, went much farther. These fell to earth as far north as Canada and Washington state, as far east as Nebraska, and as far south as Nevada, the eruption must have endured several changes of wind direction.

Our own experience tells us that wind direction can change hourly, or sometimes take several days to change. If that is so, then this is not only one of the most powerful and voluminous eruptions in North American history, but one of long duration as well.

The volume of debris discharged has been estimated at more than fifty cubic kilometers, enough to fill a football stadium to a height of 9,000 miles.

If Mount St. Helens destroyed enough trees to build 150,000 homes, how much higher must have been the forest toll at Mount Mazama?

In short, Mazama gutted itself. With a thoroughness matched by few other volcanoes. Yet some volcanoes in geologic history certainly exceeded the output of Mazama. ***See Side Bar: Mazama Squared.*** Some volcanoes affect life around the planet, sometimes sending up clouds that reduce temperatures and cause crops to fail. The 1815 eruption of Tambora Volcano in Indonesia, which ejected more than twice the amount of material that came from Mazama, killed 92,000 people from a variety of causes: pyroclastic flow, ash fallout, famine and disease.

Just the same, Mazama was an unprecedented event in the long history of the Cascades since the Ice Age blanketed the mountains with glaciers.

When the energy that sent all that debris miles into the sky finally dissipated, some of the particles suspended in midair fell back onto the slopes or into the crater (and can still be seen today in those historic walls around the lake). The weakened rocks, bereft of pressures from below, collapsed. A gaping, steaming, red-hot crater thousands of feet deep had been created, very likely filled with acrid fumes.

What would it have been like to walk down there after the ground cooled?

Well, when the volcano of Teneguía erupted in the Canary islands in 1971 (only a fraction of Mazama's size) you could walk into the crater a year after it erupted. If you did, your shoes crunched sharp rocks coated with sulfur, and you skirted the edges of deep holes emitting pungent vapors. You passed whole cliffs of bright yellow sulfur crystals in blister form, and on the way down the side of the crater you passed hundreds of football shaped volcanic bombs resting where they fell on black glassy cinder slopes.

Volcanic bombs, giant by any standard, fell out of the upward-flying clouds of Mazama, too. One of them has been found near the cafeteria on the rim in Crater Lake National Park. It measures nine feet in diameter and eleven feet in length. Imagine the energy required to lift that many tons into the sky.

Mazama's eruption and collapse reduced its summit from twelve thousand to eight thousand feet elevation above sea level.

It had a giant pit, measuring hundreds of degrees in temperature. As time went by, it cooled. A few small volcanoes erupted on the floor, post-climactic gasps from what was left of the magma beneath the crater.

Tiny chambers of gas within falling lava explode, leaving the rock full of holes and light in weight.

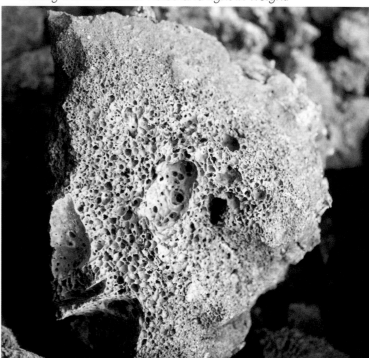

Ann and Myron Sutton

Sulfur-coated vent of Teneguía Volcano, La Palma, Canary Islands, Spain, a year after it erupted in 1971.

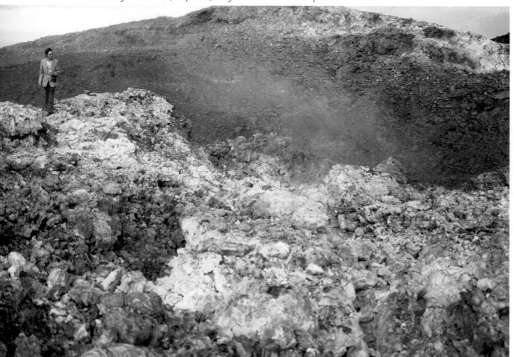

Ann and Myron Sutton

But then a long period of quiet settled over Mazama, which has now lasted for 4,000 years.

We may think that such a powerful eruption and discharge of cubic miles of debris would have left Mazama so exhausted that it could never erupt again. Yet that very sequence of blow-out-and-fall-in has occurred elsewhere twice in the same place. ***See Side Bar: Mazama Squared.***

As the first snows fell into the still-steaming caldera of

Mount Mazama, they sizzled, fizzled, and evaporated into steam. But as the crater cooled, snow piled up faithfully every winter and melted every summer. Instead of boiling away, water began to accumulate in the bottom.

A century passed as the lake level slowly rose. Then another century. Then a third. No one knows how much water leaked out through cracks in the walls. Eventually, the lake rose to within six hundred feet of the rim.

Had it risen to the top and flowed over the side, it could have eroded a canyon through the volcanic rock and cut a gash that would have drastically reduced the level of the lake. Or it could have forced the opening of some crevice or tunnel through the walls and depleted itself. Says park historian Steve Mark: "One hypothesized reason why the lake level went no higher is the presence of unconsolidated glacial till in the caldera walls on the north side of Crater Lake. A difficult thing to prove, however, given the location."

The erosion of a deep canyon happened in what is now Caldera de Taburiente National Park, on the Canary Island of La Palma, Spain. Taburiente is a huge caldera, too, but the deep canyon in its side allows the waters that fall within the crater to flow out as a river. Filled with pines, mists and deep shadows, Taburiente is a breathless sight and spectacular caldera. But it has no lake.

Aniakchak Volcano in Alaska is another example of a Crater Lake-sized caldera that once contained a deep lake, which drained away in a catastrophic flood.

The lake within Mazama found a level two-thirds of the way up the walls and stayed that way (with only minor variations in lake level). We look down upon it now as a giant blue body of water in a rocky bowl six miles across. After all that could have happened here and didn't, with so much potential for the water to drain away in cracks, fissures, springs and underground passages, we should feel fortunate that the caldera still contains any water at all.

MAZAMA SQUARED

Batur Volcano, on the island of Bali, Indonesia, has erupted in much the same manner as Mount Mazama, but with greater fury, blowing out cubic miles of debris, and then collapsing to form a huge caldera. And not once, but twice. The first eruption occurred approximately 50,000 years ago. Later, another eruption sent out megatons of ash and debris, then collapsed, producing a caldera within a caldera.

The volcano still erupts periodically, though less violently. In 1984, lava flowed from fissures on the peaks in the center across the caldera floor (black band in center), where people had built roads and dwellings inside the caldera. Note a portion of the crater lake at the upper right.

Indonesia sits astride the Sunda Arc where the Asian tectonic plate of the earth's crust collides with the Indian-Australian plate. Along that line is some of the most volcanically violent terrain on the globe. Toba volcano, in Sumatra, is said to have issued 2,000 cubic kilometers of volcanic material, 10,000 times more than Mount St. Helens in 1980.

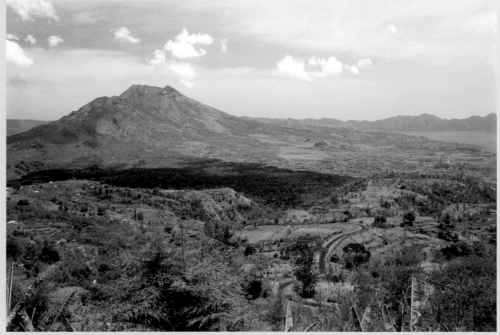

Ann and Myron Sutton

This giant canyon has been cut in the wall of the Caldera de Taburiente, a national park in the Canary Islands of Spain. Through this canyon flow the waters that fall within the caldera. Had this happened in the history of Mount Mazama, there would be no Crater Lake today.

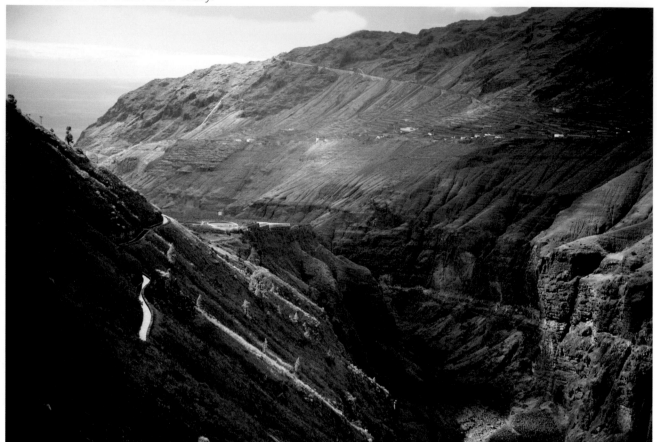

Ann and Myron Sutton

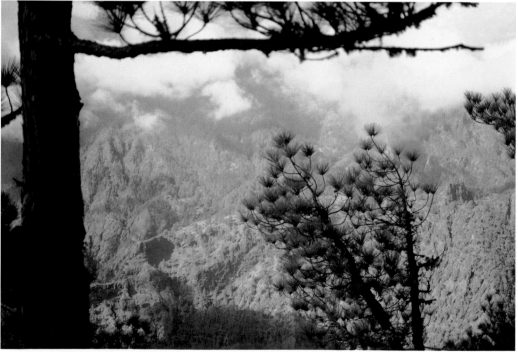

Portion of the Caldera de Taburiente, Canary Islands, Spain.   Ann and Myron Sutton

Two – Eruption

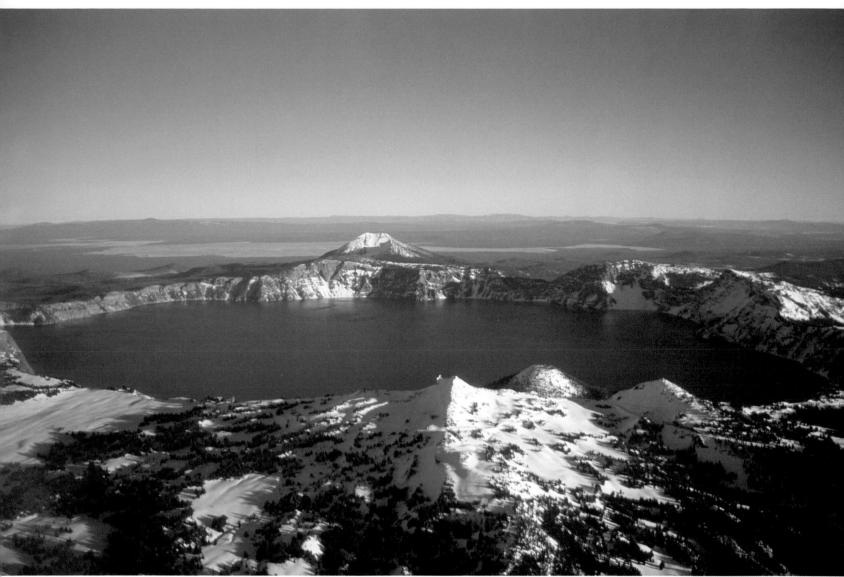

Ann and Myron Sutton

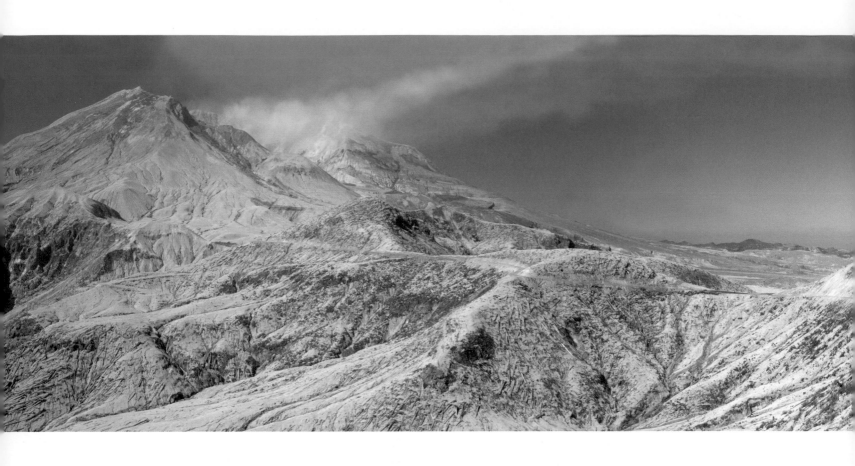

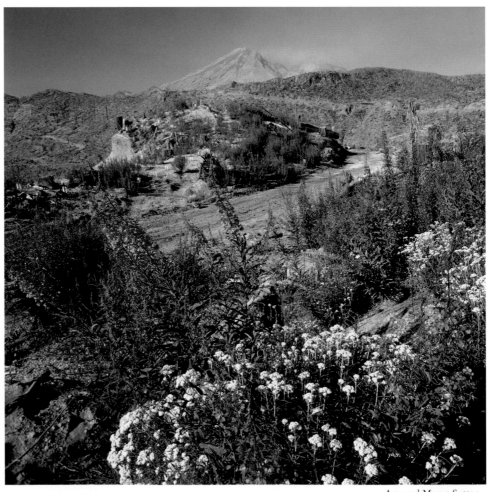

Ann and Myron Sutton

Three
AFTERMATH

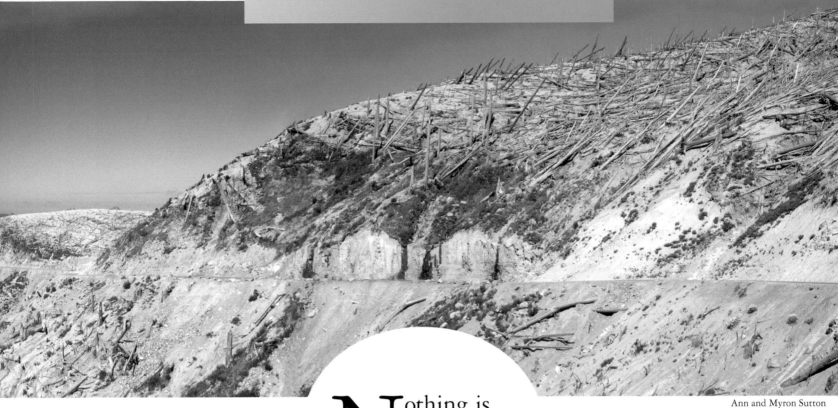

Ann and Myron Sutton

The panorama above was made four years after the eruption of Mount St. Helens on May 18, 1980. It shows the huge, sturdy trunks of Douglas fir blown down by a cloud of rocks and ash. The U.S. Forest Service estimates that the cloud measured up to 600 degrees Fahrenheit in temperature, and traveled up to 600 miles an hour. The branches of the trees were torn off, their needles vaporized. From the look of grim destruction, Nature has not even started on the comeback trail.

But that isn't true. The photograph at the left was made on the same day, less than a mile away. It shows a thriving community of lavender fireweed and white milfoil growing out of the almost barren pumice.

Nothing is certain, not even that.

Arcesilaus

Indeed, for miles around, great banks of fireweed and milfoil sprang into bloom with a vigor that has fascinated ecologists. Where once was pumice at hundreds of degrees temperature, the pioneers of a completely new forest started to grow.

What is astonishing is that the volcanic clouds did not kill everything. Seeds and bulbs buried in the soil survived. So did ground-burrowing animals, like gophers, mice, insects and spiders. Says the Forest Service:

Plants that sprouted from buried soil and late-lying snow banks have gradually spread, transforming a gray-brown landscape to green. Over time, these initial survivors have been joined by legions of colonizers as wind-blown seeds of weedy plants like fireweed... have taken root on shattered hillsides. In spring, the Monument glows with the purple blossoms of penstemon and lupine... The once silent blast zone is punctuated by the calls of kildeer and red-winged blackbirds... Red-tailed hawks can be spotted hunting for abundant mouse populations...

Fireweed is one of the great colonizers of the American West. Go to Glacier Bay National Park in Alaska, and see vast flats of it springing up where glaciers melt. In such nearly sterile lands as those and the ones at newly erupted volcanoes, pioneer plants find the enriched soil they need for a new cycle of growth to begin.

Now we ask, did any of this happen during the recovery at Mount Mazama? Who can say? Few were there to observe it, and they left no records of ecological research. Time has obscured or erased the evidence. About all we can do is guess. Guess that fireweed somehow got down into the gaping maw of Mazama and started to grow as soon as the caldera cooled off. No one knows, but these photos at Mount St. Helens tell us that it could have been possible. Eventually, rising water within the

RECOVERY IN NEW ZEALAND

The volcanoes in Tongariro National Park erupt so often that the vegetation has little chance to restore itself. The picture at right shows the volcano of Ngauruhoe (pronounced naru-hóey), which nearly always has plumes of ash and/or water vapor rising from its summit, and occasionally goes on a real rampage. The slopes are virtually devoid of forest, while in the foreground, miles from the crater, are rich vegetative communities along Whakapapanui Stream.

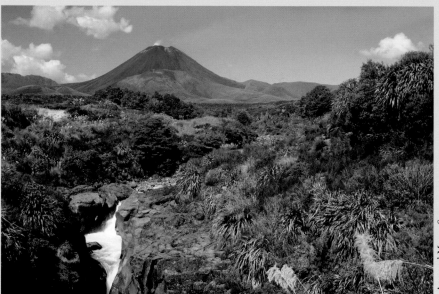

Ann and Myron Sutton

The volcano of Ruapehu (roo-a-páy-hoo), not far away, erupts every twenty years or so and throws out its crater lake. The photo below shows a 1995 eruption hurling out fountains of ice, snow, and mud. The picture at left, made along Wairere Stream near the base of Ruapehu, shows how grass and shrubs come back for a while…until ash smothers life again.

Ann and Myron Sutton

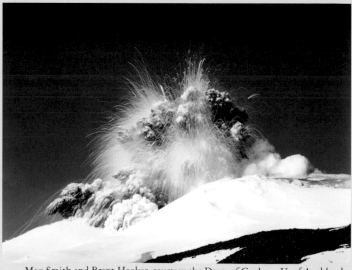

Meg Smith and Brent Hooker, courtesy the Dept. of Geology, U. of Auckland

Three – Aftermath

caldera would overtake any terrestrial plants growing on the floor.

Thus did surface vegetation begin to recover the barren ground. Buried roots, if any, survived and grew. Seeds got transported by birds and mammals, and by the wind. Plants grew and died. Soil accumulated. Trees rooted. Animal life may have survived in burrows, as well as moved in from the outside.

How many years this took, we can only judge by how long it takes the forest at St. Helens to regrow completely. None of us will live that long. The return of the giant trees and mature woodlands usually takes hundreds of years.

Meanwhile, as a vegetative covering slowly began to clothe Mazama and vicinity, and as the lake within it filled to its maximum level, the other volcanoes of the Cascades were having their turn. A lot has happened since Mazama threw out its contents.

St. Helens has been the most active volcano in the Cascades since the time of Mazama's eruption. It has produced many high-speed avalanches of hot ash and rock (pyroclastic flows), and mudflows of volcanic ash and debris (lahars) that may flow 50 miles down a river. It has also had eruptions more violent than the one in 1980. Shasta is a strong second, having erupted on average every 300 years, the last in 1786.

Scientists maintain histories of Cascade eruptions. Mount Baker, they say, erupted in the mid-1800s for the first time in several thousand years. Activity at steam vents (fumaroles) in Sherman Crater, near the volcano's summit, increased in 1975 and is still vigorous, but there is no evidence that an eruption is imminent. Glacier Peak erupted with such energy that it sent volcanic ash to Wyoming.

VOLCANOES OF THE CASCADES

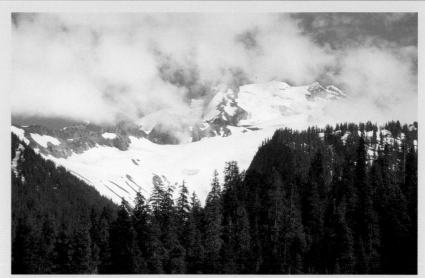

Glacier Peak. Ann and Myron Sutton

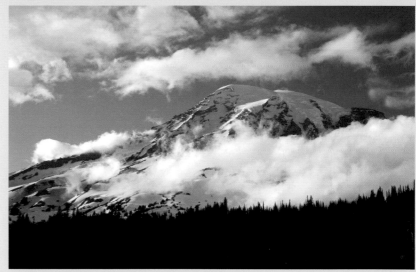

Mount Rainier Ann and Myron Sutton

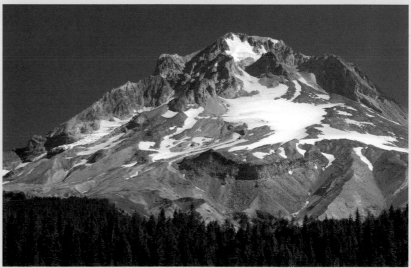

Mount Hood Ann and Myron Sutton

VOLCANOES OF THE CASCADES

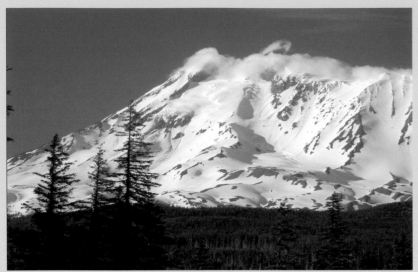

Mount Adams.   Ann and Myron Sutton

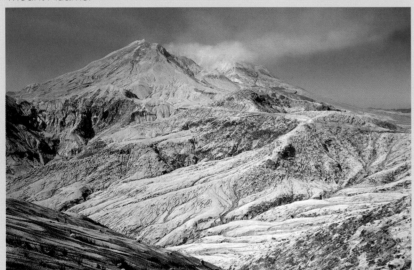

Mount Saint Helens.   Ann and Myron Sutton

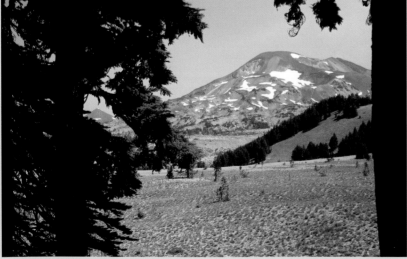

South Sister.   Ann and Myron Sutton

Mount Rainier, which towers above Seattle and Tacoma, has erupted four times in the last 4,000 years and sent down mud flows, also a recipe for death and disaster.

Mount Adams has had only minor eruptions.

Mount Hood, which overlooks Portland, Oregon, last erupted about 200 years ago. A series of steam blasts took place between 1856 and 1865.

Mount Jefferson is not known to have erupted in 20,000 years, but the wise course here is "never say never again."

The Three Sisters complex, which includes Broken Top and Mount Bachelor, are paced by the South Sister, which erupted 2,000 years ago. However, as of this writing, geologists

VOLCANOES OF THE CASCADES

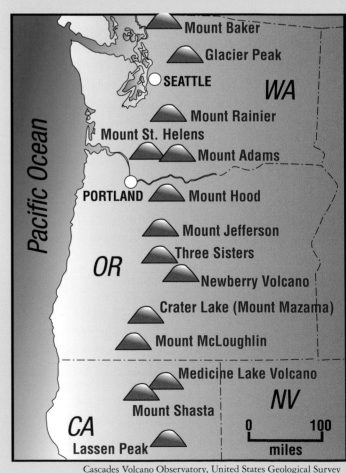

Cascades Volcano Observatory, United States Geological Survey

have reported ground swelling in that region.

Newberry Volcano erupted 1,300 years ago. Lassen Peak last opened up almost a century ago, in 1915, ejecting ash as far away as Elko, Nevada.

Of Crater Lake, scientists say that its eruption of ten cubic miles of magma was ten times as much as in any other eruption in the Cascades in the last 10,000 years. There were also smaller eruptions at Mazama: Wizard Island formed very soon after the climactic eruption, about 7.500 years ago, and a rhyodacitic dome, called Merriam Cone, 5,000 years ago, both on the lake floor.

"Of the 13 potentially active volcanoes in the Cascade Range of the Pacific Northwest," says the United States Geological Survey, "11 have erupted in the last 4,000 years and 7 in just the past 200 years. More than 100 eruptions, most of which were explosive, have occurred in the past 4,000 years, making the volcanoes of the Cascade Range some of the most hazardous in the United States."

Reports on hazards relating to these volcanoes are available on the Cascades Volcano Observatory web site. Crater Lake is fairly benign, but scientists don't leave anything to chance. They have instrumentation in place to track the movements of volcanoes long before anything happens on the surface. If that imparts a feeling of ease to visitors and residents of these regions, it does not mean that they should let down their guard completely.

It is one thing for experts to have their eyes and instruments locked on the most dangerous of these mountains, but quite a different matter for citizens to obey their warnings. Anyone who is inclined to say "It can't happen here," or "It won't happen to me," had better move now to some

VOLCANOES OF THE CASCADES

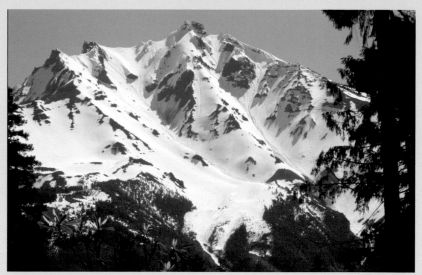

Mount Jefferson. Ann and Myron Sutton

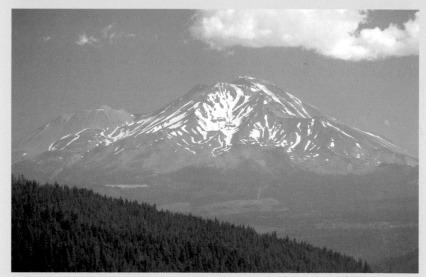

Mount Shasta. Ann and Myron Sutton

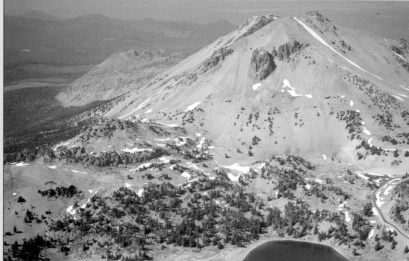

Lassen Peak. Ann and Myron Sutton

37

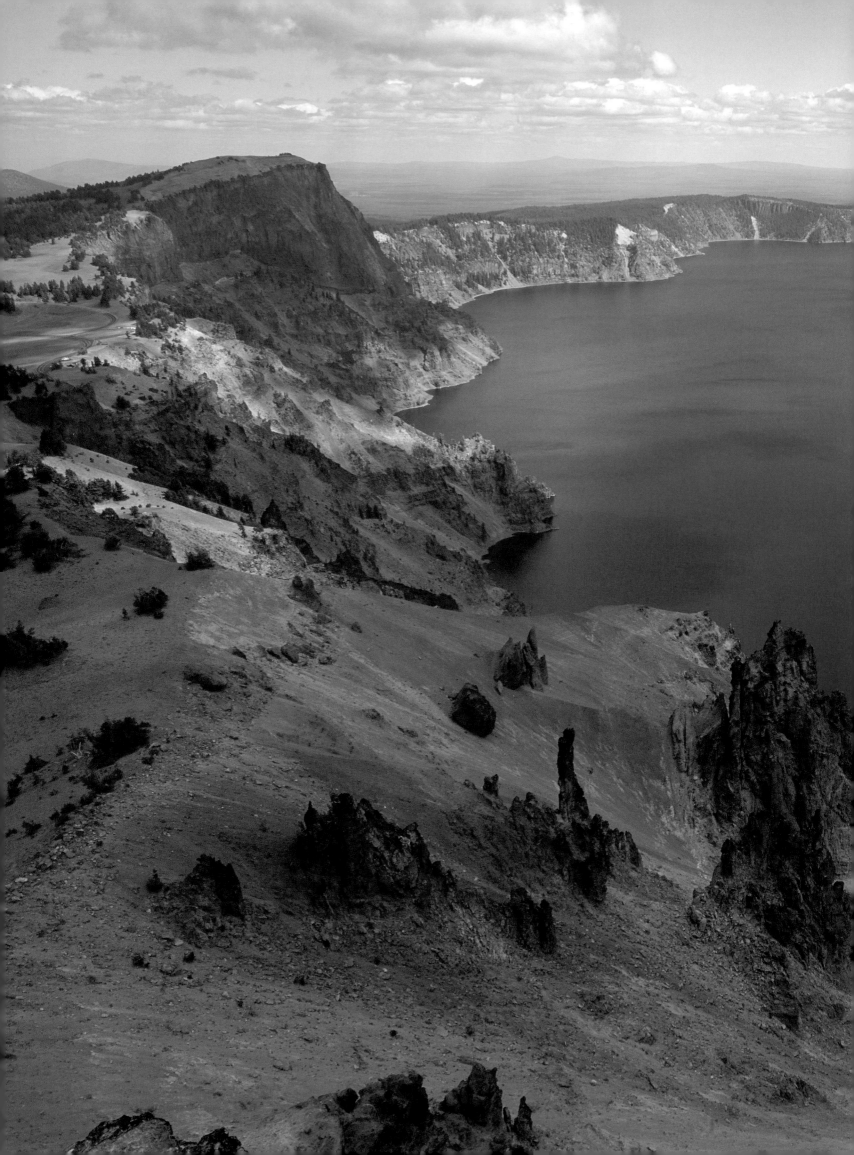

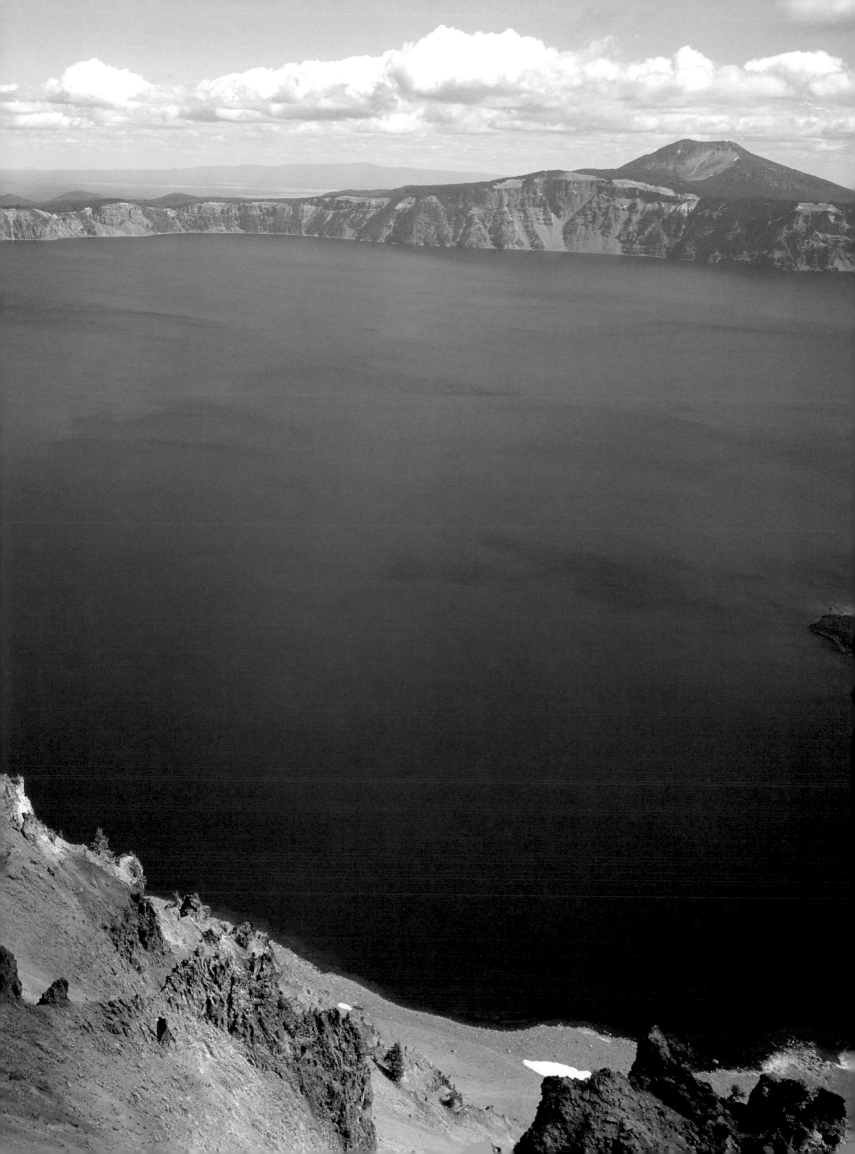

region far from the Ring of Fire, that line of active volcanoes that surrounds the Pacific basin.

In an era of instant communications, which didn't exist a century ago, it is now often possible to notify the world when an eruption begins to build up.

Considering what happened at Mont Pelée in 1902, we now know not to sit around with a curious look on our faces when ash falls and sulfur chokes our breathing. Warnings that come from scientists are based on instruments able to measure earth actions. They are tracking. Their sensors pick up signals that human beings, with limited vision and hearing, cannot. In the next chapter we follow geologists to set up instruments designed, in a sense, to keep us safe.

For the time being, we can finally answer that question about future eruptions at Crater Lake. It is contained in a 1997 report by Charles Bacon and others on volcano hazards at Crater Lake: "A large pyroclastic eruption, such as the one during which the caldera formed, or the (smaller) 1991 eruption at Mount Pinatubo, Philippines,

is not considered likely for many thousands of years in the future because the magma reservoir which fed the climactic eruption of Mount Mazama has not had sufficient time to regenerate a large volume of gas-rich magma…"

And one other note: draining of the lake "is an extremely unlikely event but one which would have disastrous consequences for downstream lowlands…"

Like Arcesilaus, we may have to concede that nothing is certain, but that is about as close as hard-working scientists can predict the future at Crater Lake.

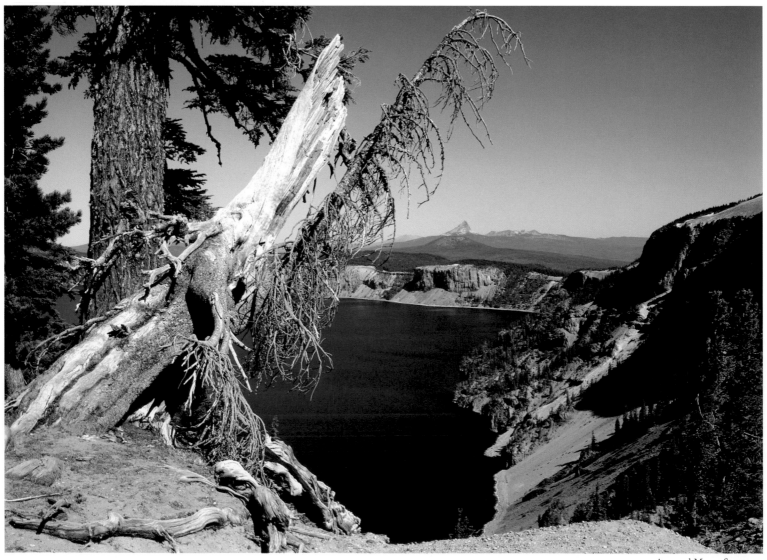

Ann and Myron Sutton

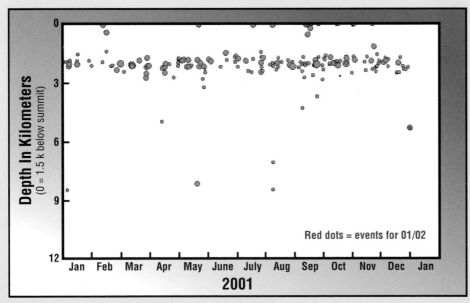

A plume of ash, observed from Pumice Plain, Mount St. Helens.

Cascades Volcano Observatory, United States Geological Survey

As long as the earth's tectonic plates still move and still ram into each other, there is not going to be any cessation of activity around the Ring of Fire. That includes the Cascades, and that includes Crater Lake. The earth was born of fire and the fires are by no means out yet. The earth is still very hot, and much beneath the outer crust is molten. Coping with violent reactions in the earth's crust, and trying to avoid disaster, is now the order of the day for fragile human beings because at last—at long last—they are able to do something about it.

With so many visitors attracted to Crater Lake there must be, somewhere behind the scenes, an outpost of electronic sensors standing sentinel to give warning if this crown jewel of the earth reawakens.

Whatugnarognaro te tangata toitu te whenua.

("Man passes but the land endures.")

Maori exhibit
Bay of Islands Maritime Center,
Russell, New Zealand.

Any "minor matter," such as virtually undetectable sinking, rising and other offsets on the earth's surface, can become major threats to human populations. For most of human history, it has been impossible to foresee such things and understand the depths of the earth by little more than analyzing rocks thrown out of it. To understand what goes on beneath volcanoes like Mazama, human beings waited for the ground to tremble and ash to pour out before predicting and fleeing an eruption.

All that has changed. Within the span of a few years, scientists have been equipped with remote sensing devices that tell them not only when earthquakes occur, but how many there were, how strong, how deep, how frequent, and how far away.

This may seem of little consequence to visitors who listen to the song of the chickadee, snap their enduring

MOUNT ST. HELENS SEISMICITY—TIME vs. DEPTH

Depth In Kilometers (0 = 1.5 k below summit)

0

3

6

9

12

Red dots = events for 01/02

Jan Feb Mar Apr May June July Aug Sep Oct Nov Dec Jan

2001

The green dots indicate earthquake epicenters beneath St. Helens over a period of time. The red dots show activity within the last week or month.

Cascades Volcano Observatory, United States Geological Survey

images of the lake, and go on their way. In the first hundred years of Crater Lake National Park, managers have been sensitive to how little is known about this place and how much knowledge is required to take good care of it.

The era of fantastic information has dawned. Congress oversees such matters, and has provided funds for the increase of knowledge here. Moreover, knowledge comes from a variety of sources, including the Smithsonian Institution, and universities. Says Willard Scott of the Cascades Volcano Observatory, "Many organizations around the world have the responsibility to monitor the volcanoes in their countries... Japanese scientists... probably have more experience than we."

All this has provided a remarkable flow of new knowledge about what is beneath the surface at Crater Lake National Park and other volcanoes of the Cascades. So effective are these accomplishments that human beings, unaware for so long of the hidden workings beneath the surface of the earth, may feel like the blind gaining sight for the first time.

Example: with a few clicks of a computer mouse, anyone can bring up on his or her monitor screen a picture of certain volcanoes, updated every ten minutes. They can see a map of earthquake activity several kilometers beneath the surface at Mount St. Helens.

A great deal of activity at the end of the twentieth century focused on Mount St. Helens because that's where the most recent action has been. But whatever is learned there can apply elsewhere. Modern eruptions, such as that at Mount St. Helens, help reconfirm, revise and update our knowledge of volcanic eruptions.

Of course, it has long been possible to draw up a map showing cracks in the earth (fault lines) directly beneath Crater Lake National Park. A few modest earthquakes have been felt here. At this writing, the most recent was in 1995.

As long as the possibility of any earth movement exists, especially in populated areas, geologists are going to be watching, if only by remote sensing. And that means artificial eyes, electronic and otherwise: the science of monitoring.

What is new about tracking these volcanoes is the ability of modern technicians to patrol the Cascades with tools their predecessors at the turn of the nineteenth century never dreamed of. Crater Lake is today part of a monitoring system set up by various agencies. Tourists and local residents need never be concerned about these

efforts, but there is a sense of comfort in knowing about them.

For example, ground deformation, such as swelling or tilting, could mean that magma is on the move again. One way to watch such changes is through sensors installed inside craters as well as around them.

As long as the landscape at Crater Lake remains quiet and peaceful, there is no need for a complex system of tracking stations, and perhaps not much more than a seismograph to measure earthquakes and a device to measure tilting of the surface. In the future, however, if limited sensing detects activity, the park could be surrounded by tracking stations.

For a while after the eruption of Mount St. Helens, the crater smoldered and a dome bulged. Geologists helicoptered to points within the crater,

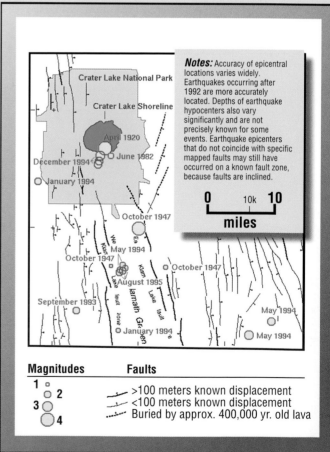

CRATER LAKE FAULT LINES

Crater Lake National Park

Crater Lake Shoreline

April 1920

December 1994 ○ June 1982

○ January 1994

○ October 1947

May 1994

October 1947

Klamath Graben

○ October 1947

August 1995

September 1993

Klamath Lake fault zone

Klamath Lake fault

○ January 1994

May 1994

○ May 1994

Notes: Accuracy of epicentral locations varies widely. Earthquakes occurring after 1992 are more accurately located. Depths of earthquake hypocenters also vary significantly and are not precisely known for some events. Earthquake epicenters that do not coincide with specific mapped faults may still have occurred on a known fault zone, because faults are inclined.

0   10k   **10**

miles

Magnitudes	Faults
1 ○	
○ 2	——⊢— >100 meters known displacement
3 ○	—ꞁ— <100 meters known displacement
○ 4	····· Buried by approx. 400,000 yr. old lava

Cascades Volcano Observatory, United States Geological Survey

These lines indicate known fractures of the earth's crust in Crater Lake National Park.

walked into the steam clouds on top of the dome, and placed or adjusted their instruments.

Then the crew helicoptered out, and the instruments they deposited or adjusted work day and night to gather, record and transmit information.

The United States has several Volcano Observatories, including the David A. Johnston Cascades Volcano Observatory in Vancouver, Washington, across the Columbia River from Portland, Oregon, and within sight of towering Mount Hood. David Johnston was a USGS scientist on duty at the Coldwater II Observation Post when St. Helens opened up, and was one of 57 people killed in the eruption.

The Observatory provides access to information about hundreds of volcanoes and volcanic fields worldwide.

In the years before computers, such information would have seemed not only impossible, but incomprehensible. We have seen how residents of Martinique climbed to the summit of Mont Pelée to find out what was happening. Today, lives need not be placed so much at risk. When something happens elsewhere, skilled rapid response teams may be invited to assist in monitoring, warning, and saving human lives anywhere on the planet. Indonesia, for example, is the most volcanically unstable country on earth. Japan is not far behind, but they have their own response procedures.

International assignments improve skills and experience among American team members. The pay-off is that they can then apply their world-class expertise to handling local volcanic events.

Since highly skilled geologists are available, the managers of Crater Lake National Park need not expend time, effort, and public funds to train their own staffs in monitoring techniques. They rely on the experts, and if any emergency arises, the rapid response teams are there.

NETWORK OF MONITORING STATIONS

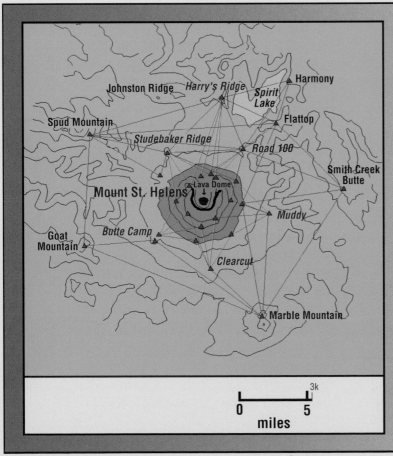

Network of monitoring stations around Mount St. Helens.

Cascades Volcano Observatory, United States Geological Survey

NW SEISMOGRAPH NETWORK

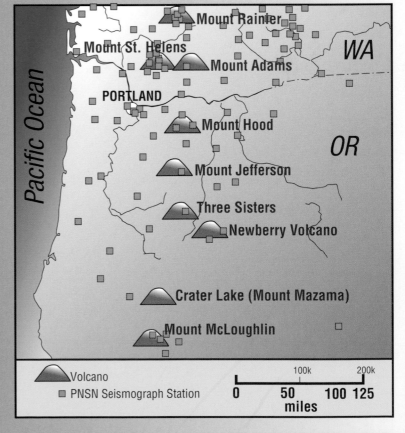

Sites being monitored in the Pacific Northwest.

University of Washington and Cascades Volcano Observatory, United States Geological Survey

Working with highly trained geologists, the park staff can assess the problems and, if necessary, issue orders for evacuation of tourists and staff until things quiet down again. Such teamwork helps to assure that visits to Crater Lake or any Cascade volcano are worry free year round.

As Will Steel, father of Crater Lake National Park, learned a century ago, you cannot establish a national park and leave it completely alone.

The problem is that the pressures of expanding human populations have forced people to settle on the slopes of many volcanoes, and even build villages *within* active craters.

Today, millions of people have settled near Cascade volcanoes, and there are even a few settlements near Crater Lake, creating a potential for local disaster. The burning memories of Mont Pelée's incandescent cloud in 1902, and the horrendous loss of life, have not been lost. What happened in Martinique isn't likely to be repeated in Oregon, but the events at Mont Pelée, if nothing else, constitute a relatively recent, vivid and enduring picture of how dangerous volcanoes can be to human life.

Will Mazama rise again? Surely with all the cubic miles of rock Mazama disgorged, there is nothing else to erupt. Is there?

Make of these nervous questions, what you will, but geologists take nothing for granted. The processes of volcanism are ongoing. If some day we have to set up scanning devices in the mode of the intergalactic drones of *Star Wars*, at least the technology has been developing during Crater Lake National Park's first century. The scientific community has moved in on the target question: Which volcano is going to erupt next?

Welcome to Crater Lake's second century!

The old and outmoded instruments of yesteryear have been replaced with digital tracking devices that can peer not only across the earth's surface, but far beneath it. Miles beneath it. No longer do we have to be content with visual scanning of fumaroles at the summits to see if a mountain is alive. Or, Heaven forbid, take an excursion to the top during an eruption, as they did at Pelée. When a volcano is issuing clouds of rock and dust at high temperature and high speed, that is definitely too late to be walking toward its summit—with volcanic bombs falling all around.

Geologic history tells us that eruptions in the Cascades are usually hundreds of years apart, and so far they have been relatively remote. Nevertheless, says the USGS, "the next eruption in the Cascades could affect hundreds of thousands of people."

And not just by lava or suffocating ash. Water is a problem, especially in the form of snow and ice packed atop Cascades volcanoes. Eruptions can melt large quantities of ice and snow and send the results downhill in rivers of steaming mud and rocks.

These *lahars*, an Indonesian term, can kill any living creatures in their paths. A number of Cascades volcanoes have year-round snow and ice. That's where it is possible for boiling hot eruptive mud flows to roar downhill. That has happened at Mount Rainier and left seventy-feet-deep deposits of mud and rock in the lowlands. One such flow in Colombia, South America, left 23,000 people dead. A lahar at Mount Rainier once was powerful enough to flow all the way to Puget Sound. Evidence has been found of more than sixty such mudflows during the last ten millenniums on that mountain alone.

Today scientists have set up monitoring sites across the Pacific Northwest. Devices at these sites measure such data as earthquakes, tilts in the earth's crust, swelling, magnetism, and spreading of such gases as sulfur dioxide.

At Crater Lake, experts make periodic slope and vertical angle measurements, as well as continuous seismic observations. Gathering such information provides baselines for future measurements, because it is often very important to note not just whether a movement is occurring, but how much since the last examination.

Crater Lake has been included in almost all of these geodetic baseline monitoring set-ups. So far, (well, up to the last five minutes anyway) no deformation of the scenery has been

Four – Tracking

noticed. If magma starts to move up the old conduits beneath Mazama, it will trigger monitoring instruments.

Where little or nothing is happening, as at Crater Lake, it may not be necessary to have round-the-clock measurements. Scientists need only check in periodically to see if there has been any movement. But because this is one of the most heavily visited volcanoes in the region, the periodic measurements are watched with care.

Field instruments are delicate, and solidly installed, but they have to cope

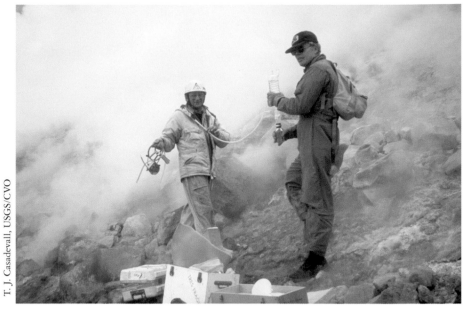

Collecting samples of gas on the smoking dome inside the crater at Mount St. Helens.

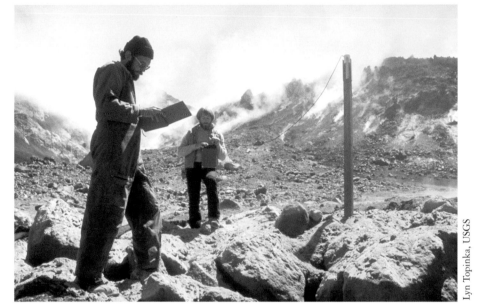

Geologists measure the magnetic field within the crater at Mount St. Helens. Changes in the magnetic field may signify changes in volcanic activity.

boxes. "After years of use," boasts the USGS, "no damage has occurred to any of our cases."

That is remarkable, considering that some measuring devices have to be left in bear country. As some park visitors have discovered, bears are experienced at getting into cars, backpacks, and camp boxes. Maybe it's because there isn't any food in instrument boxes.

For interested observers, monitoring equipment includes leveling devices, global positioning instruments, digital

with high velocity mountain winds that can make a machine think an earthquake is taking place. It is also nice to have small devices that can be backpacked in to spots unreachable by helicopter. So complex are the instruments that reading a description of them is like reading something in a foreign language. But they work, and work well, and are being improved as time passes.

The instruments are encased in airtight, corrosion resistant, foam resin

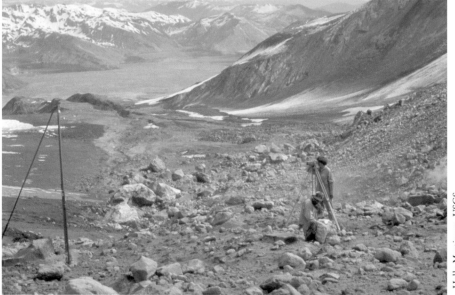

Measuring changes in the shape of the crater floor at Mount St. Helens. Movements of magma beneath the earth change the surface. These changes are measured electronically by tiltmeters. Results are transmitted to the Cascades Volcano Observatory.

telemetry systems, and night thermal instruments. *See Side Bar: Monitoring Devices.*

If Crater Lake seems to be sleeping for now, high tech sentinels, wide awake around the clock, are on hand to let us know when Mazama shows any signs of coming to life again.

Measurements have never been this good.

MONITORING DEVICES

Steven Brantley, USGS/CVO

Lyn Topinka, USGS/CVO

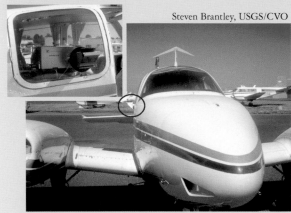

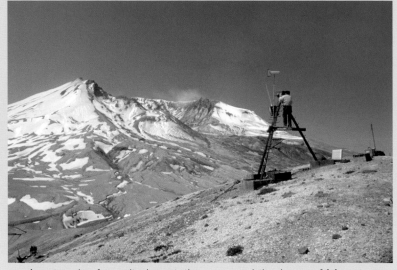

An airplane-mounted SO² gas measuring instrument, which uses a telescopic device to read ultraviolet light from the sun.

A network of monitoring stations around the base of Mount St. Helens keeps watch for deformations. Bulging at the surface means expanding magma, steam and gases below.

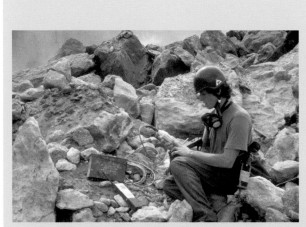

Installing a seismometer atop the dome, Mount St. Helens.

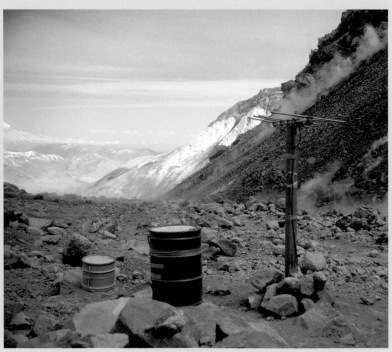

A tiltmeter station on the west crater floor, near the base of the dome, Mount St. Helens.

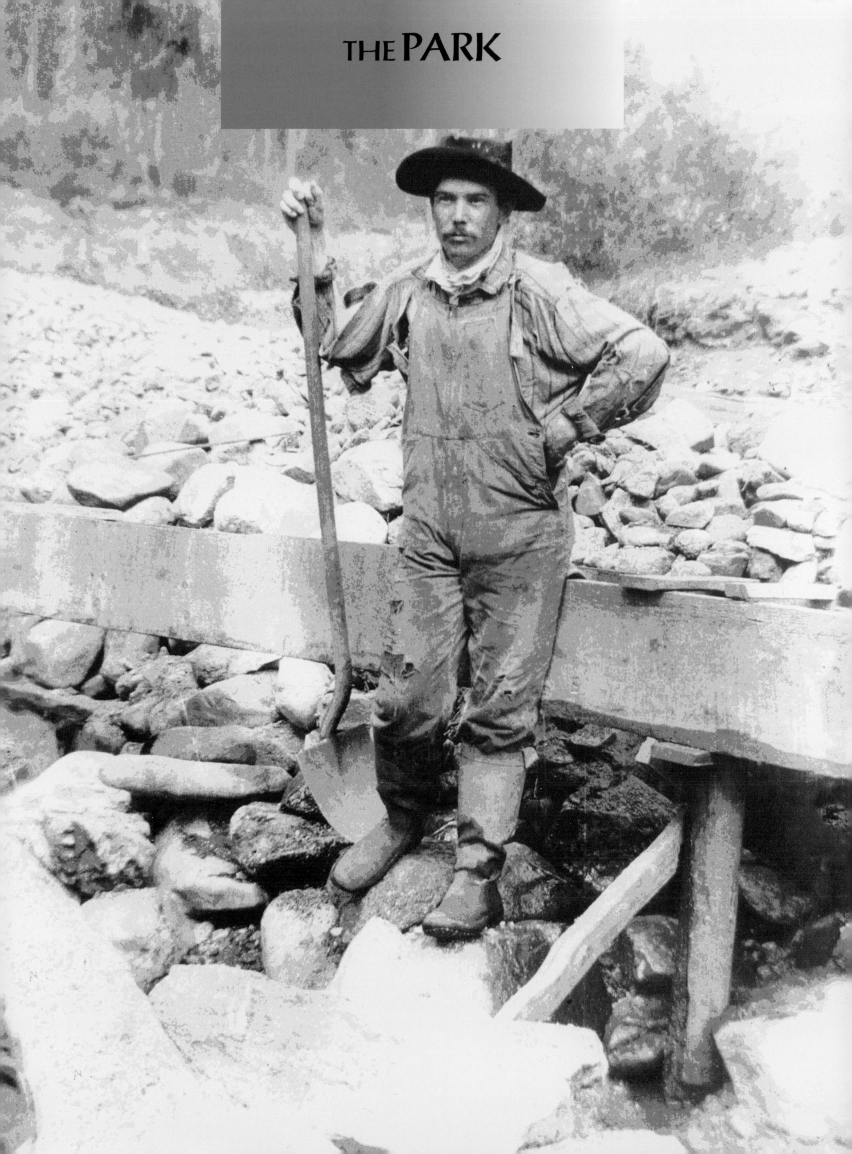

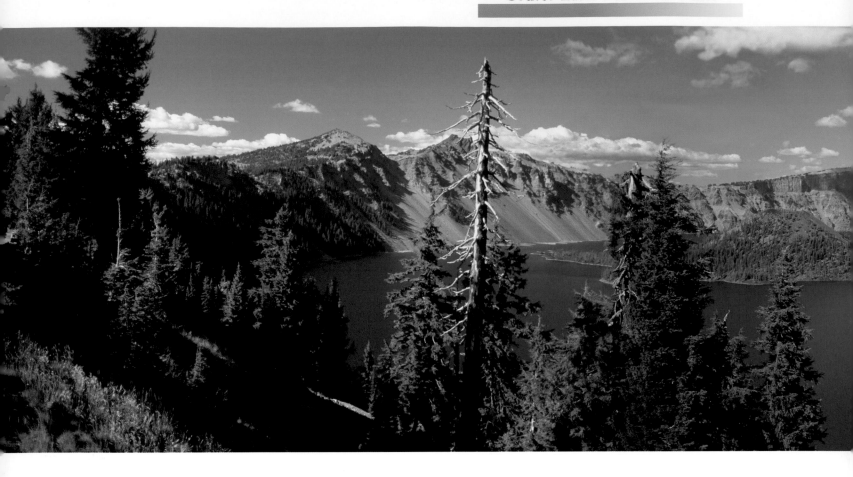

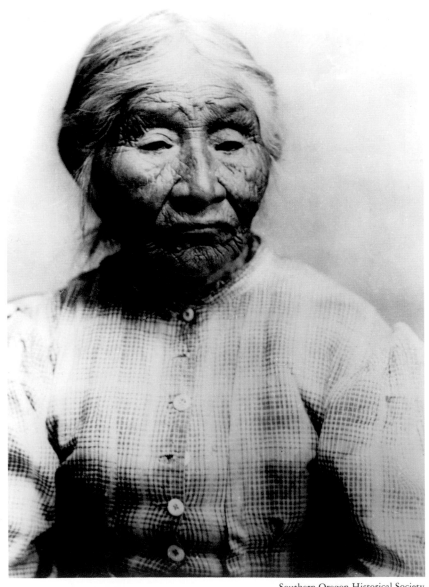

*Klamath Indian woman,
born about 1835.*

Southern Oregon Historical Society

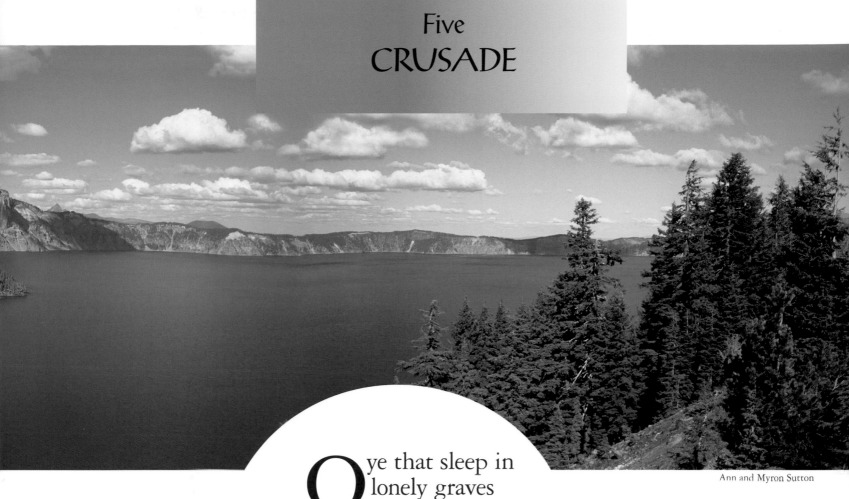

Ann and Myron Sutton

Five
CRUSADE

For seven thousand years after the eruption of Mount Mazama, Crater Lake survived without any guidance from human visitors. Forests and flowering plants on what was left of the once mighty mountain began to grow again from seeds brought in by wind and animal life. New generations grew up. Ducks and geese flew in and out. Owls perched in the hemlocks. Martens leaped from limb to limb. And squirrels built their burrows on the rim.

When lightning struck, the surrounding forest burned at will and there was no way to put out the fires, except by rain or snow.

Oye that sleep in lonely graves
by distant ridge and plain,
We drink to you in silence now
as Christmas comes again,
To you who fought the wilderness
through rough unsettled years—
The founders of our nation's life,
the brave old pioneers.

A. B Paterson

And that was fortunate, for ashes added nutrients to soil so sterilized in the eruption. Fire opened glades for grass to grow and deer to feed. Branches of trees collapsed from heavy snow. Trees fell, decayed, and enriched the soil with a little help from beetles, ants, fungi, or bacteria.

Animal populations thrived and left their droppings, which fertilized the forest soil even further. Before long, perhaps three hundred years, the blast zone had become recolonized with thick, rich woods, and abundant wildlife.

The Early People

A great many native people knew Crater Lake long before newcomers of European descent arrived. On the east side of the mountains lived the Klamath-Modoc speakers, and on the west the Takelma speakers.

They hunted and gathered wild foods, but probably more significant to them was the lake as a place of power, demanding preparation on the part of any visitor.

Native tribes visited Crater Lake sporadically, not living here, perhaps, because of the heavy winter snows. But they existed all around. They thrived on fish from lakes and streams and abundant plants and animals in the meadows and forests. Nearby were deposits of flint, chert, and obsidian, a volcanic glass, from which to fashion blades for tools and self defense.

During the climactic eruption, the streams for miles around had no doubt been choked with pumice. Fish died. Forests were devastated, and had to start growing again. As the centuries passed and the forests restored themselves, descendants of the native people once again entered the region and utilized its resources as their ancestors had.

Gold-seekers

The first settlers of European descent arrived to utilize other resources: timber, grass for grazing sheep, and metals mined to expand their private fortunes. When great numbers of miners flocked to California during the Gold Rush of 1849, newly arrived settlers in Oregon likewise rushed to the Sierra foothills. After a while, though, some soldiers of fortune came to Oregon in search of wealth.

In those days, information did not travel very rapidly unless, of course, the news dealt with gold discoveries. The veins in California granites held gold, and the sediments left over from erosion were full of golden specks. Those fragments could be precipitated in a placer pan and dropped into a small unobtrusive pouch.

The miners came north, and it mattered little that Oregon was mostly made of lava, and hence less endowed with gold than the granites of the Sierra Nevada.

Yet, the advance contingents of explorers seeking gold and silver spread out through the forests and into canyons, probing the streams for telltale signs of mineral wealth. Placer gold was found along Rich Gulch, in the vicinity of present-day Jacksonville, and later on the Illinois, Rogue and Applegate Rivers. Millions of dollars worth of minerals were eventually brought out. In the heyday of searching, towns grew up, and places like Jacksonville became social centers for the exchange of news.

Historians call these newcomers footloose and impoverished gold seekers. But some had other places

in the destiny of the American West. As told in Harlan D. Unrau's 1988 Administrative History of Crater Lake National Park:

"While drinking in a saloon, John Wesley Hillman, a 21-year-old New Yorker and his friends, were

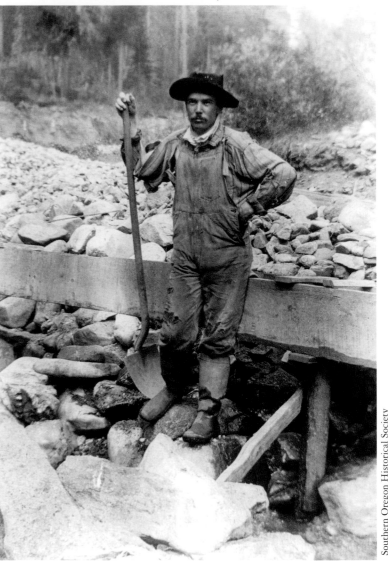

Gold miner.

Southern Oregon Historical Society

told by a party of Californians that they possessed secret information that would lead them to a rich Lost Cabin Mine in the rugged mountains of present-day Josephine County. Hillman formed a party...to trail the Californians. Thereafter, both parties played a game of hide-and-seek until their rations began to get low. Hunting mineral treasure gave way to hunting

Five – Crusade

Breathtaking views were pleasant surprises in the midst of arduous climbs for early explorers. Today, this dramatic view of Vidae Falls is a roadside attraction.

wild game, and soon the two parties agreed to work and hunt together. Several more days of floundering drew them further off course and soon they were hopelessly lost."

Oregon, alas, was not exactly designed for this kind of exploration, especially for newcomers. The forests were too thick. The streams difficult to cross or navigate. The mountains too high, canyons too deep and steep. Landmarks almost impossible to find or follow.

Anyone who hikes a trail through Oregon forests today can appreciate the problems faced by Hillman and company. Seldom can you see more than a hundred yards unless you follow a river or come out on a mountain glade. There weren't any roads and few trails. Without maps it was impossible to know what river you encountered, where it came from, or where it went.

Unless, of course, you were a veteran traveler in these regions. Some led emigrant parties across the plains and into Oregon. Others worked for decades as guides familiar with the terrain. For newcomers, however, landmarks could serve as guideposts across the prairies along the Oregon Trail. Trees weren't a problem until west of The Dalles, where travelers either used rafts and portaged down rivers, or took established trails around Mount Hood. Elsewhere, anyone who veered off the Oregon Trail and didn't have an experienced guide, would have to rise above the confining trees to get his bearings.

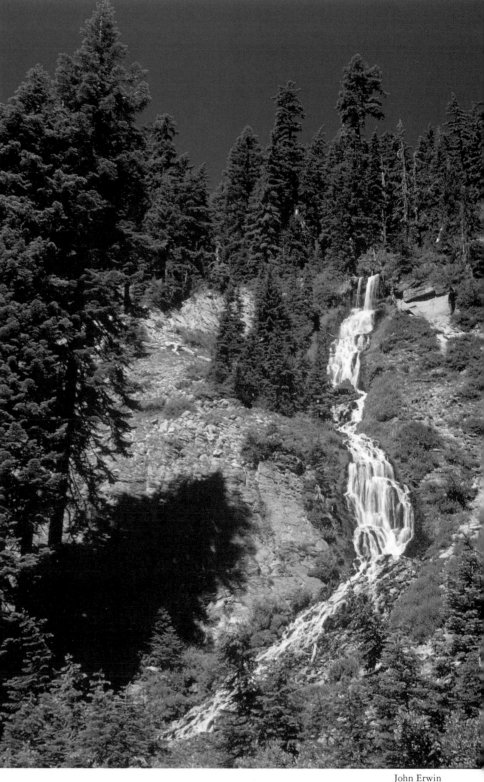

John Erwin

Overlooks, what few there were, revealed a route to the next destination. Rarely could travelers glimpse the towering shoulders of Shasta to the south, McLoughlin to the east, or Jefferson farther north. The only way these travelers could get the "lay of the landscape," and plot the route ahead, was to climb a mountain and use it as a lookout. You didn't have to climb all the way to the top. You could go up part way, find an opening through the trees, and look out across the terrain below, selecting a promising course.

That is what Hillman did on June 12, 1853, and on that ridge he found the surprise of his life: a massive blue lake cupped in a huge mountain.

"Every man of the party," he later wrote, "gazed with wonder at the sight before him, and each in his own peculiar way gave expression to the thoughts within him…We discussed what name we should give the lake. There were many names suggested, but Mysterious Lake and Deep Blue Lake were most favorably received, and on a vote, Deep Blue Lake was chosen…"

Thus did explorers of European descent, as far as is known, first look upon what would become one of the most famous lakes in the world. Word spread slowly, because the region was so sparsely settled and so difficult to travel through. Eventually, the press found out about this new lake and newspapers published descriptions of it. Thus tourism, as such, really commenced about 1868.

Then began one of the most energetic, frustrating campaigns in American history to embrace and protect a stunning segment of the landscape for others to come and see.

Steel's Crusade

In the history of world parks and equivalent reserves, there has often been a single human being who stood above all others in devotion to a specific place. One who, with unstinting hard work, not only told a disbelieving world about it, but launched a campaign to publicize and protect it before the place was lost to commercial development. Nathaniel Langford had succeeded in the 1870s at Yellowstone. John Muir was trying to do this in Yosemite. Enos Mills is a name linked to the Rocky Mountains of Colorado. And, much later, Marjory Stoneman Douglas took on preservation of the Florida Everglades. This is a distinguished pantheon, people working behind the scenes often with great resistance.

Crater Lake National Park historian Stephen R. Mark, in writing a chronology of William Steel's life, makes a very cogent point: "Over the past century, activists have done much to stimulate legislative action for national parks and equivalent reserves. Their efforts have been a key factor in the national park system's continued expansion…"

Will Steel was a sixteen-year-old farm boy in Kansas when he first read newspaper accounts of Crater Lake.

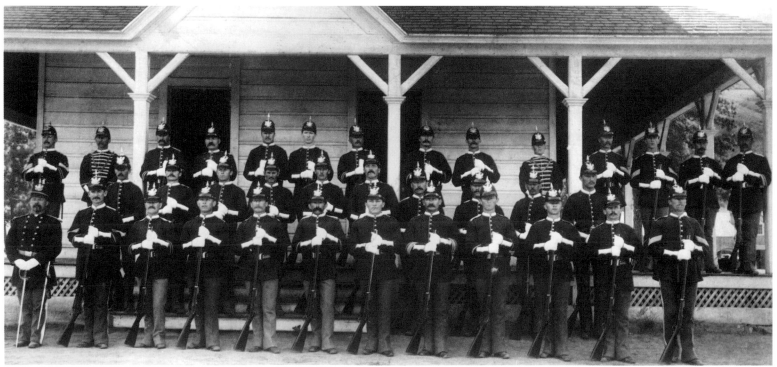

Soldiers at Fort Klamath.

Southern Oregon Historical Society

Five – Crusade

Impressed, he vowed to get there as soon as he could. His family moved to Oregon in 1872 but it wasn't until 1885 that he got to the lake for his first glimpse.

National parks were scarcely known in those days. In 1872, Congress had been persuaded to set aside Yellowstone, but not yet as a "national park." It was simply called a "public park and pleasuring ground." The words national park were not embodied in Yellowstone legislation until 1883.

The name, however, was less crucial than the idea. After Steel saw the lake for the first time, he wrote, "An overmastering conviction came to me that this wonderful spot must be saved, wild and beautiful, just as it was, for all future generations, and that it was up to me to do something. I then and there had the impression that in some way, I didn't know how, the lake ought to become a national park."

However noble and patriotic, this idea was being swamped in the aftermath of the discovery of gold in California in 1849. The potential of gold rendered western lands sacrosanct, paradise for miners. Extensive forests, so basic to construction of camps, villages and towns, gave lands great value to the timber industry. And the abundance of grass meant forage for livestock.

You would think that if a stunningly beautiful lake were discovered amidst these sacred lands, there would be leeway to protect the lake and surrounding lands and keep them undisturbed. Not so. Steel's plan may have sounded simple. "Wyoming has a national park, what are we waiting for?"

It may seem hard to fathom nowadays, but opposition rose at the first suggestion of such a wild idea. Steel met the objections head on. With journalistic skills and newspaper experience, he knew how to write, and he knew important people.

The more he was met by opposition, the more he responded with politics and persistence. Skills of cajolery came into play, especially with friends in high places.

The job became very complex, and is too long to go into detail here. Suffice it to say that Steel met with members of Congress, State officials (Oregon became a state in 1859), and anyone else he could find. Letters, news stories, petitions and proposals flew.

All to end in failure.

Some Congressmen in the 1890s felt that it might be acceptable to set aside a national park at Crater Lake, but you could not rule out mining. The minerals, if any, must not be "locked up." Maybe when the lands around the lake had been divested of their assets, then it could be made into a national park.

There wasn't much high-quality saw timber within the proposed park area anyway, and it would have been difficult to haul out. "The main problem in Congress," says Steve Mark, "was the willingness to appropriate funds for something considered both useless and exclusionary (only the rich might be able to afford a visit)."

From Portland, Steel sent a thousand letters to nearly all the newspapers in the United States seeking their support for a Crater Lake National Park. He got Oregon leaders to sign petitions, which made their way to President Grover Cleveland. The Oregon Legislature submitted a petition to Congress. This stimulated a blizzard of testimonials. Steel sought, at the very least, withdrawal of the land from the public domain.

A bill was introduced in 1886 to set the park aside, but it contained those fatal words: no mining, lumbering or other private enterprise.

Since the land asked for included Mount Thielsen and Diamond Lake as well, it was a pretty big chunk of real estate to remove from private enterprise. When that reached Congressional committees for consideration, the battles began. On the positive side came support from national magazines and newspapers. One of the best accolades was written for the magazine *Science* by Clarence E. Dutton, a noted geologist of the time.

"In the heart of the Cascade Range there is a little sheet of water which is destined to take high rank among the wonders of the world... It was touching to see the worthy but untutored people, who had ridden a hundred miles in freight-wagons to behold it, vainly striving to keep back tears as they poured forth their exclamations of wonder and joy…"

Steel solicited testimonials from eminent people, and got one from Gifford Pinchot, first director of the U.S. Forest Service:

"You asked me why a national park should be established around Crater Lake. There are many reasons. In the first place, Crater Lake is one of the great natural wonders of this continent. Secondly, it is a famous resort for the people of Oregon and of other States, which can best be protected and managed in the form of a national park. Thirdly, since its chief value is for recreation and scenery and not for the production of timber, its use is distinctly that of a national park and not a forest reserve. Finally, in the present situation of affairs it could be more carefully guarded and protected as a park than as a reserve."

John Wesley Powell, the famed one-armed Civil War veteran who had led the first boat trip down the Colorado River through Arizona's Grand Canyon in 1869, was at that time the first director of the United States Geological Survey. There is no record that he ever visited Crater Lake, so the passage was almost surely drafted by someone else. It says:

"There are probably not many natural objects in the world which impress the average spectator with so deep a sense of the beauty and majesty of nature. Although Crater Lake is the dominant object of interest in the proposed reservation the whole tract is eminently fit to be 'set apart forever as a public park and pleasure ground and forest reserve for the benefit of the people of the United States;' and I might venture to add for the benefit of the people of the world. There is not a square mile within the proposed tract which does not contain something which would add to the attractiveness of such a park either in the way of varied beauty or of instruction and entertainment of visitors."

Despite such high-level praise from within the government itself, Oregon lumber, ranching and mining interests prevailed again. Oregon Senator Dolph finally threw up his hands. The majority on the Public Lands Committee, he wrote to Steel, were "opposed to the creation of any more National Parks, and there is no possibility of securing the passage at the present session of Congress, and I fear not at any future Congress, for a bill creating such a park."

That was a hopeless note if there ever was one. It would have been easy just to give up in the face of such finality.

But Steel kept up the pressure. A proposal came to set up the area as a State Park, but Steel said no—the state could not afford to manage such a large and complex area. Historian Steve Mark says that Steel had three reasons for opposing state park status: he saw Crater Lake as a truly national area; the state park at Yosemite was attracting much criticism…as an

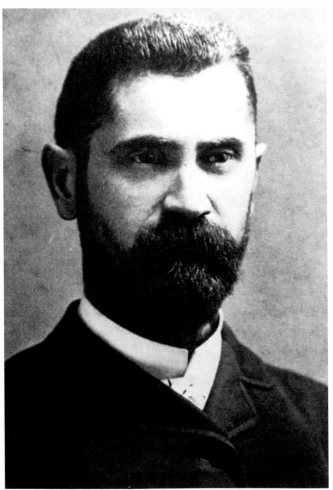

William Gladstone Steel.

National Park Service

area badly managed; and Steel knew Oregonians well enough to know that the legislature would never appropriate the kind of money needed to develop Crater Lake.

Steel wrote a book on the natural beauty of the mountains of Oregon, thus launching new efforts to get the public to pressure Congress. More bills were introduced, only to pass one house and die in the other.

All this merely underscored the fact that Americans were not yet ready to push en masse for conservation. It was on the way, however, and as efforts grew, pressures grew. The ideas of Henry David Thoreau, George Perkins Marsh, and Frederick Law Olmstead began to take hold. Yosemite and Yellowstone had been set aside. So had Sequoia and the General Grant redwoods.

Good precedents. Disappearing forests began to alarm people. Ohio was about to lose 85% of its original woodlands, and the more this happened, the more it became obvious that the people had to take control over their natural resources or lose them altogether.

Out here on the frontier there was a different focus. Those resources were needed to build the West, to make America the great country it was destined to be. Never mind that the national parks would take up only a tiny per cent of the land area of the nation. They were a harbinger of things to come, and if too much of the country were "locked up," as they liked to say (and still do!), then America would never achieve greatness. Time had not yet demonstrated what a powerful economic lure the national parks would be, and how many millions of people would visit them... thus enriching the surrounding area from travelers' expenditures. Without

that, it is little wonder that Steel had such a difficult time getting Crater Lake established as a national park.

Yet those other parks were beginning to showcase America the beautiful, to which was added: "And let's save some of it!" Parks, too, could help make America great, and the voices of Thoreau and Marsh produced a rationale for doing so.

With American conservation policy being so powerfully articulated, pressures began to rise on the other side, to set aside natural areas before they were destroyed. As Forest Reserves began to be set up, Steel supported efforts to establish a Cascade Range Forest Reserve, which was done in 1893. This, at least, gave some measure of protection to Crater Lake.

That didn't sit very well with the opposition. Notices posted by the government were torn down. Forests were deliberately burned. The government responded by hiring federal agents to administer the laws.

By 1898, more than 40 million acres had been set aside as forest reserves.

This gave vent to cries of too much land being locked up.

Steel persisted in lobbying, created a mountaineering club to help, organized outings, and got as many notable people as possible, scientists especially, to raise the issue with Congress. He promoted articles and feature stories in the local and national press.

On this issue, incidentally, something Steel could not have known, it was the press, in the coming century, that would play crucial roles in similar battles around the world, from Latin America to Australia. Quite often, as the 20th century arrived and progressed, the press would issue scathing indictments of how "neglect" was letting the national heritage be lost (Costa Rica in the 1960s is one of the best examples in world history). Such articles angered citizens and got the attention of legislators and presidents.

Very effective...and Steel knew how to use it.

More negotiations. More proclamations, rules, regulations, studies, surveys. The national psyche was now trending toward protection, and Steel took advantage of it.

In 1895, another bill was introduced to make Crater Lake a park, and it got closer. But still it could only pass if mining restrictions were deleted. The park bill died again.

In 1899, another bill. Another failure.

By now, however, a lot of people were at work on this project. The final bill was introduced in 1901, promoting help for "scientists, excursionists, and pleasure seekers," and allowing for restaurants and hotels to be set up.

This bill looked like it had a good chance when the Speaker of the House stopped it because there were a number of park bills before the House, and he refused to recognize any of them.

Pinchot went straight to President Theodore Roosevelt, a staunch supporter of wild land preservation, who asked the Speaker to let the Crater Lake bill come up.

Debate ensued in the House, mostly about the location of mining claims within the park. Back to Committee the bill went, where language allowing mining claims was inserted. That did it.

On April 21, 1902, after more debate, the Senate passed the bill.

Steel wrote to President Roosevelt: "Please accept my sincere thanks and grateful acknowledgment for the great assistance rendered in this matter by you. When I tell you I have labored for seventeen years to bring this to pass, paying every expense, except one single item, and all as a matter of love for the grand region in question, you may comprehend the depth of my gratitude."

Roosevelt signed the law on May 22, 1902, and America's sixth national park finally became a reality, seventeen years after Steel began his long crusade.

Steel was a precursor and, though he couldn't have known it, his campaigns would later be matched by such as Howard Stanley and Len Smith in Australia, Mario Boza in Costa Rica, José Rafael Garcia in Venezuela, and Maria Buchinger in the rest of South America. Their goals were very much like Steel's: get the land set aside by law, then prepare the place for tourists.

People trying to establish national parks in the twentieth century often ran into all kinds of stiff resistance. Fortunately, Steel did not have to clash with campaigns to rip up the land for petroleum exploration, spilling oil into native streams, a problem common in tropical regions, such as Ecuador. Nor did he live in a country where voting was compulsory, as in Costa Rica. Had that been the case, Steel's efforts would have been even more complicated than they were. The question would have dogged him: "What good is a national park," went parliamentary debates in other countries, "if the poor, our greatest block of voters, can't afford to get there?"

Still, the activist of 1902, with help from other activists, won by dogged determination, and he had every right

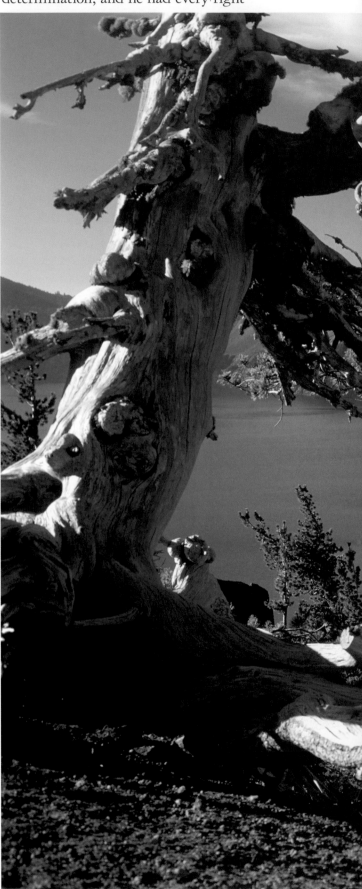

An early morning view of the lake from the west rim, just 50 feet from the rim road.

to be proud. It was, however, just the beginning of an experiment, for him, and for Crater Lake.

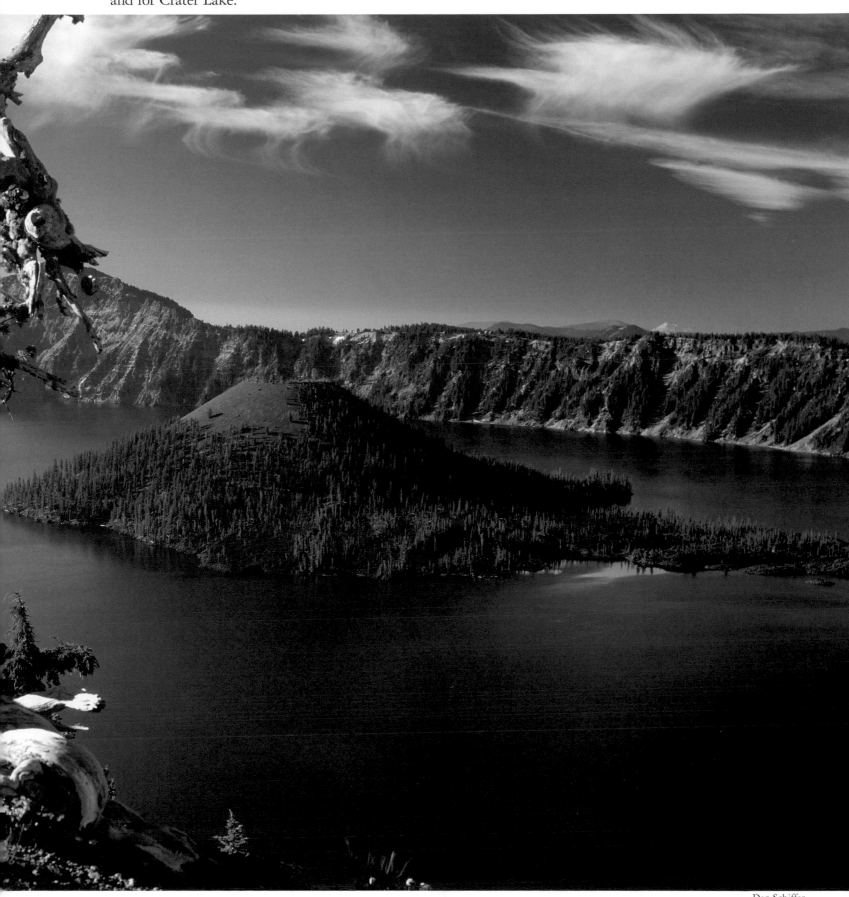

Dan Schiffer

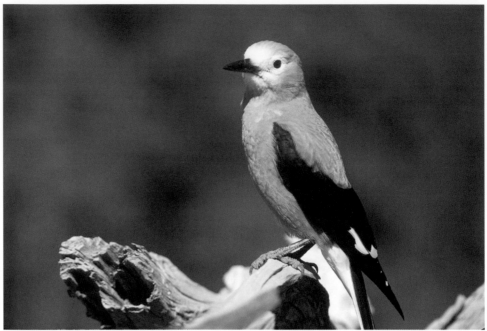

Clark's Nutcracker.

John Erwin

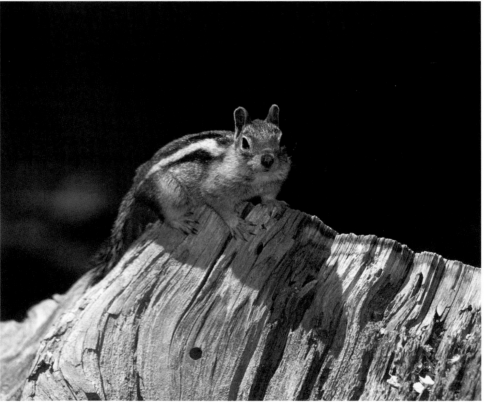

Chipmunk.

John Erwin

*Campers in Crater Lake
National Park, 1913.*

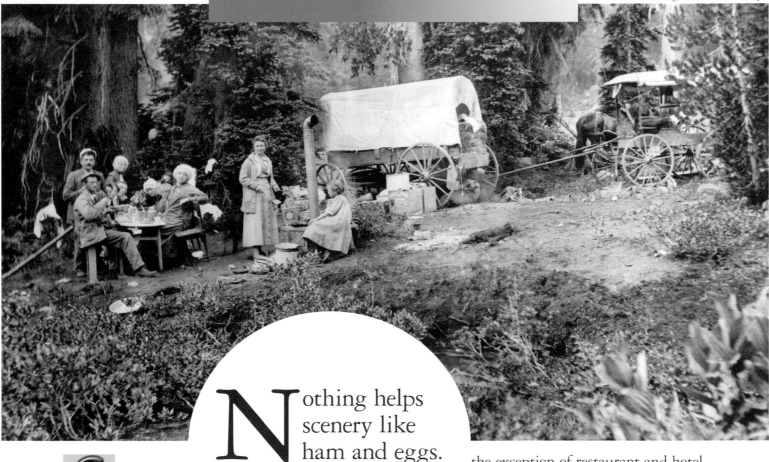

Nothing helps scenery like ham and eggs.

Mark Twain

So—now that we have a park, what next?

The only specific guidelines were in the Congressional Act itself. The land was withdrawn from settlement, occupancy, or sale, and "set apart forever as a public park or pleasure ground for the benefit of the people..."

The Secretary of the Interior was ordered to set up regulations for "preservation of the natural objects... protection of timber from wanton destruction, preservation of all kinds of game and fish, the punishment of trespassers, the removal of unlawful occupants and intruders, and the prevention and extinguishment of forest fires."

There was to be no settlement, no lumbering, no business at all, with the exception of restaurant and hotel keepers who would establish 'places of entertainment'."

Mining claims? Yes, but not if they wrecked any of the natural features and processes. The Act itself was scarcely a page and a half in length, but that was enough to start the buildup of rules and regulations.

For the first eleven years, the superintendent of the park was William F. Arant, a Klamath Falls rancher whose family had crossed the plains to reach Oregon fifty years earlier. If you think he was merely the caretaker of a patch of undisturbed wilderness, consider what he faced.

He was supposed to encourage travel to the park. The very fact that the lake was given such honorable treatment by the United States Congress meant to many that "we must go see it as soon as we can." The lake, of course, was available for all to see. But how do you protect the forest and wildlife around it when people are scrambling to cut firewood, set up tents, build fires and stay for weeks? In the beginning, the park was not prepared for even a small influx of visitors.

Getting Ready

To understand what this public desire to see Crater Lake National Park as soon as possible meant, we must reset our minds back to 1902. There were no paved highways, hamburger stops, service stations, telephones, or rangers. The main artery of transportation was a military "road" from the Rogue Valley to Fort Klamath. And that road was merely a passage in which stumps of trees were barely low enough for wagons to get over them.

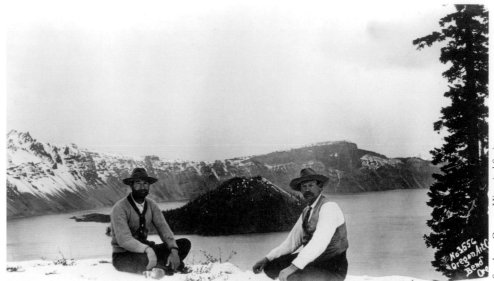

Arant (r.), and unidentified man at rim of Crater Lake.

Southern Oregon Historical Society

Anyone who tried to reach the park had a real adventure: horses and wagons to carry people and provisions. Stops along the way to renew provisions at ranches and feed horses. Tents for camping out.

When visitors arrived at the lake, they occasionally encountered loose livestock with no fences to keep them out. Sheep grazing had ceased in 1896.

Congress allocated $2,000 a year to run the park, which meant subsistence levels of operation, and little else.

So Superintendent Arant had his hands full. He needed help, and he had to start moving as fast as possible.

First task: improve the road up to the rim, hire workers, survey the route, start construction, and haul lumber with which to build bridges. All in the scant time between melting of giant snow banks in July, and heavy new snowfall in autumn.

Then came the building of roads to other parts of the park, and a trail inside the crater to the lake.

Though the park was closed in winter, it still had to be patrolled on account of poachers and other lawbreakers. The snow might be twenty feet deep, but by spring it had compacted to four feet and had the consistency of granular ice, making it easier to walk on, but tricky nonetheless.

Access was a critical point with nearly every park established in those days. If loggers and grazers saw the parks being underused, they might pressure Congress to open the parks for other uses. Park officials had to attract substantial numbers of visitors with every means they had, take good care of tourists when they arrived, and entertain them royally once they were there.

All this had a certain logic. Cutting off such large segments of land to commercial uses might have adverse effects on the economy of the region and the well-being of miners, loggers and their families. These people voted, so they had rights.

Park officials knew the power of this logic, and it must have been in the backs of their minds during more than half of Crater Lake's first century. If this experiment didn't work, the park could be lost. Conversely, the more visitors, the more voters out there promoting the park.

With all the hundreds of millions of people who visit the national parks nationwide today, it is difficult to grasp this philosophy of a century ago, but it was real, and it drove park pioneers to extra hard work.

The Interior Department acted quickly to give Park Superintendent Arant detailed rules and regulations. Three months after the park was established began a flow of fine print that dealt with everything from destruction of natural features to prohibition of barrooms.

Six – Experiment

Yet the overriding question that has applied to practically every effort in the world to get national parks up and running was simple: what good are regulations without someone around to enforce them?

In those early days, if the roads weren't dusty, they were muddy. Tents set up in summer for primitive hotel accommodations got crushed by snow in winter.

If any worker or tourist got hurt, it was a long way to the nearest hospital (a situation that still prevails in places like Canaima National Park, Venezuela, home to Angel Falls, the world's highest waterfall).

Then there was the problem of public safety in dangerous territory. Wherever human beings untrained in wilderness travel are introduced into parks that have steep cliffs and wild forests, there are inevitably cases of victims trapped on ledges, falling over the edge, or clashing with dangerous animals. People in parks can get into trouble very easily.

Then the park officers who have to go rescue them run the risk of getting trapped themselves, falling in, or clashing with an 800-pound bear.

With the improved roads came more visitors, even though getting to Crater Lake National Park remained very difficult. A family from Portland, say, had to make its way to Medford or Klamath Falls, where they would hire a team of horses and a wagon, and outfit themselves with blankets, tents and food. It took three days to get to the park. Along the way, they stopped at ranches to restock their supplies of beef, milk, eggs and fresh vegetables.

On the rim, they would cut a supply of firewood and lay out a camp for a few days or a week. Without roads and trails there wasn't much to see beyond the lake. The nights got cold. And another week would be required for the return home.

This was also a time when the automobile was coming into existence, first steamers and then internal combustion types. The effect of these noisy contraptions on teams of horses pulling wagons was pandemonium. Autos had to move to the outside of a road, and come to a stop if necessary, to keep teams from bucking and stampeding. Vehicle drivers had speed limits of five miles an hour. On a straight stretch of road, with no teams in sight, they might increase to a blazing fifteen miles an hour.

Some of the early roads were also virtually one-way. When a family wanted to start up the final narrow switchbacks to the rim, there was no guarantee they could pass another rig if one came downhill at the same time. Accordingly they sent a scout up the road. When he arrived at the top he fired a rifle to signal that the way was clear.

The same procedure was applied in reverse when a team was ready to go down the switchbacks. There was one small variation however. A log had to be attached to the rear of the wagon so as to help brake its descent on the downward trip.

Before proper safeguards such as railings and retaining walls could be installed, cars with poor brakes would start rolling down the slope at the rim. In one case a mother lifted her child out of the car and walked away, only to turn and see her car rolling over the edge.

Getting Crater Lake ready for the public was a complex task for a few people, given all the new arrivals each summer. Perhaps it would have been smarter to close

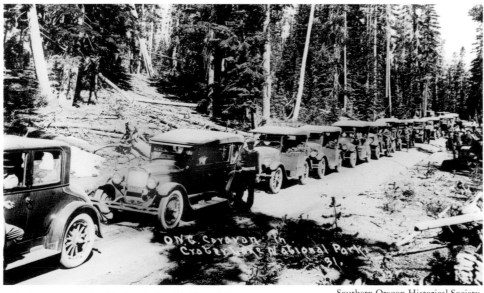

Auto caravan in Crater Lake National Park.

Southern Oregon Historical Society

the park entirely until roads, trails, railings, staffing, and accommodations were ready. That would have caused an uproar among people clamoring to get in, a politically untenable situation. And park people wanted as many visitors as they could get. By contrast, in today's China, a new tourist site remains closed until staffed and made ready for public use. Then it is beset by thousands of visitors a day, if not an *hour*.

Construction crews at Crater Lake National Park worked hard, and accidents were to be expected. Arant himself slipped accidentally through the slats of a bridge under construction and fell twenty feet to the rocks below. Giant machines to ease the construction of roads in rocky ravines either didn't exist or couldn't be brought to the park. Blasting road cuts through hard basaltic lavas sometimes hurled rocks down on construction workers, crushing them to death.

And even in these cool mountains, summer temperatures could rise to 90 degrees F. Forest fires started but were put out before much damage could occur.

The good news was that during those earliest years traffic to the park reached 2,000 tourists a summer.

The experiment was working!

Moreover, when asked how they would like the park to be managed, these early visitors replied that it should be kept in its natural state for the enjoyment of all.

No words could have been more welcome to Arant. No pronouncements could have better rewarded all the workers for the dangers, injuries and tough times they were going through. They were dealing with their country's heritage. As history has shown for more than a century, patriotism has been almost universally the most powerful driving force in the preservation and management of national parks and wildlife reserves.

So the trials and tribulations were worth it.

Meanwhile, with the onslaught of visitors, tents and hotel accommodations were furnished and meals served. Park rangers had their hands full with tourists downed by strokes and heart attacks, hikers

trapped on ledges, and people parking on the rim without setting the brakes of their car. One boy sledded over the rim and his body was never found. Another person skied to her death. Hikers on the trails misjudged their footing and fell. At one point, the chief ranger died while trying to walk through a vicious snow storm.

Vandalism began early, as soon as tents and hotels were built. Because of friction on the roads between teams and wagons and those new-fangled automobiles, it was once proposed that two roads be built around Crater Lake, one for cars, one for teams.

The park staff had to rule on whether domestic dogs and cats, brought in by visitors, should roam free or be restricted. They had to develop some kind of ranger uniform so that the increasing thousands of visitors would know a ranger when they saw one. The presence of uniformed personnel, they found, encouraged obedience to park rules and regulations. Once visitors knew what rules to follow, they became diligent in obeying them, and it was not unknown for one visitor to reprimand another for some infraction.

Following the Congressional dictum to "entertain" visitors, the staff sometimes concocted pretty wild

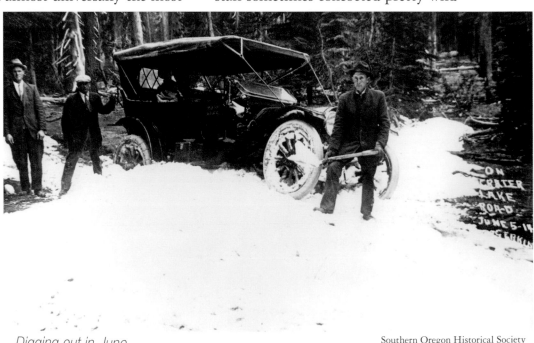

Digging out in June.

Southern Oregon Historical Society

schemes. It was reported in 1923 that the park staff placed explosives in the crater on the summit of Wizard Island. The staff had told visitors that the island was warming up and an eruption could be expected in a few days. Then with visitors watching from the rim, the simulated eruption was staged. This was an example of the resident staff testing ways to entertain visitors. Eventually, the rangers would settle on the park's features themselves as the most exciting aspect that needed no pranks or elaboration. The learning process was alive and well.

The story is told that one day in the late 1920s some rangers were preparing buckets of fingerling fish to be planted in the lake. A lady came up to ask why the lake was so blue, and they answered that if she watched on the morrow, she could see them dumping buckets of laundry blueing into the water.

They were joking, of course, but she complained all the way to Washington about how the rangers were destroying the lake by coloring it artificially.

When the National Park Service was established in 1916, it helped to standardize policies from one park to another across the country. It also set guidelines about what publicly staged events could be held and what could not. And the idea of misleading visitors became a thing of the past.

The Steel Era

No one was more closely allied to Crater Lake National Park than William Gladstone Steel, and when the time came for a second superintendent, he pushed himself vigorously for the job. Other candidates had surfaced for this political plum, but Steel's coterie of friends in high places helped usher him in.

He had been involved in establishing the park, then creation of the Crater Lake Company as a concessioner, putting in floored tents and a dining room for visitors. Soon there was a "tent city" on the rim, accommodating 50 persons. Now in charge of the park, Steel was responsible for handling a cascade of challenges during his tenure from 1913 to 1916.

The roads were still not up to standard. Every spring, they were washed out and rutted anew from all the

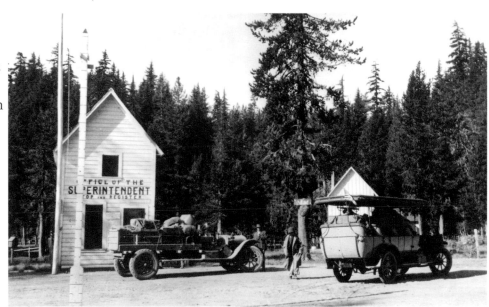

Early travelers arriving at the Superintendent's Office.   Southern Oregon Historical Society

snow melt and runoff, and obstructed by rock slides and falling trees.

Visitors intent on immortalizing themselves reveled in carving, painting and writing their names on rocks, trees and railings. Park managers were still troubled by the passage of herds of cattle through the park.

Steel stayed with it. "All the money I have is in this park," he once said, "and if I had more it would go there, too. This is my life's work, and I propose to see it through...We are now building a cut-stone hotel on the rim of the lake from the veranda of which you will be able to look down upon the waters 1,000 feet below."

It was very difficult for a concessioner with a five-year contract limit to operate a business in the park on the basis of a short summer, so he managed to get contracts extended to 20 years.

It was all the stuff of operating a growing business, and growing service to the public.

Steel was plagued by inadequate appropriations to accomplish his goals, a common lament in those days. Visitors were now coming in at the rate of 5,000 a year, and still getting covered with dust—a fine dark lava dust that penetrated ears, eyes and clothing.

Steel called for more rangers, and for expansion of the park. Wild animals from the park went down to lower elevations in the autumn, right into the hands of hunters, so Steel wanted the surrounding area to be set aside as a reserve so that native species would have some protection during migration.

He cleared the road banks of potential forest fire hazards, built water lines, and sold permits to the ever-increasing numbers of automobiles entering the park.

In 1915 he hosted an eminent visitor, William Jennings Bryan, recently United States Secretary of State. Steel took him down the trail to the lake for a launch trip. On the climb back up out of the caldera, Bryan suggested that a tunnel be dug from the lake to the rim and a system provided for easier access to the water.

Steel took up this idea because of the difficulty of hiking by trail down to the lake and back. Many visitors, he said, couldn't make the trip and were disappointed by not being able to get to the lake. In requesting funds from Congress to start a survey for the tunnel, he wrote: "A lift or other installation within the rim is wholly impracticable, for the reason that every spring enormous slides of snow and rocks would sweep any sort of framework into the lake. Under such conditions I would suggest the construction of a tunnel from a convenient point on the road several hundred feet below the rim, to the surface of the water..."

The project had a lot of support but never succeeded.

With the establishment of the National Park Service in 1916, Crater Lake National Park started the long process of coming of age. The new director of the service, Stephen T. Mather, galvanized the whole system. He promptly visited Crater Lake and at a subsequent meeting in Portland said: "I have just come from the Crater Lake Park, and I am free to say that I believe it has probably the greatest possibilities of any scenic park in the world."

As national parks gained public esteem, Crater Lake shared in the superlatives expressed in newspaper articles. The park was variously described as fascinating, enchanting, wonder among wonders, and as one of the most beautiful spots in America.

All these floods of superlatives had their effect on travel. By the time Steel's superintendency ended in 1916, there were nearly 12,000 visitors a year to the park.

Steel was then appointed park commissioner, whose job was to rule on matters of law within the park. This post he kept until the end of his life in 1934.

Thus ended a remarkable and enduring devotion to a national park, a single-minded dream to establish, a fight to create, and then diligent efforts for years to assure success of the park he loved so much. Today he rests on a knoll in the Siskiyou Gardens in Medford, his grave site shaded by a multitude of trees in whose boughs songbirds provide a fitting tribute to a pioneer who led the fight to protect an American crown jewel.

Parking lot, May 1932.

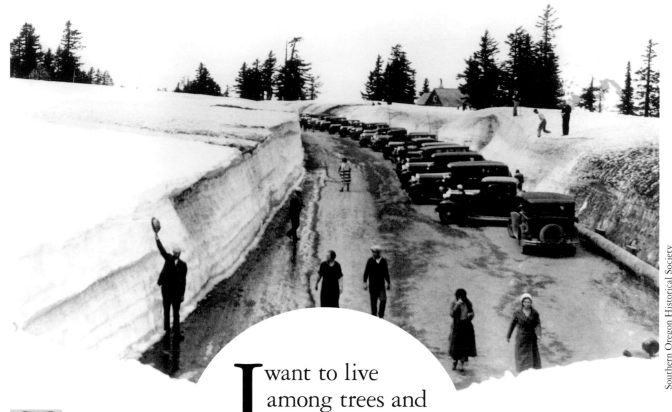

Southern Oregon Historical Society

I want to live among trees and bushes,

Silent friends who respect my state of nerves.

Alfred Nobel

The experiments in managing

T he experiments in managing national parks did not end, even with the establishment of the National Park Service in 1916. The Service refined and adjusted its management procedures at Crater Lake right up to the end of the park's first century.

The task, however, became infinitely more difficult, even with well-trained staffs and modern equipment. The better the roads, the more visitors came. The more visitors, the greater publicity.

Travel to the park rose from 7,530 visitors in 1913 to 273,564 in 1941.

Travel plummeted during World War II because of gas rationing and so many people gone to war. By 1950, travel was back on track, setting a new record of 328,041 in that year. That nearly doubled in 1962 when droves of travelers headed for the Seattle World's Fair.

If there were no more clashes between teams of horses and lines of Model Ts, other problems arose. For example, in the 1940s, movie companies began in earnest to shoot films on location throughout the U.S.A. The studios recognized that this was more difficult and expensive than staying in Hollywood, but the authentic, spectacular backgrounds and the coming of color in the 1930s made it worthwhile.

Filming the Parks

Since many desirable backdrops were located in national parks, the pressures arose to bring casts and crews into delicate wild places. *Journey to the Center of the Earth* was filmed in Carlsbad Caverns National Park, New Mexico, for example, and *North by Northwest* at Mount Rushmore Memorial in South Dakota.

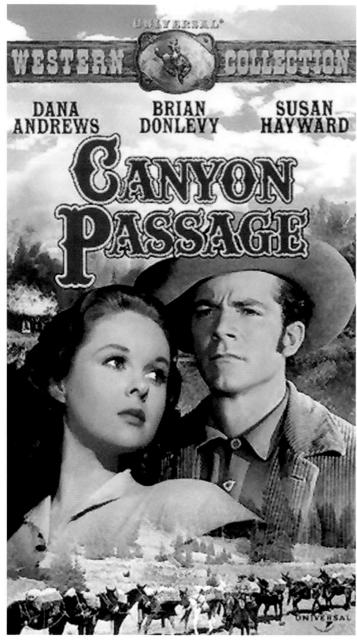

Three films were partially shot at Crater Lake National Park.

In 1941, *Sundown*, starring Gene Tierney, Bruce Cabot, and George Sanders, a story set in Africa, was produced with only a few scenes filmed within the caldera. Materials for the set, a boat dock, were slid over the rim and let down to the lake's edge. An amphibious plane brought in the crew and supplies. Public activities on the lake had to be canceled during the filming of those few scenes.

There was no reference in the film to Crater Lake National Park, and no credits to the park staff for assistance in making the film there.

Walter Wanger's 1946 film *Canyon Passage* was another of those popular stories brought to the screen from the pages of the *Saturday Evening Post*. Starring Dana Andrews and Susan Hayward, it was set in the mining town of Jacksonville. Crater Lake appears in only a few scenes, and is shown as little more than a place from which Indians come forth to attack settlers.

Once again there was no mention of the lake, and no credit to the National Park Service for assistance.

The IMAX super-large-screen program on the Eruption of Mount St. Helens, released in 1990, contains magnificent views of Crater Lake and briefly discusses Mount Mazama.

Prima facie, the incorporation of American national parks into films was an idea with promise. But merely to use Crater Lake as an African locale without credit began to set up the notion that the parks could be unduly abused, even if inadvertently.

In 1950 came *King Solomon's Mines*, filmed partly in Carlsbad Caverns National Park, New Mexico, a picture—like *Sundown*—with an African setting. The educational value of the parks, for their own sake, was almost nil.

As time went on, the National Park Service became a little edgy about protecting natural features from the onslaught of crews, Klieg lights, and crowds of curious onlookers.

The 1953 production at Montezuma Castle National Monument, Arizona, of a film called *Flaming Feather*, proved a turning point in motion picture policy for the entire national park system. The sight of Cavalry troops riding up under an ancient and fragile cliff dwelling and thrashing native shrubs of creosote bush at the base was too much.

From then on, filming was not prohibited, but studios had to agree to stiff provisions. For example, they would pay for rangers to stay on the set at all times to prevent damage to park features. And they would shoot at night, if possible, or in out-of-the-way locations, to avoid disturbing or distracting park visitors.

Policy Making

All this refinement of policy is easy to describe, but it is not easy to bring about. Every time any change is proposed as to how the parks are managed, it has to go through crucibles of controversy—first inside the National Park Service, and then outside.

You are dealing, after all, with prime real estate that belongs to every citizen. There was a time when most people gladly left the management of national parks to the staffs in charge. Park officials had it easy. They often had it their own way. They were the recognized authorities and what they said was the law. What they proposed was done without public interference. Even so, they dared not make a glaring mistake, lest they damage the public's domain, but they were free to carry out plans more or less on their own.

From the middle of Crater Lake National Park's first century to the end, however, the public became far more aggressive in its attitudes toward parks. New magazines and conservation organizations formed. Devereux Butcher, of the National Parks Association, was especially effective. Readers alerted to controversies helped put pressure on Congress. With the coming of television, the issues could be brought into living rooms.

One divisive issue that simmered and boiled behind the scenes for many years, and would have had quite an impact on Crater Lake, was whether some kind of vertical transport should be installed to simplify traffic within the parks.

Will Steel, you recall, was a strong proponent of that idea. He wanted to drill a tunnel down through the rim in order to get visitors quickly and easily to the surface of Crater Lake. Any superstructures for tramways above ground would be crushed under heavy winter snows.

Steel also backed construction of a road down to the lake, and was impatient with people who said that would mar the natural scene.

"Crater Lake belongs to the people," he said, "and if they want to deface the wall, they can do it. What good is scenery if you can't enjoy it? Every person who visits Crater Lake wants to go to the lake shore and out on the beautiful lake in a boat." In reporting this, the Portland *Oregonian* backed Steel in his "visionary project."

The whole idea of tramways in the national parks almost succeeded. Nationwide, America's historic predilection toward locating railroads, hotels and other visitor facilities as close to the sites of major interest as possible very nearly passed on to other forms of transportation.

As it was, roads were almost universally built where drivers and passengers could see the major features while driving. Grand Canyon is a good example, as is Crater Lake. Roads and parking lots were built to within yards of major features, most notably a lodge at Yellowstone's Old Faithful Geyser.

A natural extension of this would be to construct means of transportation to go down into canyons or lake basins on cable cars, or up onto mountain peaks in chair lifts. The benefits would be enormous. Roads would not have to be constructed. Revenue could be collected. More people could be served.

None of this was lost on foreign governments, and the building of tramways, teleferiques, and cable cars in national parks took place in earnest. As the director of Canadian national parks once told us, "We gave up early on that one."

Chair lifts were built on the rim of Teide Volcano in Teide National Park, Spain, up the side of El Avila National Park above Caracas, Venezuela, into Uludag National Park, Turkey, on Mount Ruapehu in Tongariro National Park, New Zealand, and elsewhere.

Over the years, such facilities were proposed for the American national parks, but found very difficult going. Reasons: Americans bent on saving natural beauty balked at yet another form of human intrusion; and in a country so large, such devices could be built in places outside national parks. For example, a ski lift adjacent to—rather than inside—Grand Teton National Park in Wyoming.

Still, the urge remained. Why not a tramway up El Capitán in Yosemite National Park? What a thrill that would be! Or down into the Grand Canyon? A superintendent of that park once told us that he was planning *eight* such devices into the canyon.

Every time this sensitive matter was raised, alongside efforts to build dams in national parks, it polarized public opinion. "As well flood the Sistine Chapel," said opponents, "so we can go out on a boat and get closer to the ceiling." Each time the matter was dropped.

But not forgotten. In the 1960's it was raised again with more vigor than ever. Congress, after all, had made it federal policy to provide the means for visitors to access and enjoy the national parks. A concerted effort was made to provide more facilities for more visitor use, including roads and alternate forms of transport, all under the banner. "Parks Are For People."

Opponents promptly dubbed that: "Parks Are For Motors—With People on Them." The effort became very serious and proponents argued, not without logic, that such devices, discreetly located, would eliminate road construction—which marred the landscape far more than tramways would.

As the argument heated, it was subjected to vigorous debate within the National Park Service. At a high-level long range planning meeting in Williamsburg, Virginia, during the first week of April, 1963, the matter was discussed with Interior Department advisers to get their reaction. Tramways were presented as a means of giving the aged and disabled access to more places within the parks. "Think about these people," went the argument. "You can't rule them out of society. Give them a chance!"

Sigurd Olson, an adviser to the Secretary of the Interior, and long-time author of such books as *Runes of the North*, answered without hesitation.

"They've *had* their chance!"

The room became suddenly silent. It was not the kind of language some government planners had ever heard.

Sig went on. "Let there always be some places on this planet that are not easy to get into. We need to save places for the young and the young at heart who want to

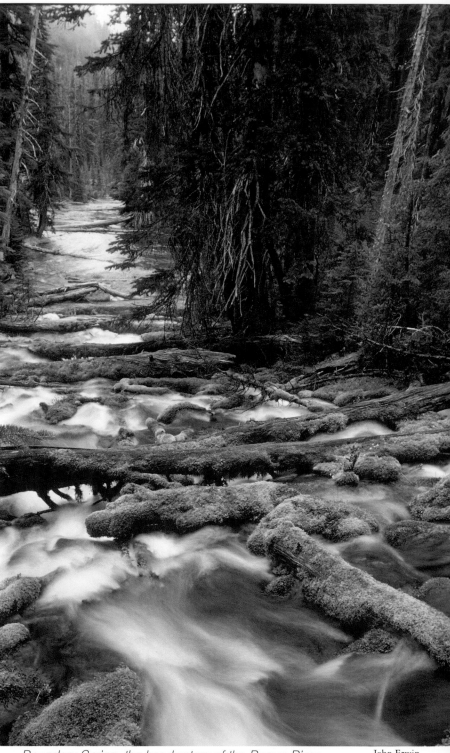

Boundary Spring, the headwaters of the Rogue River.   John Erwin

shoulder a backpack and put their faces to the wind and struggle under their own power to reach a destination. Give them a chance! Give them places that have no other means of access but toil of muscle and sweat of brow."

Despite Olson's spirited comments, and almost overwhelming public opposition, the Interior Department took the matter to Congress, along with requests to authorize more roads in the parks.

Always in the background was the hope, in distant quarters, that some day there would be tramways, chair lifts, cable cars or tunnels down from the rim in such places as Crater Lake.

On April 25, 1967, government policymakers tested before the Senate Interior Committee the idea of an aerial tramway for access to a major new national park.

It never left the ground. Senator Clifford P. Hansen, of Wyoming, pointed out very simply that other parks would seek tramways, too, and such a trend would "do great violence" to the traditional policy of preserving the pristine character of the parks.

Access

End of tramways. But as time went on, these efforts were swallowed in a major nationwide campaign called accessibility. Congress passed legislation mandating easier access for the disabled from streets and sidewalks into public buildings. That applied also to access to visitor centers, cafeterias, and other buildings in the national parks. In places, this process became very difficult. For the big question was: where do you stop? Do you turn every hiking trail in the national parks into a pathway suitable for wheelchairs and scooters? If so, you would have to redesign a great many trails in order to eliminate steep grades and modify access to hard-to-reach places.

This problem popped up on a grandiose scale along the 2,000-mile Appalachian Trail, between Mount Oglethorpe, Georgia, and Katahdin in Maine. To provide for the disabled, would the national hiking trail systems have to be turned into national riding

trail systems? Many people hike the entire 2,000 miles of The Appalachian Trail in a single year. Surely the disabled couldn't do that, the way the trail was.

But, oh yes, they could. One of the early through hikes of the entire trail was made by a 67-year-old grandmother. She was obviously not disabled, but neither was she in her youthful years. The 2,000-mile trek was made in 1990 by a blind man with a white cane and guide dog. Depending on the disability, not all disabled are immobile, and they, too, are attracted by outdoor challenges. For wild land managers, however, there are nightmarish visions of such people falling off the edge where the trail becomes a ledge on a cliff and one misstep could spell disaster.

One solution in the national parks, including Crater Lake, is to develop special trails for the disabled.

Still the matter remained, and how it was decided along The Appalachian Trail could affect the future of Crater Lake.

As Crater Lake National Park's first century came to a close, these matters were being subjected to new buzz words in the halls of public planning: "Scoping," for example, and "viewshed."

The trend seemed to be that you must use a wide approach when planning for recreation in units of federal park and recreation systems. If a watershed was a mountain valley saved for production of clean drinking water, then a viewshed was a landscape preserved in its natural condition because the public view of it was more important than anything else.

That would suggest that if any unit of the national park system were set up to preserve an outstanding scenic masterpiece like Crater Lake, then nothing, no special trails or roads or access, would be considered if it endangered the "viewscape" that is, the original reasons for setting aside that area. Such things will go right on being debated in the park's second century.

Safety

For many years it has been general policy to provide better access for disabled visitors, improve safety in hazardous areas such as thermal basins, and plan for more efficient movement of increasing numbers of park visitors.

For example, trails with rolling rocks on them can be hazardous, and sometimes officials have to decide whether to relocate the trail or to construct special safety features, all short of vertical transport by cable or cog railway. To reduce congestion some parks are modifying auto traffic by arranging visitor parking outside the boundary and using bus transport within.

Now consider another modern twist on park activities.

Suppose you are the Superintendent of Crater Lake National Park, and a group proposes to conduct a marathon run around the rim. You ask the staff to bring forth any problems they foresee, along with solutions. Close the rim road for a few hours? How? Set up first aid stations for runners at 8,000 feet? Bring in doctors? Nurses? Rescue helicopters? Portable water fountains?

In what is sometimes called the Age of Litigation, the federal government can be sued even if a tree falls on a car. The government has invited visitors and is therefore concerned about what happens to them. That is extreme, and things don't always work out that way, but it is something to keep in mind.

So, what would you do? Okay, maybe it's a lot of trouble for park staffs, but they are here to serve the public. It is a delightful setting for a major sport event. Won't harm resources. Might even entertain visitors.

So you approve it. In actuality, rim runs have been held since 1976, when the park's chief ranger, Dan Sholley, actually encouraged them as a Bicentennial event. They are still going on every second Saturday in August.

Performance

Now suppose some one comes to you and suggests that a popular music group perform on the brink of the lake. What would you do?

At this the park staff foresees problems. Not about music, but about the crowds that would likely arrive. If a hundred thousand people arrived in forty thousand cars, where would they park? Out in the forest? On the delicate, fragile meadows? What about traffic control?

The park, much as it might want to, simply could not handle so huge an onslaught. From past such events in the national parks, rangers have memories of facilities damaged by exuberant but rowdy crowds, with undertones of drug abuse.

So this time, to protect the park, you say no and wish you could help.

Thus it is clearly a different world out there now with new age challenges. As Crater Lake National Park glides into its second century one thing is sure; other problems will surface from time to time, the Superintendent will call in the staff, and decisions will be made.

Another inescapable fact is that it costs a great deal more to manage a national park today than it used to. In 1902, Congress allocated $2,000 to run Crater Lake National Park. In fiscal 2002 the draft budget was nearly $4,000,000. Part of that is inflation, of course, but you see how times have changed.

Congress oversees management of national parks. Increasingly, so does the public. It is the public which has to pay for such operations and citizens are keeping an eye on wild lands management. In Crater Lake's next century wild lands managers can count more than ever on support of the people. With greater public involvement, sophistication and vigor of opinion, the national parks have come to be not only of the people and for the people but by the people.

In the final analysis, what do Oregonians think of the national park today? We asked this question of John Dellenback, who for many years in the State legislature and the United States Congress represented the district in which Crater Lake National Park is located. His answer:

"Today the economy of Oregon has four principal legs: forestry, agriculture, tourism, and light industry. Crater Lake brings many tourists to Oregon and is therefore an important factor in the state's economy. But more importantly, we're extremely proud to have in this state such a wonderfully beautiful place, and a truly world class national park."

RUNNERS ON THE RIM

T he 25th annual rim run, in the year 2000. Runners gather beneath The Watchman at the starting point, then take off on signal. Some will run around the lake, some just portions of that distance. An ambulance follows them, as a precaution. The elevation is 8,000 feet and some runners may overestimate their abilities.

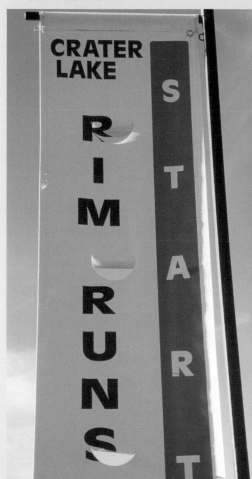

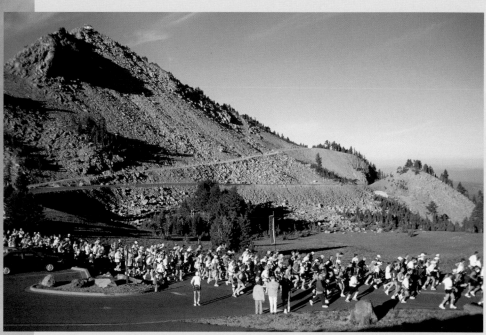

Runners starting.   Ann and Myron Sutton

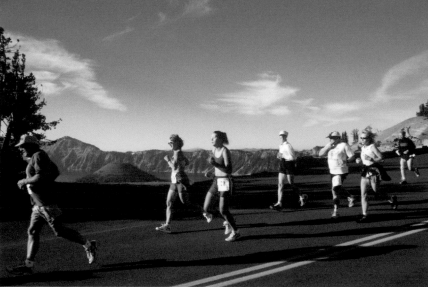

Runners on road.   Dan Schiffer

OTHER CRATER LAKES: EXTREMES IN THE TROPICS

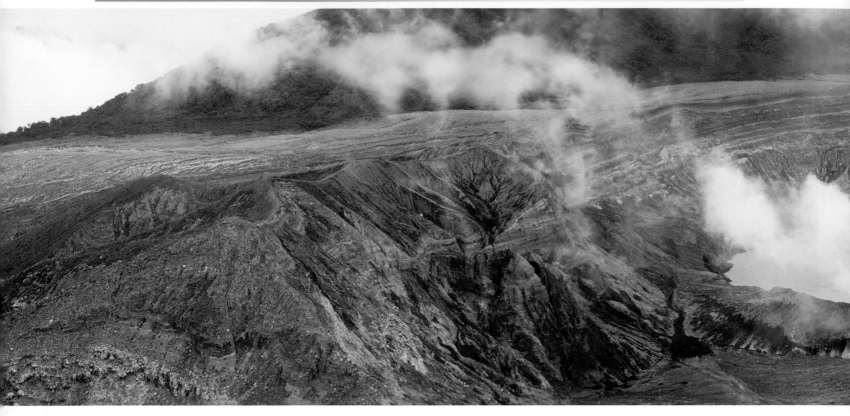

The muddy lake in Volcán Poás National Park, Costa Rica, often erupts and sends out clouds of steam. By contrast, a few hundred yards away, is Lake Botos, a cool and delightful crater lake surrounded by tropical forest.

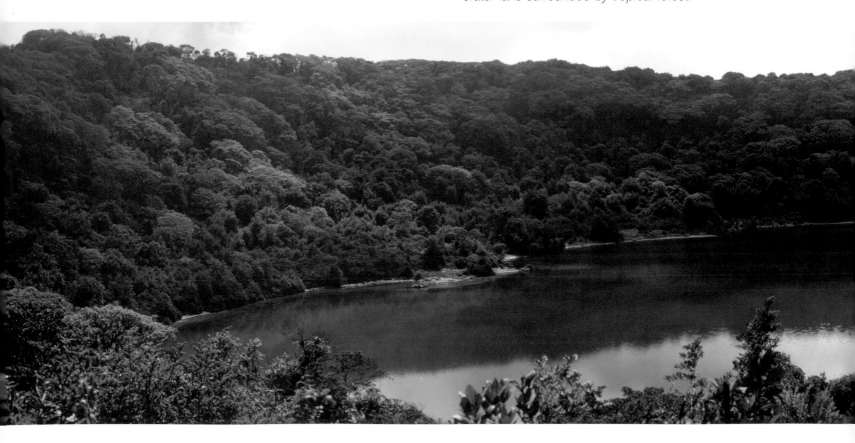

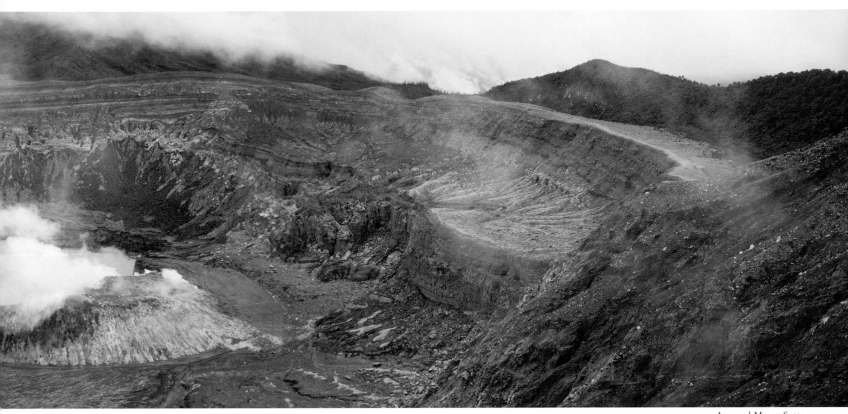

Ann and Myron Sutton

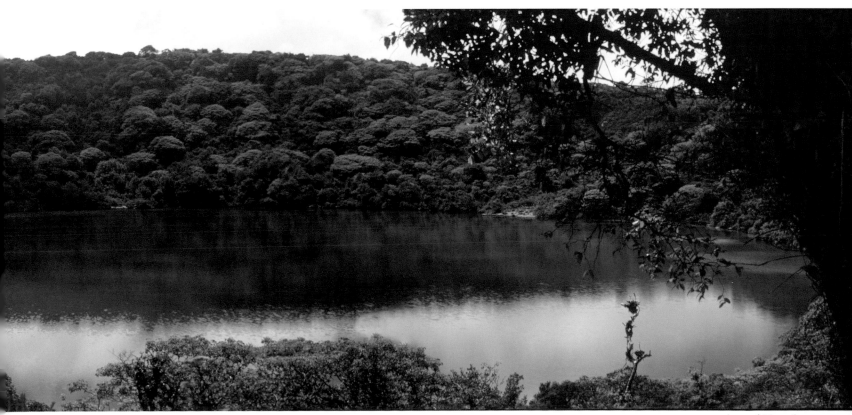

Ann and Myron Sutton

Paintbrush in bloom along trail up Wizard Island.

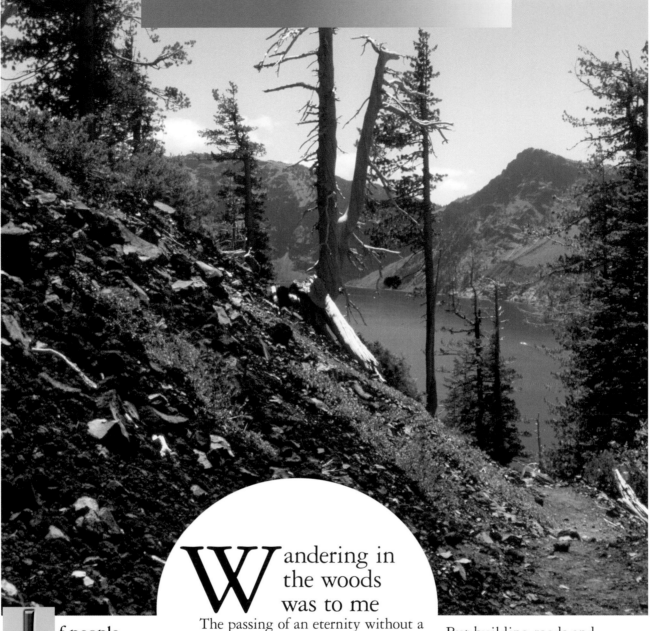

Jim Phelan

W andering in the woods was to me

The passing of an eternity without a weary moment.

Jean-Jacques Rousseau

If people were going to wander through the woods of Crater Lake National Park, right after it was established, they had to be able to get there, and then have some kind of protection after they arrived. Accordingly, the first important task was access. As a park for the people, no one could deny that these wild places had to be provided with amenities—and roads were first on the agenda.

But building roads and other types of construction in national parks called for some pretty special rules. Visitors to national parks are sometimes so dazzled by the scenery that they become mesmerized, confused, inattentive to danger. This is supposed to be the way for them to react, so if they are wandering around in a blissful daze, it is up to the foresight of construction engineers to think ahead, anticipate the troubles people can get into, and head off disaster.

First problem: how can a tourist drive along the rim and watch the lake without driving off the road? Or how can a tourist hike along a rim trail and keep to the path without falling over?

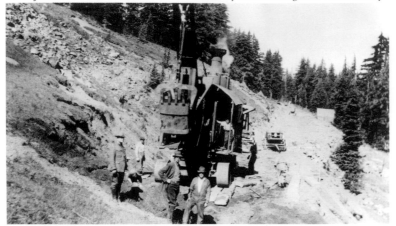

Early road construction.

You may say that it is up to the tourist to watch over self and family. That's true, of course, but this is an unfamiliar environment and the managing agency must take some responsibility for public safety.

Result number one: rock walls along the outer edge of roadways.

Result number two: walls or railings along the outer edges of rim trails.

Lest you think this is a simplistic task, have some pity for the poor engineer. Before anyone can construct a road anywhere, the nature of the underlying rock must be thoroughly examined, even if it calls for outside experts. It is not unknown in places of unstable rock for whole sections of steep cliffs to slide down into the valleys below. That might not happen for centuries, but the engineer has to assure that it *never* happens.

Every rivulet that drains from a slope must be provided with a bridge or culvert. The bed beneath a road must not be allowed to soak in water, lest you soon have a sump and a sunken road bed.

The planners try to avoid close encounters between tourists and yawning chasms, preferring to steer the road away from any place that might frighten drivers. Traffic patterns, if any, have to be analyzed. If visitors, for example, habitually try to park in a certain place to get a good picture, that tells the engineers to put a parking turnout there.

This may seem a bit imprecise, but a brilliant plan takes into account the public's desires and habits, and forestalls potential accidents. Given that the attention of drivers is often diverted in scenic places, the planners must avoid such things as sudden, unexpected sharp curves, distracting signs, and cliffs with falling boulders.

Then the approaches to cafeterias, hotels and other places of congested traffic may have to be repeatedly revised if travel to the park increases. That is reflected in the current revision of how a visitor arrives at the rim of Crater Lake and where he parks. The idea is to move the parking lot back from the rim.

To be sure, it is impossible to plan for everything. If a tourist wishes to disobey signs and leave the trail to clamber over cliffs, that is a self-induced invitation to death and transfiguration. Those railings along the edge of the rim—rangers get prematurely gray when they see young people balancing themselves on top of those railings.

Now you see the problem. The only way to curtail every problem might be to erect a 20-foot-high electrified fence completely around the rim. That's not a solution, of course, but it points up the fact that park managers can go just so far in trying to keep the public out of danger.

A visitor once remarked: "I never read signs; you can get in trouble that way."

But here we are dealing with extremes. The vast majority of visitors will do exactly as they are required to do, and are glad to have regulations to obey.

Bad Ideas

Planners, ever trying to be helpful to visitors, dream up a lot of "brilliant" ideas that never succeed. For example, noting a busy overlook somewhere along the rim, a planner might say: "Why not build a little rustic amphitheater there. Some hollowed-out logs for people to sit on, all facing the lake. Then the interpreter can stand on the rim and explain what they see."

On a list of bad ideas, that one would rank among the top ten. The interpreters themselves would be first to nix it.

For experience elsewhere has shown that in such a situation, the dozen or so visitors sitting on those benches would fidget uncomfortably all the time the

Eight – Construction

talk was in progress. And when the ranger swept his arms widely and moved backward a step, the audience would rise up white-faced and gasp in fright.

One would say: "Ranger, would you get away from the edge. You're scaring me to death."

Fearing that the ranger would fall backward over the edge, the audience would scarcely hear a thing he said.

Here's another one. The planners might design a museum with an open-air patio so that they can display old wagons and vintage autos as examples of early transportation to the park. When the summer season ends, they move the wagon and autos elsewhere, but then snow fills up the patio. Come spring, it melts and water runs over the floor of the museum, out into the lobby, and down the steps outside. Somebody forgot to put a drain in the patio.

You may laugh, but mistakes are very good teachers.

Next, the planner goes wild over exhibit ideas. "Why not," he asks, "build an exhibit in which we have a big screen showing volcanic clouds rising during an eruption? On each side of the viewing area, we'll build walls and install in them a dozen powerful woofers and tweeters. These high-tech loudspeakers will reproduce the loud explosions, lightning blasts, and multiple shrieks of projectiles falling to earth.

"Visitors will love it!"

Once again, the interpreter, with his understanding of human nature, will kill the plan. Such noises would distract visitors so much that they would not be able to concentrate on the other exhibits in the museum. And any employees sitting nearby at an information desk, hearing

that exhibit 250 times a day, would be basket cases by quitting time.

So then, hook up headphones, you say. Well, you'd want to discuss with health authorities the possible transfer of germs from one visitor to another. Then consider how children love to play with such "toys." And whether you would be creating a nightmare of electronic maintenance.

Better, perhaps, to capture sounds from live volcanes and put them on CDs or audio cassettes. That way, visitors can buy one to take home for audition at top volume. Some years ago, while on assignment in Yellowstone National Park, we were impressed by all the different sounds made by bubbling mudpots and erupting geysers. We decided to put microphones down into these cauldrons and record the burbles, sputters, and blurps. Then we collected these in a "Mudpot Concerto," which became an instant hit and was used in lectures worldwide. A concert of sounds is a neat idea in any national park.

Maintaining

Now for the hard part. Whatever the planners, engineers and construction workers install in a national park can't just be put there and forgotten. Everything from roads to trails to buildings has to be maintained in good condition. And this often entails a fight with Mother Nature herself. Especially at Crater Lake.

Which prompts us to ask, how does anyone cope with snowdrifts forty feet high? Blizzards that bring human activity almost to a standstill? And buildings that collapse under tons of snow?

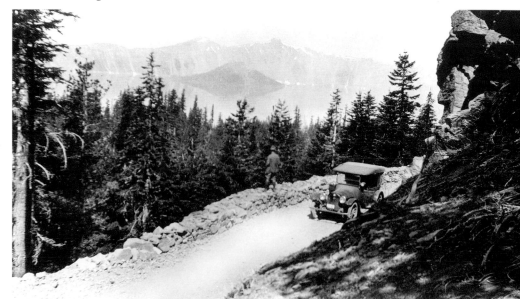

Early rim road with protective rock wall.   Courtesy Southern Oregon Historical Society

You might guess that maintenance employees at Crater Lake have a rapid turnover, but that would be a very wrong guess. One member of the maintenance staff worked at the park for *26 years*.

To get some answers, we interviewed Gordon Toso, Chief of Maintenance at Crater Lake National Park, who had been at the park for nine years.

Q. *Gordon, how can you possibly cope with all that snow, year after year? Isn't it hard work? Don't you feel worn down and worn out?*

A. Well, we get snow every month of the year. It is stressful.

Q. *Of course! Buried under all those mountains of snow...*

A. No. By stressful I'm not referring to winter.

Q. *(Pause.) What?*

A. It is stressful in summer, not winter.

Q. *You're joking. You meant the reverse?*

A. No. Winter's not the problem.

Q. *Gordon, you're defying every bit of logic an outsider has. He or she sees you up here buried in hundreds of inches of snow eight months out of the year, fighting to remove megatons of that stuff from the roads. Most homeowners are stressed when only a foot falls. If winter isn't stressful, you've lost us.*

A. (Smiling.) Summer is when we start *removing* all that snow. Of course, we plow all winter to keep the access road to the rim open. But the rest of the roads have to wait until summer.

Q. *Then why is that stressful?*

A. Because the snow has reached its maximum depth. It has compacted. It is as hard as ice. Visitors are arriving. They want to drive around the lake. The sun doesn't melt the snow fast enough to let them through. So we have to remove it by snowplows. Seventy per cent of our maintenance budget goes for snow removal.

Q. *Now wait. We're not talking fluffy stuff. You're saying that all snows are not born equal. By spring this stuff at Crater Lake turns into granular ice? Looks like you'd need saws or picks to cut the ice away.*

A. We use three snow-throwers, the largest 930 horsepower. Once the ice is cleared away, we only have a short period in which to repair, recondition and service all of our equipment before the snow begins to fall in early autumn.

Q. *Okay. That's stressful. But when you are clearing the snow away from roads, don't you find other things that have accumulated during blizzards, shifting snow, etc?*

A. We have to cope with fallen trees on the roadway, rocks, picnic tables, trash cans, signposts snapped off...

Q. *Stop! We understand. But what if you undercut a high drift, and cause a few tons of ice to fall on you?*

A. Well, we try first to undercut any cornices above so that it's safe to plow at the bottom. We've never had snow fall on us.

Q. *Do you find the remains of bears or other animals that died and got buried on the roadway? Or hungry bears just out of hibernation?*

A. No.

Q. *Do visitors ever slide off the road?*

A. Yes, maybe a roll-over into a ditch. That's all.

Q. *You must have a lot of people on your staff to cope with all this?*

A. We have 20 permanent employees and up to 20 seasonals.

Q. *And they like their work?*

A. Sure. But there's one problem. The work is so intense a lot of the time that they can't take any days off. Our work is a continuous operation.

Q. *No days off each week? No vacations?*

A. Not in the busy season. We depend on them, and they do a good job.

Q. *Obviously. On another subject, some parks have whole sections of road fall out once in a while. Does that happen here?*

A. No. The road has porous volcanic rocks and good drainage under it.

Q. *What do you do for a vacation in winter? Go to Alaska?*

A. (Laughs.)

Q. *Must be awfully stifling for families closed in all winter. Do you have a school bus come up here?*

A. Yes.

Q. *What do you do for recreation?*

A. Ski. Snowshoe.

Q. *(Laughing.) What else? Snowball fights?*

Eight – Construction

A. Potlucks. Parties. Card games. Some families live in nearby cities, and employees commute to the park.

Q. *Have you solved the problem of buildings being crushed by snow? Looks like these high pitched roofs wouldn't let any snow accumulate.*

A. Well, snow can pile up against them. Depending on its depth it can weigh 490 pounds per square foot. Sometimes snaps big rafters within.

Q. *One last question: what do you do with sewage and garbage from so many visitors in lodge, cafeteria, campgrounds etc?*

A. We have sewage lagoons. Garbage is recycled and eventually hauled to landfills in nearby towns.

Q. *Thanks, Gordon. Give your hard-working staff our very, very best regards.*

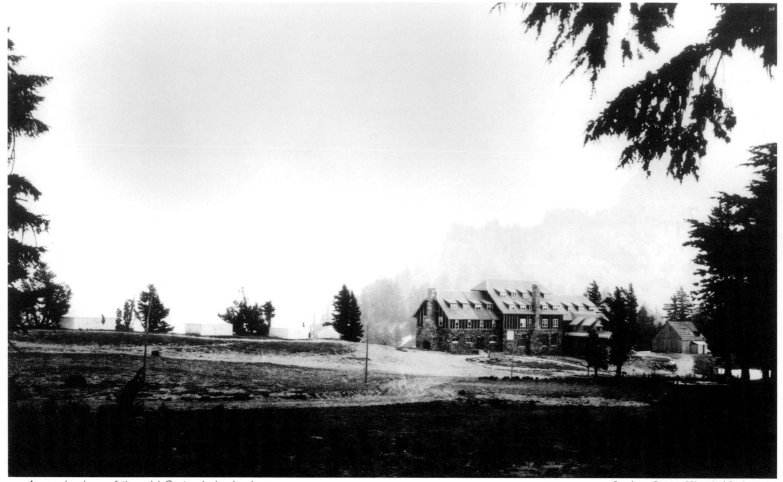

An early view of the old Crater Lake Lodge.

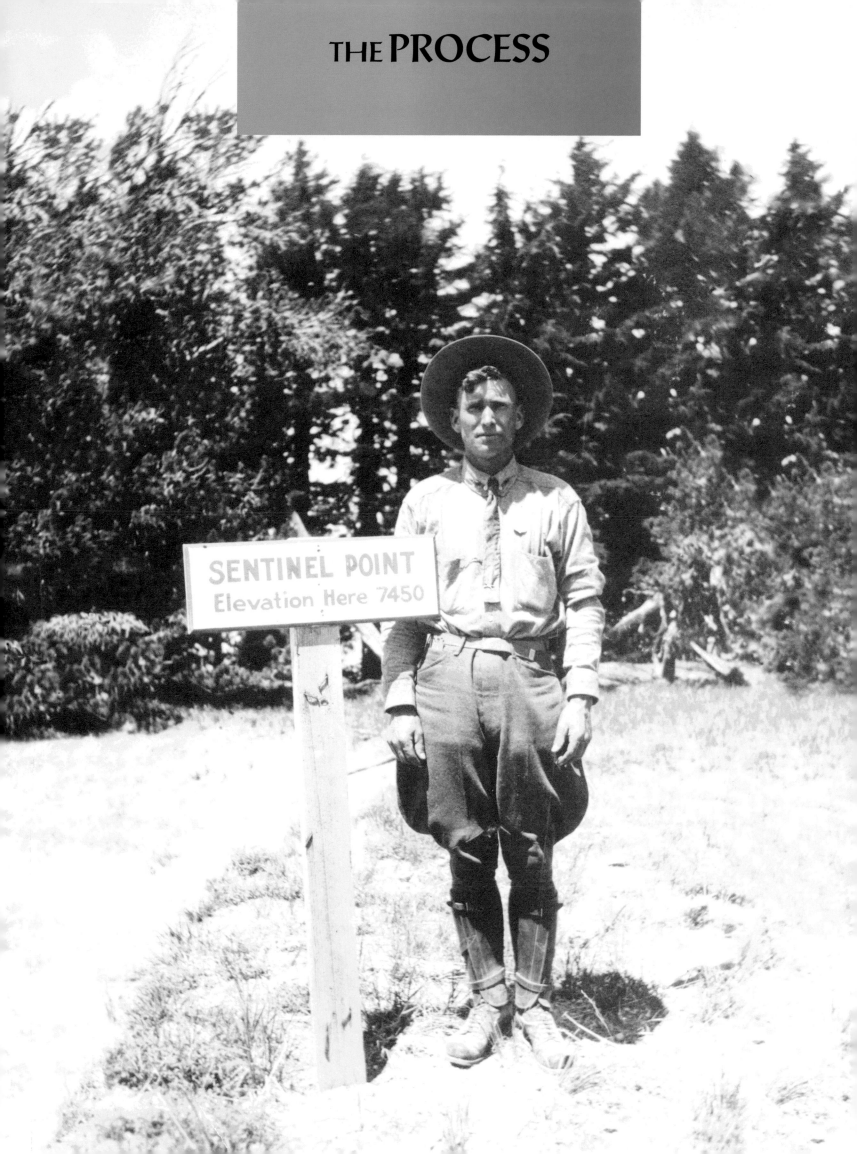

SENTINEL POINT
Elevation Here 7450

Nine
RANGERS

Anyone who perceives the lives of national park rangers as riding mountain trails and singing *Ah! Sweet Mystery of Life* is overdue for a dose of reality.

It is true that serving visitors as a ranger is one of the most satisfying jobs on earth. Parks are exhilarating places in which to live. Pure air, spring water, and forests fragrant with the aroma of pine and fir are very enticing. So is the snow. Many young rangers would almost sell their souls for an assignment to a snowy park. Said one ranger newly assigned to Crater Lake National Park, "I feel like I've entered heaven."

Some visitors envision rangers spending their winters with feet propped up to the fire. That notion also needs updating. There is, in fact, never a dull moment. One common question is, "What do you rangers do in winter?" A pat answer would be "Catch up on things we didn't get done in the summer." But that doesn't work at Crater Lake.

For insights on the life of a ranger in Crater Lake National Park, we talked with George E. Buckingham, long time chief ranger at the park. He answers that question about what the rangers do in winter this way:

"Winter at Crater Lake is so different from summer that there is little comparison. The things we need to get done in the summer cannot be done in the winter. It is an entirely different approach to work and to life. Summer is a mad dash to deal with visitor problems, try to cover the backcountry,

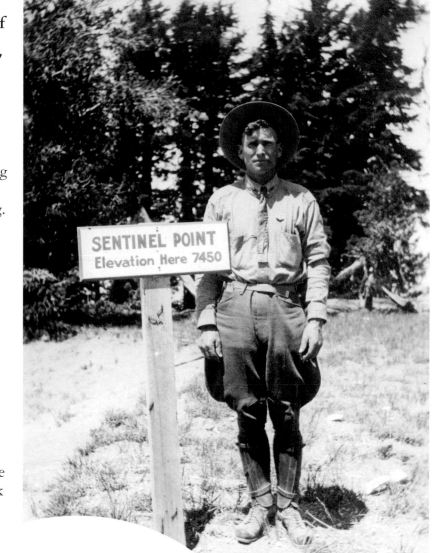

John Maben, courtesy National Park Service

We do not go into the woods to rough it; we go to smooth it.

We get it rough enough at home.

George Washington Sears

see some backcountry, etc. Winter is dealing with snow and snow related visitor problems. Stuff that didn't get done in summer has to wait until another summer, just like winter stuff has to wait until another winter."

The rangers live and work amid an endlessly changing panorama, and it is not unusual for them to feel that summertime visitors miss most of the excitement. At lower elevations, outside the park, there are brilliant yellow aspen trees and vivid

Woman in ranger uniform, 1950s.

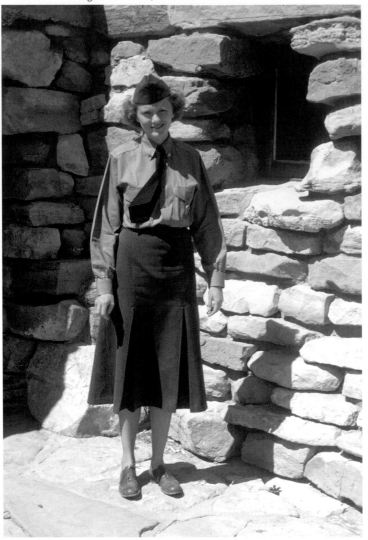

Myron Sutton

scarlet maples along the Rogue River. Up in the park, there just isn't any autumn, and no spring either. "There are two seasons," Buckingham says, "a long, long winter and a short glorious summer. The change is rather abrupt."

All this does not a paradise make, but it's close. The other factor that enriches rangers' lives is the people they meet. Travelers from every state, province and country come to Crater Lake to see the scenery, and if the startling views raise multiple questions, the visitors know exactly where to get answers. Rangers are not only buddies, pals, and friends in need, they are also walking encyclopedias. No wonder they are looked upon as heroes.

Enter another factor. In the early half of the 20th century, the ranger's job was thought to be too rough and dangerous for women. It was not until the 1950s that females began to be widely accepted on all-male ranger staffs. When they were, they had to wear not very flattering uniforms designed for men. And they still seemed out of place to some eyes. It was not unknown for a young boy to sidle up to a lady ranger, scowl, and snarl in disgust, "You're a *woman!*" That has changed, and indeed, some visitors feel more at ease talking to a woman ranger.

Over the years, these men and women in green and gray have earned a reputation as some of the friendliest and most helpful people in the public service. That distinctly does not mean, however, that they are casual in enforcing the law. Thieves who might have thought so at Crater Lake have found themselves behind bars in the nearest county jail. For this is federal property. It belongs to all the people, and any offense committed on it gets attention far beyond the expectations of the average felon.

It may seem incongruous that in such peaceful and inspiring surroundings there should be any laws at all, much less lawbreakers. But no park is a Shangri-La. With more and more visitors crowding into national parks worldwide, modern society is such that people sometimes bring their evils with them. A traveler who ignores this could be victimized.

Prowlers are delighted to discover station wagons with windows that showcase everything inside. They surreptitiously peek in the windows of any car and rejoice to find cash, cameras, and credit cards lying on the seats in plain sight. That is an open invitation. Sometimes, a brief window smash makes the visitor's property theirs. More often they will utilize a slim Jim or lock punch.

Such "car clouting," however, is more of a problem elsewhere than it is at Crater Lake. But such theft happens, and it doesn't take much effort to guard against it. For rangers, more common problems at Crater Lake include dealing with emergency medical services, search and rescue, resource protection (poaching), and motor vehicle traffic.

However distasteful it may be to contemplate crimes in public parks, the problem is universal. A modern sign in many parks reads, "Unsafe to leave valuables locked in your car."

So what's to do with them?

Rangers can't be in a thousand places at once. If they have their hands full with a heart attack victim at the edge of the lake, or a child trapped on a rocky ledge, or a forest fire, the disappearance of your credit cards sinks into pretty low priority. No one protects possessions better than you yourself. Precautions you take in crime-ridden urban neighborhoods near home could apply just as well to wilderness areas. Never rely on someone else to protect your valuables. Hide them. Take them with you. Shun fancy, saddle-stitched camera bags that brand you as super rich.

If you come and go without any problems, no one will be happier than the rangers. They have simple rules to keep your travels safe and pleasant, *(see Ranger Rules at end of chapter)* but

to cinch this matter and achieve your own peace of mind, apply a little creative thought yourself. For example, if you are going on a very long hike and will be gone for days, find some place other than your car in which to leave valuables.

There's another challenge unique to nature reserves such as this. If you take a small car to a trail head, and leave some fresh beef steak inside in a cooler, you may discover what hungry, omnivorous bears can do to cars to get inside. They have opened enough coolers to know what these ice chests contain. This is the animals' domain, not yours, and the laws they obey are theirs, not yours.

At Crater Lake, coolers are the most popular items sought by bears, especially in the Mazama campground. As Buckingham puts it, "Rangers spend a lot of time educating campground visitors. They put up signs, hand out leaflets, talk and talk, confiscate coolers and write violation notices. We have a saying, 'An habituated bear is a dead bear.' [Meaning that if any bear becomes a problem bear by repeatedly attacking coolers left out by visitors, the bear may have to be relocated or eliminated.] Our job is to keep the bears alive. If we have to confiscate coolers and write tickets to protect the bears, that is the lesser of evils."

A Ranger's Life

There is no such thing as a "typical ranger's day," but we can call up a fictitious one that could be close to the mark.

Driving down the road in a patrol car, a ranger comes upon a car parked in the middle of the highway, its doors wide open, its occupants dashing wildly into the woods to photograph a deer and fawn. That's unsafe, but the visitors are too excited to realize what they are doing. If by any chance they are trying to photograph a bear, that adds another layer of danger and foolhardiness.

The ranger flicks on warning lights to slow

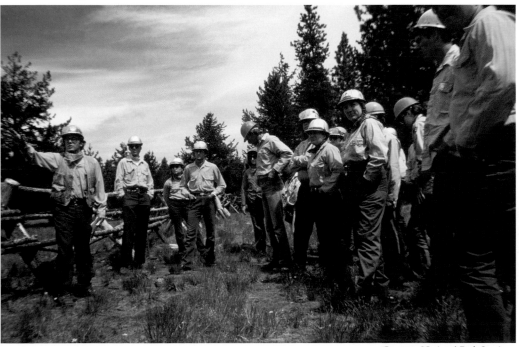

Forest fire training at Crater Lake National Park.

Courtesy National Park Service

85

down traffic, gets out, closes the doors of the travelers' car, and calls for the family to come back. Time for a short and friendly lecture on highway safety and wild animals.

Actually, this scenario occurs more often in winter than in summer. Buckingham says that "typically that vehicle belongs to snow boarders, surprised that anyone would mind them blocking both lanes of traffic. After getting through that issue, the ranger will begin talking about winter survival, having noticed a lot of cotton clothing. Often these are very young people with no knowledge of dealing with winter. [Synthetic insulation materials, unlike cotton, insulate even when wet, and synthetic outerwear that effectively sheds water while transpiring perspiration, can and does mean the difference between an enjoyable experience and a deadly one.] Education in progress."

Farther on, a chunk of basalt has fallen on the roadway, and rocks that size could cause accidents. This especially occurs after thunderstorms and during snow melt, when lots of rocks are coming down. So the ranger parks the patrol car carefully, then removes the rock, and goes on.

Around the bend, wisps of smoke are observed back in the woods. A lightning storm last night. Tree hit. Beginning to flame up.

It is often quite difficult to find such a small fire. In densely forested areas like Crater Lake National Park, rangers and fire-fighters can search for hours or days and still not find the fire. Perhaps it has gone out by itself. But if the ranger is first on the scene, he or she knows that you don't just go over and slap a few shovels full of dirt on the snag or tree. Or get out a fire extinguisher. Or douse the fire with a pail of water. You call the park's fire crew and they will arrive in special protective clothing so that they can cope with any sudden breakout of flames. The ranger sticks around until the fire crew arrives.

Next, there's a group of young people playing games of devil-may-care on the rim. The ranger's mind is filled with recollections of poor souls who have accidentally gone over the edge. What follows plays out something like theater.

RANGER (walking up): You're a little close to the edge.

DAREDEVIL: We don't mind heights.

RANGER: I don't either. What I do mind is going down to the bottom of that cliff and scraping up the remains. Takes about eight hours.

DAREDEVIL (surprised): People fall from here?

RANGER: Rock's deceptive, crumbly. The slope is very steep.

DAREDEVIL: Looks pretty solid to me.

RANGER (looking downward): See all those rocks at the bottom of the slope down there?

DAREDEVIL (peering over): Yeah.

RANGER: Those were once up here, right where you're standing.

DAREDEVIL (grinning and shifting away from the edge): Ruins your day, huh?

RANGER: Yeah. If you don't mind, fellas? (Exits.)

DAREDEVIL (Calling). Thanks ranger. Appreciate that.

Buckingham's comment on such an event:

"This is indeed a common occurrence. It isn't so much that the rock breaks under their feet. Usually they misjudge how steep and slippery the slope is. It can be deceiving. Starting out doesn't seem too bad, but then the rock gradually gets steeper until the visitor either slips and falls or stops, unable to go up or down.

"Often, the motivation is get to the lake edge. That beautiful lake can be a powerful attraction. We often will rope down to stranded hikers and belay them up to the top. Or, we find them at the bottom and will boat them across to the Cleetwood Trail. A violation notice is almost always issued in such cases. If an injury has occurred, the resultant operation can be very time and resource consuming.

"A fall in the caldera is often fatal. While I was at Crater Lake, it seemed that this happened every 2-3 years. Recovering a body is a traumatic experience for all concerned. Like rescuing an injured person, the operation can be very involved. We have had single operations involving hiking, technical rope-work getting to the scene, technical evacuation (litter, etc.), crews of people carrying a litter, supplies, etc., boat transport, ground ambulance and helicopter transport, all for a single victim.

"Afterwards, a Critical Incident Stress Debriefing is usually conducted to provide emotional support for personnel involved in the incident. Park rangers, just like any emergency services public servant, are often emotionally traumatized by exposure to such incidents. I know I was for a very long time, probably still am. We, as an agency, are better at dealing with it now than we used to be. Most people do not realize the extent of the emotional price we pay to be park rangers. These kinds of incidents impact the entire park staff for days afterwards."

At the next overlook, the ranger is accosted by travelers with puzzled looks. "Did the top really blow off this mountain?"

The ranger could reply with studious demeanor that volcanic action at Crater Lake was initiated through an arcuate set of vents, and then a Plinian column formed with widespread distribution of tephra. But not all visitors are geologists, and rangers know that. A better response: "Molten matter blew out through holes in the top, reducing pressure inside and hollowing out the mountain, so the top eventually collapsed rather than blew off."

Next the ranger comes to a car parked along the roadside at the edge of the forest. A man and woman are busy carrying a piece of lightweight pumice rock to their car. The woman points to it proudly as the ranger approaches and says, "Isn't it beautiful? I'm going to hollow it out, put a plant in it, and set it on our east patio deck. It'll be a souvenir of Crater Lake."

The ranger smiles, his golden badge glinting in the sunlight. "And all the rest of your life you'll feel guilty for having broken the law."

She turns white, her smile vanishing. The man asks, "This is against the law?"

The lady says, "A piece of rock. Look how many there are."

The ranger responds: "Half a million?"

"What?" she asks.

"If word got out, all the other 500,000 visitors to the park this summer might want one."

She looks at his badge and slumps. "You're a ranger?"

"Yes, ma'am. And this is a national park."

They drop the rock. "Are you going to take us to jail?" she asks with a trembling voice. "We didn't know—."

"I tell you what," replies the ranger. "Why don't you just take it back where you got it?"

They carry it back, drop it, and return.

"Oh, ranger," the lady says, subdued. "I'm so sorry…"

The ranger smiles and pulls a park folder from the patrol car. "I'm going to autograph this folder and give it to you as a souvenir of Crater Lake."

The lady takes it, giving the ranger a warm and vigorous handshake..

"Hey!" says the man. "That's probably against the law, too!"

They depart laughing. The ranger watches until they disappear around a bend.

This may seem trite, but it is a composite story edited from real life. Such things happen. The ranger could have delivered a stern lecture, taken them to a magistrate, and made them feel like enemies of the state. But park rangers know the complexities of human behavior. It's part of their job. They won't give in when it comes to obeying park regulations. But, with a little kindness, they can turn potential violators into lifelong champions of the American heritage.

On a more serious note, the parks are locations of all kinds of vegetation, and as the first century of this park ended, society at large was taking very seriously alternative medicines from wild plants. A ranger could come upon poachers searching for specific plants, or, believe it or not, gangs preying upon the poachers. Rangers can use stakeouts and other methods to capture suspicious characters, and these methods are very effective. This is a dangerous game, of course. The parks are not designed to be battlefields, but throughout the American national park system, four National Park Service rangers have been murdered in the line of duty since 1973. Others were killed before 1973 as well. A heavy price to pay for eternal vigilance.

Rangers at Crater Lake, understandably, have a close attachment to this "people's park", and patrol it day and night. They have a lot of friends in the FBI, Sheriff's Departments, Oregon State Police, National Guard, and Forest Service—all of whom are very good neighbors. And if those agencies are ever needed to back up the rangers, their personnel can arrive within minutes or hours. Prospective poachers on these hallowed grounds could find their mission interrupted, and arrests can be made.

Back to the visitor. If you knew how many times people come to a ranger for advice on cameras and photos, you'd know why they are trained in photography. They are also trained in public speaking. Getting up and giving a talk the first time may be a little scary, but the rangers soon find themselves comfortable in this and it is their job. Throughout their careers, they must speak with authority, whether it's to a pair of visitors or an auditorium filled with people.

And woe be unto them if they are insensitive to contemporary feelings on race, gender and religion. The slightest misstatement could send their careers into a tailspin. Expect them, therefore, to be completely neutral, respectful, and admiring of human diversity.

Rangers carry guns, and they know how to use them. "It's part of the uniform," says Buckingham. "We are pretty good marksmen, and hold our own in interagency competitions."

If that is a reminder of the evils of urban life, from which travelers are trying to escape, don't blame the rangers. Their job is to keep this place as close to paradise as humanly possible, to protect the park as well as visitors. They are trained at the Federal Law Enforcement Training Center. At the park they learn more about on-site techniques of pursuit and arrest as well as search and rescue, and have the help of full-time experts if a case gets nasty.

To put it in the contemporary vernacular: "Don't mess with the rangers."

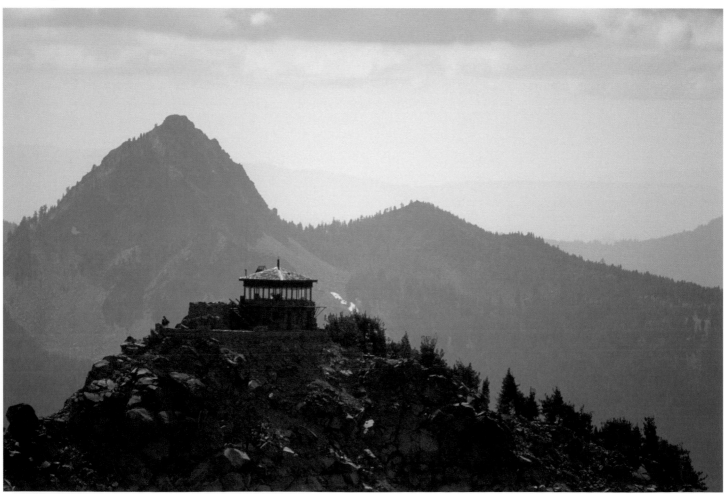

Watchman lookout with Union Peak in background.

Jim Phelan

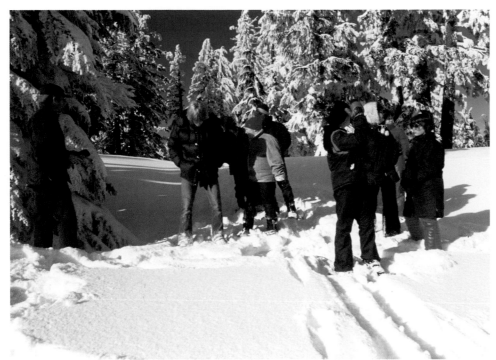

Winter outing with ranger.   Courtesy National Park Service.

He was so grateful (the bag contained all of his group's cash, passports, etc.) that he wanted to give us $100. We, of course, would not accept the gratuity, but he happily put the $100 into our Emergency Medical Services donation box. That is a great 'help'."

Down through the years, rangers in Crater Lake National Park have been involved in sometimes bizarre and deadly tasks. They have had to deal with such challenges as avalanches, murders, drug abuse, poaching, trees blown down across highways, clashes between wagon trains and automobiles, fires in buildings, capture and removal of problem bears, runaway youths in stolen cars, reports of wolves and Sasquatches.

They are trained in emergency medical services. They have to be involved in putting out building fires because municipal fire departments are a long way off. They collect fees, help maintain trails, and sometimes get involved with tort claims. One ranger is an expert in educating young people to seek other life styles. The program he teaches is called "D.A.R.E." which stands for Drug Abuse Resistance Education.

They have secret ways to uphold the law, too. One of them, not so secret, is getting help from average citizens. "I can relate lots of stories," Buckingham says, "about ordinary citizens providing help to Crater Lake rangers, often without being asked."

"For example?" we asked.

"Well, very often at Crater Lake, visitors will help us push a wheeled litter up the Cleetwood Cove Trail. We get lots of reports from visitors. These include the gamut from crime to injuries to smoke to maintenance needs, and constructive criticism. One fall an Oregon State Police volunteer hunting outside the park reported another hunter in the park and we were able to track him to an elk kill and make a good case. This was widely reported and did our cause a lot of good, both from having caught the bad guy and the fact that other hunters were serving as 'eyes and ears.'

"One time when I was at Bryce Canyon National Park in Utah, we 'rescued' a bag the French Air Force Attaché had dropped over the edge…

Then there are other problems. The most common are auto accidents on slippery roads. Vandalism began in 1912, with damage to the lodge and furnishings. In the summer of 1994 there were a record 42 forest fire smoke reports investigated and/or fought.

The matter of grazing sheep and cattle seems to have diminished. Says Historian Steve Mark, "Sheep grazing supposedly ceased in 1896 after arrests were made, with the first forest reserve ranger patrols of the park area

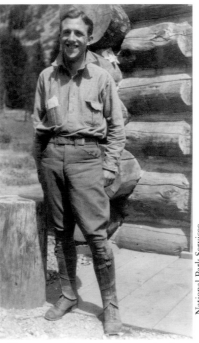

National Park Service

Ranger uniform in the early days at Crater Lake.

in 1898. Timber trespass, though admittedly difficult to confirm one way or the other, does not seem to have been a problem here, given the difficulties of transport and easy availability of good lumber elsewhere."

At first, there weren't any rangers at all, and for a long time there weren't enough to patrol the whole park. The first uniforms—breeches and leather leggings—came to Crater Lake in 1914. Not until the creation of the National Park Service in 1916 was the uniform modified and made consistent throughout the parks. There is some question about the origin of that distinctive hat. Some say that the rangers unabashedly borrowed their hat from the Canadian Mounties, and put a silver Sequoia cone on the leather band (the cone is now gold). Others trace it back to origins with the U.S. Army.

That hat, broad brimmed as it was (and is) widened a ranger's head by six inches, and whenever the hat inadvertently struck a tree, the ranger felt like he'd been hit with a sledgehammer. But the hat gave a visual notability to set park personnel apart...and has been famous ever since.

As time went on, U.S. park rangers became some of the most exalted personnel in the public service, guarding the national heritage year round, with notable bravery, insight, and devotion to duty. And don't misunderstand. However tough the job, however rough the weather, and however dangerous their tasks, they love it.

If eventually a ranger gathers rich experience, it may be time to move on up the administrative ladder. If so, it is quite a life style change. As

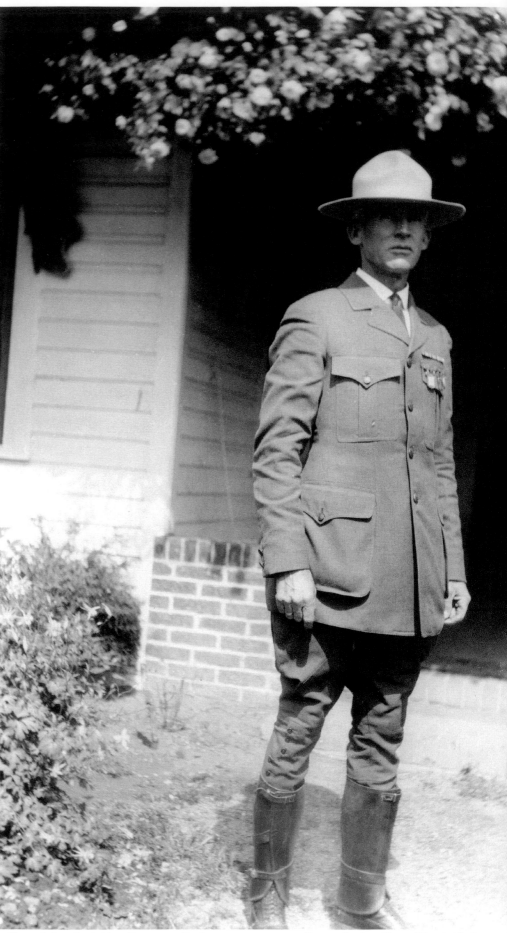

Superintendent Alex Sparrow, Crater Lake National Park, circa 1920.

Courtesy Southern Oregon Historical Society

an administrator of Coorong National Park in Australia once said, "I started out as a forest officer, and now I'm an office forester." We once chided Buck Evans, long time Chief Ranger of Crater Lake National Park, about this and got a calm response. "Not for me. I want to stay right where I am, doing just what I'm doing." And he did.

George Buckingham says that a description of the trials of park rangers may "sound like I was unhappy or sorry for my career choice. Nothing could be further from the truth."

RANGER RULES FOR A SAFE AND HAPPY TRIP

1. Drive safely. Keep to the speed limits. Wild animals can get confused in the presence of automobiles and leap across the road in front of your car. Wandering tourists, mesmerized by the scenery, can be a hazard, too, and it is up to you to avoid them when they amble across a roadway.

2. Leave your valuables home. No one expects you to wear diamond jewelry in this environment.

3. Keep cash, checks and cameras at your side.

4. Lock your car, but remember that locks merely keep out the honest.

5. When in doubt, ask.

6. When in trouble, stay where you are and call or send for help.

7. When hiking, watch your step. Rolling rocks make trails in steep places dangerous.

8. Stay away from the edge. In winter, the rim is slippery, and people have skied and snowshoed over the edge to their deaths.

9. Never pick any kind of vegetation or harm wild animals. Life in this climate isn't easy as it is. And besides, disturbing nature is a federal offense in national parks.

10. Help other people wherever you can. Such good will makes you a hero to them and the rangers. However, don't go beyond your capabilities, i.e., don't move an injured person if the problem seems to be a broken back, pelvis, leg, arm, neck, etc. Rangers are trained in First Aid, but if the case gets urgent, a helicopter flight can be arranged for trained medics to transport the victim to a hospital.

11. Report hazards such as fallen rocks or trees on the roadway.

12. Research your trip well in advance. Know what you want to do before you arrive. Nothing enriches your trip more than this. Write Crater Lake National Park, Box 7, Crater Lake National Park, Oregon 97604.

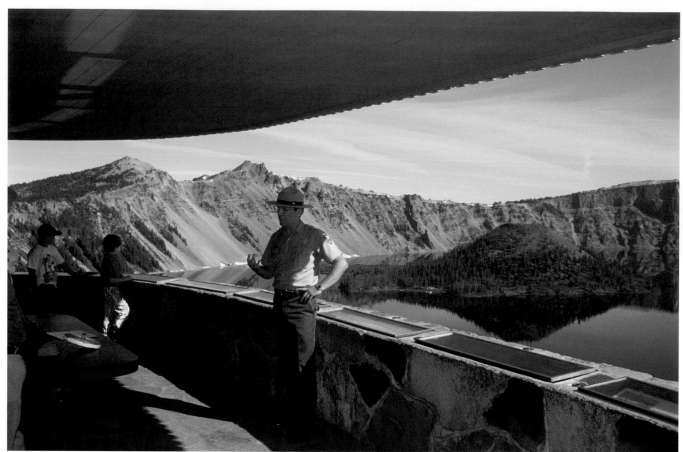

Interpreter at Sinnott Memorial.

Jim Phelan

Ten
INTERPRETERS

As we arrive at the rim, our eyes take in the scene with disbelief and, once we catch our breath, the next inquiry is logical: "What happened?"

On the ranger staff, that is the province of the interpreters, whose job it is to convert the sometimes difficult language of biologists, geologists, ecologists, and historians into terms the untrained can absorb. For a great many things happened here at Crater Lake, over a long period of time, and the interpreters represent multiple disciplines that require years of training.

It goes beyond that. An interpreter has the power to awe. By making the complex understandable, a visitor's life can be completely turned around. It is not unknown for a young visitor to decide, after listening intently to an interpretive talk, that "I've finally found what I want to study in college."

For others, the interpreter at Crater Lake can leave a visitor in head-shaking disbelief and wonder. Struck with awe that so much has been discovered about what was thought to be so "simple" a lake. That geology and ecology are so astonishing. That human beings have had the sense not to occupy this terrain and build housing developments on it, as is done so much elsewhere, but to preserve it in its natural state.

Among their ranks, the interpreters, whose fame draws so many people to their sides, have a profound and enduring maxim: Interpretation leads to understanding and understanding leads to protection.

Said one: "There are no better places to make Americans proud of their country then here in the national parks." Said another: "Once visitors see one of these parks, they want to protect them all." We would take that further by saying that there are thousands of national parks around the world where we can be very proud of the planet on which we live, and very lucky to be here.

This may seem like excessive pie-in-the-sky thinking, but it is as real as today. It undoubtedly happens thousands of times around the world each day as interpreters step up in front of an audience and begin to talk.

No thoughtful visitor can stand for long on the edge of this stupendous caldron without wondering how it was formed.

Howel Williams

We see them everywhere: on the rim of Grand Canyon, in the valley of Yosemite, on a tour of the Florida Everglades, on the rim and trails of Crater Lake, at campfire programs in the evening, slide talks in visitor centers, boat trips, club meetings in surrounding towns and cities, and at colleges and universities everywhere. They are very much in demand.

The skills required of interpreters are enormous. They must love people. They must love talking. They must love the outdoors (and often indoors at historic locations). They must be thoroughly acquainted with the vicissitudes of human behavior. They should be able to inject into their talks a little humor that sets visitors at ease.

Example: an interpreter was once interrupted by a listener shrieking in fear. "Look over there!" she shouted, pointing to a little old lady, white hair flowing down her back, starting vigorously up a mountain trail.

"Ranger, do something! She'll get hurt! Go stop her!"

The naturalist followed the woman's gaze, saw all other listeners turn and watch with trepidation, and then said: "Ma'am, I would if I thought I could catch up with her."

An interpreter must be skilled at public speaking. There is sometimes a fine line between delivering what is intelligent and understandable and what seems like baby food for the ear. Even talks delivered to young people

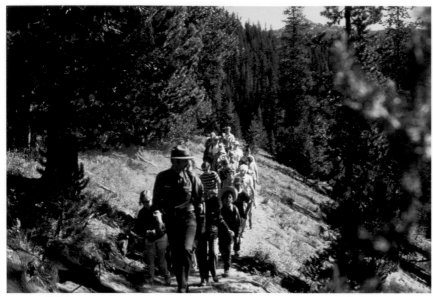

Guided walk on forest trail.

National Park Service

Reading the Trailside

Explaining something to someone else is a task as old as civilization. Ramses II did it through scribes and artists, Plato through the dialogues of Socrates, and Confucius through the Analects. The superintendents and staff in the early days of Crater Lake National Park had little to interpret: few scientific studies, few research records. Nothing on birds but heresay. Nothing on mammals but visual observation. And little on wild flowers because grazing sheep had consumed them all.

With its establishment as a national park, Crater Lake became a *destination* of major significance. As the national parks grew in number, and more people came to them, the demands for answers to questions grew. It began to

must be on a plane much higher than baby talk. An interpreter never talks down to any audience. The focus is on higher concepts that require the listener to reach upward and outward.

The interpreter's voice must reach outward, too. Like an actor on the stage, he or she must project the voice as far out as the last person in the audience; round the lips, enunciate clearly, and use a slow and easy pace that relaxes the audience. That's not easy when all that's overhead is sky, and there is no echo chamber to amplify the voice.

If it is a talk to a group of geologists, then such terms as tephra and Plinian columns can be used. Indeed, difficult terms can be used before lay audiences, providing new words are first explained. The interpreter assumes that every audience is intelligent and capable of learning new ideas.

And when illustrations are used, as in slide programs, the interpreter takes care not to use inferior pictures. In modern times, when photos of exceptional quality are seen in books,

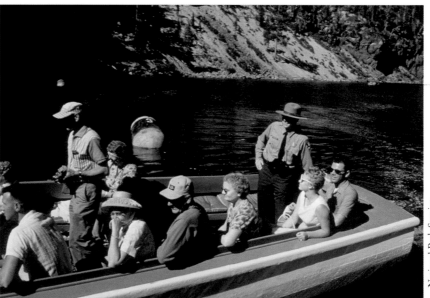

Interpreter on boat trip, Crater Lake National Park.

National Park Service

calendars, posters and on the World Wide Web, the interpreter using less than top quality images will incur laughter in place of praise.

And wherever they go, interpreters are able to fire answers to almost any question. If they don't know the answer, they will tell you where to find it. That is how they get the reputation of being walking encyclopedias.

be perceived that talking about nature is a difficult task. It takes versatile know-how to describe a butterfly nymph, volcanic eruption, aspen leaves, an ant-lion pit, a formation of cirrus clouds, and the flight of a woodpecker—all on one trip. Okay to be a graduate geologist or botanist, but this kind of leader has to be skilled in other sciences plus public speaking.

Not until after the establishment of the National Park Service in 1916 did interpretation begin to take on a professional tone in the United States. In the summer of 1917, C. M. Goethe, a Sacramento nature enthusiast, asked a noted California ornithologist, Harold Bryant, to accompany him to Montana's Glacier National Park, where Goethe noticed Bryant's special enthusiasm for the natural phenomena all around him.

Two years later, they hiked the trail from Tahoe to Yosemite, in the Sierra Nevada of California. Goethe, just back from Europe, had observed nature study operations there and wanted to try something similar in the American national parks. He and Bryant agreed that nature could best be interpreted along the trails and roadsides.

During a summer at Tahoe, Bryant marked nature trails, conducted field walks, presented campfire lectures, and entertained resort guests by showing them how to "read the roadside like a book."

The project succeeded beyond all expectations, and Stephen T. Mather, first director of the National Park Service, arranged to have this activity moved the next year to Yosemite National Park. There, Bryant worked with Dr. Loye Miller of the University of California to develop a nature guide service that caught on with remarkable speed. Bryant took it over as a full time job, saying: "With proper development, the national parks may become the great outdoor universities for which their superlative exhibits so finely equip them."

Thus was national park interpretation born, under the principle that it was more important to inspire the public

to observe carefully than to teach them facts. In 1926, Loye Miller started the Crater Lake interpretive program. Before long there were guided trail trips, rim talks and walks, campfire programs, a rudimentary library, slide collection, and a series of published Nature Notes in which to record valuable observations.

Said a superintendent of Crater Lake in 1927: "The Nature Guide Service," as it came to be called, was "beyond question the most popular and worthwhile service ever accomplished at Crater Lake."

Some interpreters from Crater Lake rose to higher callings. John Doerr, tall, stately, deep-voiced, was Park Naturalist here from 1935 to 1940; eventually he went on to become Chief Naturalist of the entire National Park Service in the 1950s.

The transcendent contributions made by these readers

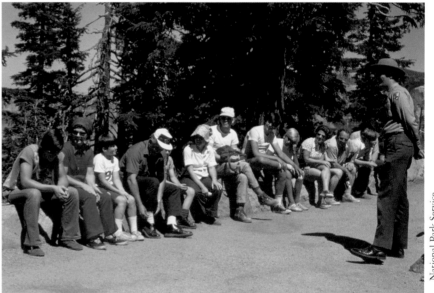

National Park Service

Waiting for the talk to begin.

of the roadside has been to make all facets of Crater Lake understandable to people who yearn for knowledge. The interpreters fill their weary brains as though preparing for a final exam, and hold there a vast resource of answers for an inquiring public. Thus do modern visitors come to Crater Lake in the expectation that someone will be around to interpret the facts in a clear and entertaining manner.

TWENTY QUESTIONS MOST FREQUENTLY ASKED AT CRATER LAKE

Experience has shown that commonplace questions (other than "Where are the rest rooms?" or "Have you seen a little redheaded boy about this high...?" or "What is wrong with my camera?") are frequently devoted to natural resources, history, and ranger activities. Here are some of the most common queries (with answers), as selected by members of the staff at Crater Lake National Park.

1. Does the lake ever freeze? (Yes. See Chapter 15)
2. What kind of bird did I just see? (Could you be a little more specific? What color? Flight pattern? Behavior?)
3. Where is the helicopter? (Refers to a helicopter that crashed into the lake and is still on the bottom because it would be too risky to raise.)
4. How much snow do you get and will it ever go away? (See Chapter 14. Yes, it goes away each summer.)
5. Where can we collect rocks? (Inside the park that's illegal. All natural objects in national parks are protected by law. Try outside the boundary.)
6. Do you live here? (Yes.)
7. Where can I get to the lake to go swimming? (Forget it. The Smith Brothers, one-time Crater Lake rangers and compilers of data on the park, described how Mrs. Lee Fourrier, a champion endurance swimmer, became the first person to swim across the lake. Swimming in the lake had been prohibited, but she was allowed to go after getting permission from the superintendent. Well-greased, she entered the water in the late afternoon on August 4, 1929 and swam the 6.5 miles in 4 hours, 18 minutes. She claimed that this was the hardest swim she had ever made. She was ready to climb out and call it quits but the crowd on the opposite shore was rooting for her and waiting, so she went on. "The water was like ice," she said.)
8. Are there any fish in the lake? Where can I go fishing? (See Chapter 16)
9. Doesn't gasoline from the boats pollute the water? (Yes, if you pour gasoline directly into the water, and nobody does that. Exhaust from the motors may pollute, but the amount is negligible and few boats use the lake.)
10. Did they ever find the meteor that made the crater? (No meteor. This crater is volcanic. See Chapters 1-4.)
11. Was there a volcano here? (Yes, see Chapters 1-4.)
12. Is it always this windy? (No.)
13. Where can I pet a chipmunk? A squirrel? (Try a children's zoo somewhere else. These animals are wild. Approaching them could be dangerous.)
14. Do you have eagles here? (Yes. Bald and golden.)
15. What do you put in the water to make it so blue? (Nothing. See sidebar in chapter 16, "Why the Lake is Blue.")
16. What is the yellow stuff floating on the lake? (Pollen from trees. See Chapter 11.)
17. How do you get the boats down there? (Lower them by helicopter, or disassemble them and take them down by trail.)
18. How cold is the water? (68 degrees on the surface in summer, near freezing in winter. Temperature on the bottom approaches freezing.)
19. What kinds of animals do you have here. (List is available at the Visitor Center. See also Chapter 11.)
20. Where can I go snowmobiling? (This sport is pretty disruptive to wild animals and has been discontinued in some national parks. At this writing it is still permitted at Crater Lake.)

Eleven
RESOURCES

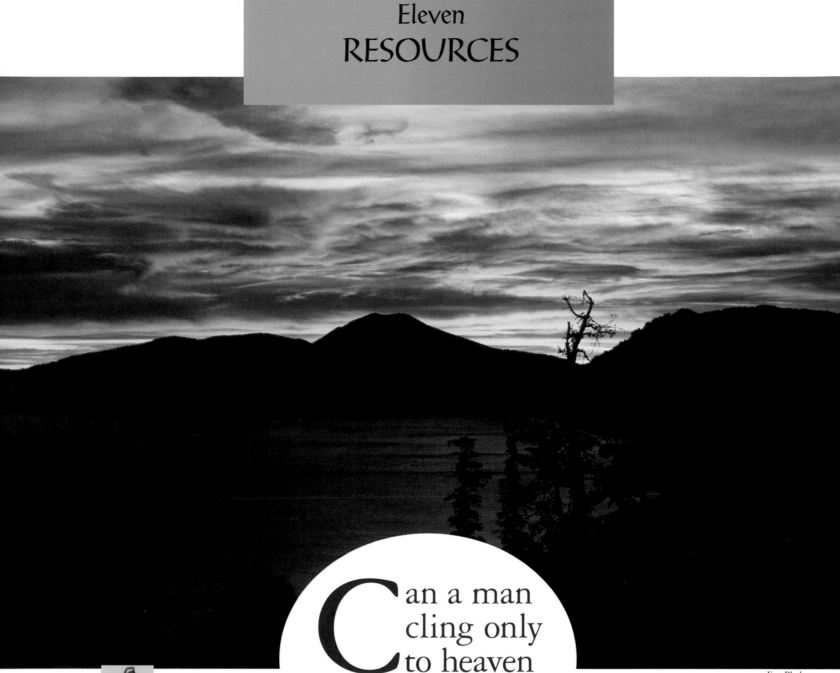

Jim Phelan

Can a man cling only to heaven

And know nothing of earth?

Chuang Tzu

A "resource" is a textbook word. Administrative, too. In tallying up resources of a national park, the most efficient way is to prepare extensive lists, and there are lists of mammals, birds, reptiles, amphibians, and plants of Crater Lake National Park.

New observations are recorded: sightings of unusual birds, discovery of a salamander heretofore unknown in the park, unusual behavior of a muskrat, extension of the range of a rare plant. Recording these observations has sometimes been haphazard down through the years, but the value of what's there is unquestionable. Censuses of black bears have been made since before the park was established, and if the history of the bear in the park has gaps, it merely points up how difficult and time-consuming is the task of tracking every aspect of nature.

There is a maxim in the world of resource management that says simply: We cannot protect what we don't understand.

If all this makes the park an outdoor living museum, that would make its founders—from Theodore Roosevelt to William Steel—very proud. In truth, however, Crater Lake National Park is more than that. It is an outdoor living laboratory for the study of the natural sciences. This includes one discipline not well known: ethology, the science of animal behavior. Not in cages, not in traps,

97

not in museums, but out here in the wild, creatures in their native habitats. Living as they and their ancestors have for millenniums. If the rest of the world's landscapes are deteriorating, the national parks become much more crucial in various forms of research. And they also constitute a source from which to replenish biological species that might be lost elsewhere.

And yet, there is one significant problem with lists. There are resources that can't be listed.

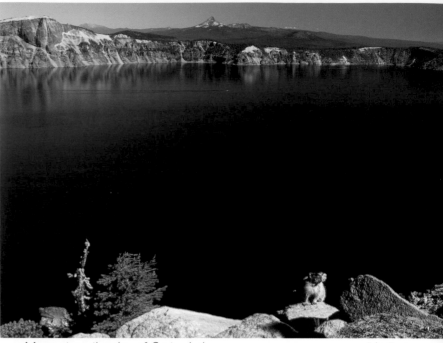

Marmot on the rim of Crater Lake.   John Erwin

Of Marmots and Bears

What of the song of the meadowlark in the grasslands? A perfume of pines in the forest? The chatter of a ground squirrel on the rim? The frantic scamper of the chipmunk as a hawk sails down from on high? Scintillations of monkey flowers in the morning sun? A rippling cascade on a forest stream?

These are triumphs of sight and sound, a hundred-year legacy of drama, adventure, dazzle, and color. They are infinite. How can we make a list of them?

Alas most visitors on a busy schedule, going from park to park, haven't time to sample these sights and sounds in the rest of the park. Seeing the lake, they move on. But for the discerning individual, it is always possible to vow a return, to stay a while, and sample more of the dramas, adventures, dazzle and color.

Anyone who does can count on thousands of dramas a day going on in this park. We know that because of the insights published over the years in *Crater Lake Nature Notes*. Here's one recounted by the photographer Ralph Welles in 1952:

Such visual images are resources, too, at least to our minds and eyes and ears.

Golden-mantled ground squirrels, among the most conspicuous of park mammals, captivate visitors for hours, pitching for handouts on the rim. The Clark's nutcracker, a black and gray bird perched on posts or limbs at the crater rim has become a familiar sight.

Periodically there are invasions of tortoiseshell butterflies, much to the culinary delight of birds and squirrels, even fish in the lake.

For visitors who return to Crater Lake on a more relaxed schedule, there are multiple destinations where different populations of wild creatures can be seen—marshes, springs, bogs, streams, craters, cliffs and woodlands. Getting advice from a ranger or naturalist will save a great deal of time, and it is possible to gain insights into animals recently spotted on patrols or research trips.

Large flocks of pintail ducks visit the surface of Crater Lake in summer, but

"I recall the particularly colorful yellow-bellied marmot that used to sit in the late afternoon on a rock in the meadow back of headquarters. We never saw him except in the late afternoon when the light was almost gone. I had watched for him there several times during the day but he never put in an appearance, so I finally realized that I would have to get him on his own terms and took his picture that evening about six o'clock. The next morning a marmot was found dead on the highway in the same vicinity, and while it may be merely coincidence, a particularly colorful marmot never appeared on that rock in the meadow again."

Welles goes on to document observations of a den of red foxes. He describes a nest of bald eagles and how he watched the parent eagle

"swoop down with breathtaking swiftness and alight on the edge of the six-foot nest and proceed to tear up what appeared to be a white bird and feed it to the young."

it might be more productive to seek small ponds in the surrounding forest, where waterfowl traditionally feed on larvae in the mud. Diligent searching may also turn up beavers and muskrats along the streams.

Always, one must be on the lookout for bears. During much of Crater Lake's century as a national park, bears panhandling along the road have been a familiar sight, almost a trademark of the national parks. That was bad for the bears, who did not evolve on a diet of cookies and Twinkies. It could be bad for visitors, too, because anyone who proffered a sandwich to a bear may have thought the act a good Samaritan deed. But the bear might not know where the sandwich ends and the fingers begin.

Even worse, bears learned to break into garbage cans, backpacks, automobiles, and camp boxes.

After years of research to build a bear-proof garbage can, the National Park Service succeeded, with the result that bears gave up and retreated to the depths of the forest, where their native foods, such as roots and grubs, are more in abundance.

Ouzels and Owls

The dipper, or water ouzel, inhabits streams within the park, dipping into pools and under waterfalls in search of insects.

Because of all the old growth forests, there are northern spotted owls in the park, some at the highest elevations at which that bird is found. At least seven pairs live within the park. Any proposed construction, such as trail extensions or road building, triggers a careful survey of spotted owl sites before the bulldozers roll.

Some birds are very hardy and can spend the entire winter at Crater Lake. Among these are the Oregon jay, raven, Clark's nutcracker, red-breasted nuthatch, chickadee, and possibly Steller's jay (named after the first naturalist of Alaska),

When spring comes, robins and bluebirds are some of the first to return.

All this may sound as though Crater Lake is a haven for winged victims from other places. To be sure, it is a refuge where human beings must live by rules designed to protect animals. But there is no guarantee that one animal here is safe from another. Example: the raven is

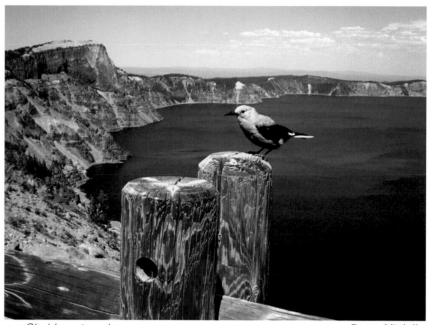

Clark's nutcracker.   Preston Mitchell

notorious for robbing nests and destroying the young of other birds.

A newcomer might ask: then why not rid the park of ravens?

Don't laugh. In the history of the national parks, and in a century of learning to manage park resources, ill-advised experiments were undertaken. For example, in the early days of Yellowstone, efforts were made to remove mountain lions because they preyed on deer. And eliminate pelicans because they fed on native fish.

Nowadays we know a great deal more about survival of the fittest, how predators fit into the scheme of things, and how they benefit the ecosystem. The result is that park managers seldom interfere. But they can, if necessary. Especially if danger comes from the outside.

Outside Dangers

The damage by world pollution has not yet been completely studied. The effects of human beings on the nervous systems of animals, and hence on reproduction in the wild, is not always known. In other places we can see with our own eyes how low-flying aircraft cause serious damage to wildlife, as when helicopters cause tropical birds to fly frantically from their mangrove nests, dumping eggs and young in the water. Could something similar happen at Crater Lake when a helicopter (which in the eyes of animals may look like a gigantic hawk) flies over the forest? Or what actually happens when aircraft buzz mountain goats in Alaska and send them panic-stricken across high meadows?

This is by way of saying that human beings haven't all the answers, but they are learning. And sometimes they focus on some species whose very existence is fragile.

To wit: the Peregrine falcon. Some resources in Crater Lake National Park are damaged by problems outside the park and far away. Peregrine falcons, a worldwide species, possess such speed of flight that they can easily capture and eat other birds. Unfortunately, however, some of the birds they eat have picked up pesticides on their own intercontinental travels, and pass this along to the peregrines. Although chemicals such as DDT were banned in North America many years ago, they have been in use since then in Mexico and South America, to which even the peregrines themselves migrate. Thus the eggs can suffer the thin shells typical of DDT intake.

Several families of peregrines have been raised within the park, with a little assistance by park naturalists.

Reports the *Crater Lake Nature Notes*: "The only known active peregrine eyrie in Oregon in recent years was at Crater Lake National Park. It was discovered in 1979, and remained active until 1983, when both adult birds disappeared. Although the birds in the eyrie successfully fledged young in 1979, they were unsuccessful in 1980. Each of the three eggs laid the second year showed high levels of a derivative of DDT.

"Nesting again took place at Crater Lake in 1987. The nest was manipulated to ensure that the pair would successfully fledge young. Four eggs were removed from the nest, three of which hatched and were fledged in California. Two captive-bred young were fostered into the Crater Lake eyrie. Unfortunately, one of the young was killed by a great horned owl... The other bird successfully fledged.

"The peregrines again used the historic eyrie in 1988. They laid four eggs, of which three hatched. Approximately twelve days later all of the young and the adult female were killed by a great horned owl."

And so it goes. Where the park staff can help biologically in the return of a threatened species, it will. That makes the park a refuge for the tempest-tossed in the avian world. But there is sometimes no way to avert natural tragedies.

Trees

Crater Lake's forested surroundings are diverse and typical of the Cascades. At the lower elevations grow lodgepole and ponderosa pines, two of the most widely distributed trees in western North America. Sugar pines, with their giant cones, grow a bit higher up, as do the white pines. With the passage of years, some trees reach good size and old age, perhaps a thousand years.

The familiar mountain hemlock grows along the rim, but the western hemlock also grows in the park, although at lower elevations.

Of the firs, the noble fir grows along the rim, the slender alpine fir especially around park headquarters, and the white fir near the south entrance.

Of the trees, the whitebark pine is one of the most interesting. Steve Mark and Ron Mastroguiseppe, writing in a 1992 issue of *Crater Lake Nature Notes*, give this report:

"The whitebark pine is a tree found generally above 6500 feet on exposed slopes in dry, rocky soils. Although Crater Lake National Park has no true timberline, whitebark pine forms the elfinwood or krummholz of timberline in many western mountain ranges.

"Whitebark pine is a pioneer species colonizing subalpine habitats as the first tree. An amazing example of its pioneering ability can be seen at the Newberry caldera where whitebark pine is the only tree established upon the relatively recent obsidian surface. At the Crater Lake caldera, whitebark pine may have been the first tree to colonize the pumice slopes of old Mount Mazama within the first century following the climactic eruption. Whitebark pine is generally encountered as a pioneer tree, as there are several places around the caldera rim where old 'mother trees' provided a favorable microclimate for the establishment beneath their canopy of subalpine fir or mountain hemlock. Whitebark pine is arranged in ribbons or bands along the contours of Cloudcap and other habitats along the caldera's edge. These sites represent slightly higher, rocky substrate for the survival of whitebark seedlings since exposed areas devoid of snow earlier in the year have a significantly longer growing season.

"Most pine seeds have wings for wind dispersal, but whitebark seeds have retained only a rudimentary wing. The dispersal agent has become the Clark's Nutcracker. These birds have learned to retrieve whitebark seeds with their specialized beaks, storing a number in their sublingual pouch, and methodically storing seeds in soil caches. Only a fraction of the seed caches are retrieved, however, so some caches sprout seedlings in clumps which may grow into larger whitebark pine colonies."

Color in the Wild

For park visitors there are thrills just for the observation. Example, around heavily visited areas may be glimpsed the western tanager, one of the most magnificent birds of all. Its brilliant yellow, red and black are seen throughout the American West. And

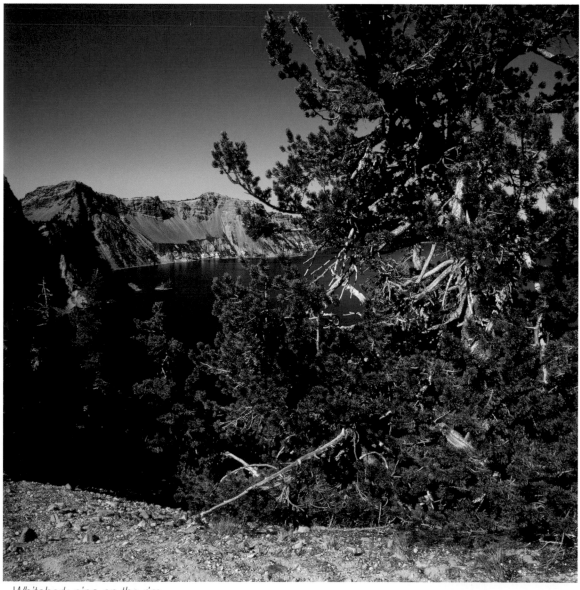

Whitebark pine on the rim.

Ann and Myron Sutton

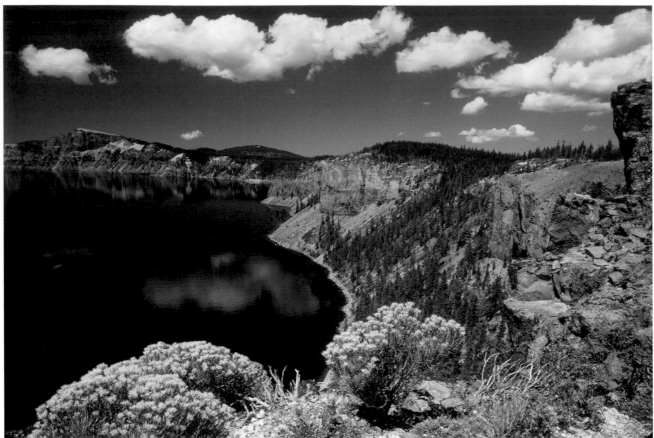

Rabbitbrush on rim.

John Erwin

when a hummingbird swoops down in spring and shows the brilliant orange of its crest, the result is a memorable sight indeed.

But the greatest color in the wild is in the kingdom of plants. The vegetation has made a remarkable recovery from the early days of grazing by sheep. And here lie some of the most magnificent encounters between park resources and park visitors.

Take, for example, the monkey flower. Not many people know about this wild member of the Snapdragon family, but it occurs from the depths of deserts in the American Southwest to high mountains of the Cascades. There are fifty species in the northwestern states alone. They are often located near springs, sometimes in a rich vegetative setting of mosses and ferns.

Seeing a cluster of monkey flowers (*Mimulus*) beside a wild spring can be one of the most exhilarating experiences in nature. At Crater Lake, this species is very popular with visitors. Photographers,

especially, can capture it in a triumph of artistic creation.

There is a wildflower garden not far from Park Headquarters where several species have been collected in an environment of springs. Here, one can sample the variety of wild flowers in the park.

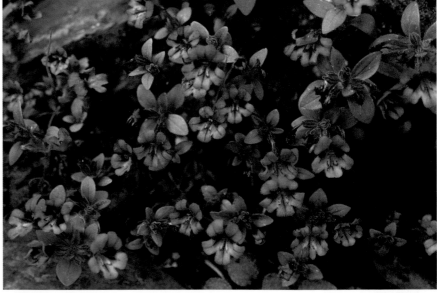

Monkey Flower.

John Erwin

Eleven – Resources

Since spring comes late to these mountains of heavy snow, there are times when the snow does not melt until June and July. In effect, this is springtime for the flowers, and some will rise up out of the soil before the snow is gone, even come up through holes in the dripping, melting snow. Because the summer is so short, they must display their flowers and produce their seeds without delay.

Twisted Species

Because snow becomes very heavy and as hard as ice after compacting itself all winter, we ask: How can the seedlings of trees survive? How do these fragile precursors of stately pines and other species breathe when they are so buried? Is it possible to grow while being crushed?

Well, when the snow at last releases them, some do seem a bit disheveled, bent and ragged. But they are alive. They have survived months of burial. You may see young trees with twisted trunks, the results of years of annual burial and pressure. Eventually, though, they conquer their environment and grow up mostly straight and tall. This is a slow process, of course, because

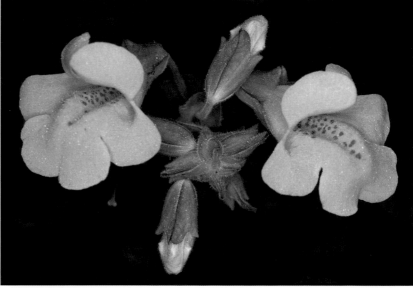

Monkey Flower.   John Erwin

of the short growing season at this elevation (6,000 to 8,000 feet).

Where the weather is most violent, as on the exposed rim high above Crater Lake, the whitebark pines manage to survive, though they retain their twisted, contorted trunks throughout their lives.

These hardy trees must withstand extremes of weather far up on the mountain, out in the open, vulnerable to high winds and freezing temperatures for days at a time. Little else in the world of plants is such a tribute to the tenacity of life.

There is an unusual spectacle visible from the rim under certain circumstances. When lodgepole pines of lower elevations outside the crater release their pollen and set it loose upon the swirling winds of spring and summer, such pollen settles

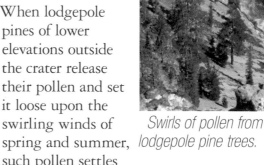

Swirls of pollen from lodgepole pine trees.   National Park Service

on the surface of Crater Lake. There it floats, producing yellow swirls that cover much of the surface.

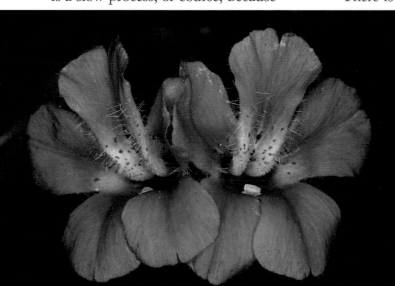

Monkey Flower.   John Erwin

FLOWERING COLOR

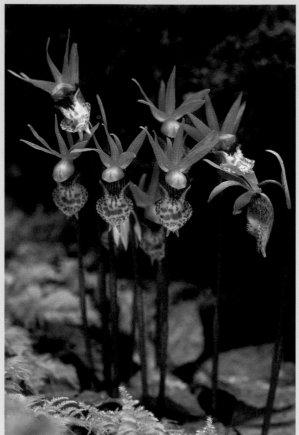

Fairy slipper orchid.

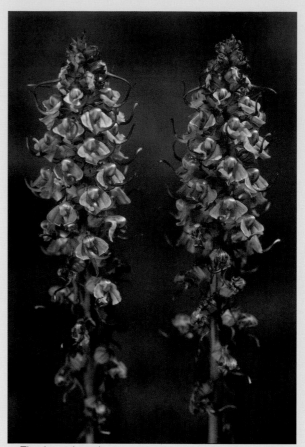

Elephant head.

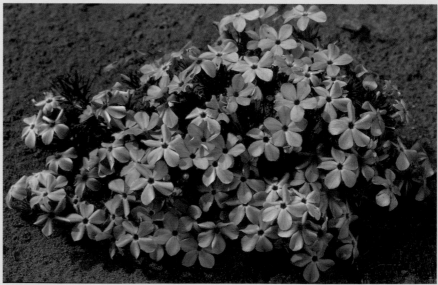

Phlox.

All photos by John Erwin.

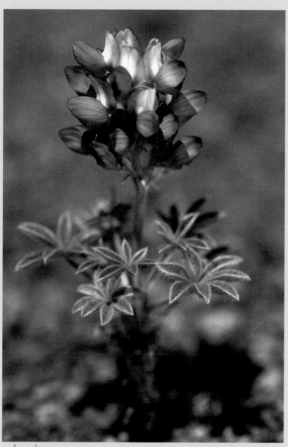

Lupine.

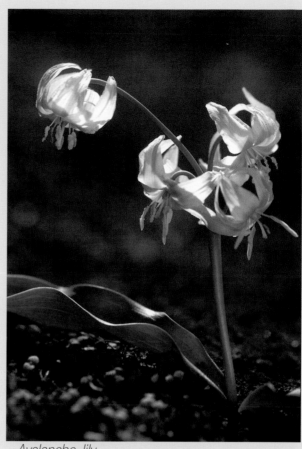

Avalanche-lily.

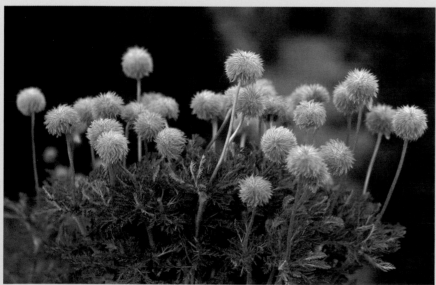

Seed heads of anemone.

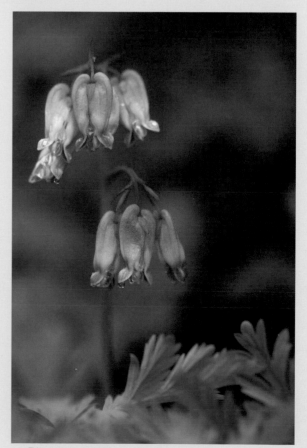

Bleeding heart.

Peter Zika is a professor of botany at Oregon State University, and here is his overview, from *Crater Lake Nature Notes*, of how the plants show up with the beginning of spring.

"The hiking trails at Crater Lake National Park will take you to elegant floral displays as the snows recede and spring seeps up the caldera walls. Botanists have found roughly 700 species of flowers, ferns, and conifers in the park. You can sample a rich diversity of plants by simply stretching your legs and setting out from the macadam.

"While snow drifts still surround Park Headquarters, western flowering dogwood, *Cornus nuttallii*, Shelton's violet, *Viola sheltonii*, and pink fairy slippers, *Calypso bulbosa*, are luring bees in the warmer depths of Red Blanket Canyon, on the lower trail to Stuart Falls. Legions of lupines, *Lupinus latifolius*, and scarlet paintbrushes, *Castilleja miniata*, greet you when summer's heat has opened the footpaths along Annie Creek and into the Castle Crest Wildflower Garden.

"You might be pleased by a walk on the south-facing Garfield Peak Trail, located east of Crater Lake Lodge. Melting snowfields water a delightful mix of plants through the summer. As you pause for yet another splendid view of the lake, you can admire the blue blossoms of squaw carpet, *Ceanothus prostratus*, or later in the season see shocking purple and pink beardtongues, *Penstemon davidsonii* and *rupicola*.

"Midsummer brings monkeyflowers into bloom on wet ledges and streamsides. Pink and yellow monkeyflowers, *Mimulus lewisii* and *M. guttatus*, form festive natural bouquets on the shores of Crater Lake and even in roadside ditches. The relentless sunshine sears the well-drained treeless expanses at high elevations. Graded paths up Mount Scott and Crater Peak take you to pumice fields tinted red with the fading and drying leaves of fleeceflower, *Polygonum newberryi*. When fleeceflower is conspicuous on the caldera and in Pumice Desert, brilliant yellow-flowering shrubs beckon butterflies along the eastern side of Rim Drive. This is rabbitbrush, *Chrysothamnus nauseosus*, a cousin to the locally rare sagebrush, *Artemisia tridentata*. Rabbitbrush draws on reserves in its deep root system to flower so late in the year. In doing so, it seems to defy drought conditions common to the upper slopes of Mount Mazama during summer and early autumn.

"Frost and early snow withers vegetation on the rim in September, but pearly everlasting, *Anaphalis margaritacea*, holds persistent white flowers at lower elevations until later in the year. Cold nights finally leach the pink from loose mist-like masses of ticklegrass, *Agrostis hyemalis*, at Spruce Lake which is located due west of Llao Rock near the park boundary. By November, new snow drifts end another season of wandering through the wildflowers."

You can, of course, find all of these if you take plenty of time to roam the trails and get into the back country. Lists of wildlife and plants in the park have resulted from people searching and recording for many years. Some of the most conspicuous plants of the park are those with richly colorful flowers, such as larkspurs, fireweed, paintbrush, marsh marigold, columbine, violet, shooting star, laurel, lupine, lily, and orchid.

Plants sort themselves by habitat. On the warm, south-facing slopes where more sunshine reaches the surface, the snow melts earlier and the plants have a longer growing season. Of course, water evaporates earlier, too, and some of the species in such places are characteristic of deserts. But the open forest glades present a good variety of flowering plants. Examples: manzanita, pussy-paws, and anemone. Within the forest, and in shady places at higher elevations, the snow stays longer, and plants there can only start to grow late in the spring or early summer. Wetland species like bog-orchids are confined to marshes, bogs and riverbanks. With the park's range of 3,000 to 10,000 feet elevation, there are obviously multiple habitats and a good variety of species.

All this is the other face of Crater Lake National Park, the land beyond the lake. To travelers it is the delight of encountering clusters of brilliant flowers. To the botanist it is a paradise of multiple species.

To the record-keeper, these are resources, a mundane word that represents some of the greatest diversity and most magnificent productions in the world of nature.

Art on opposite page based on photo by John Erwin.

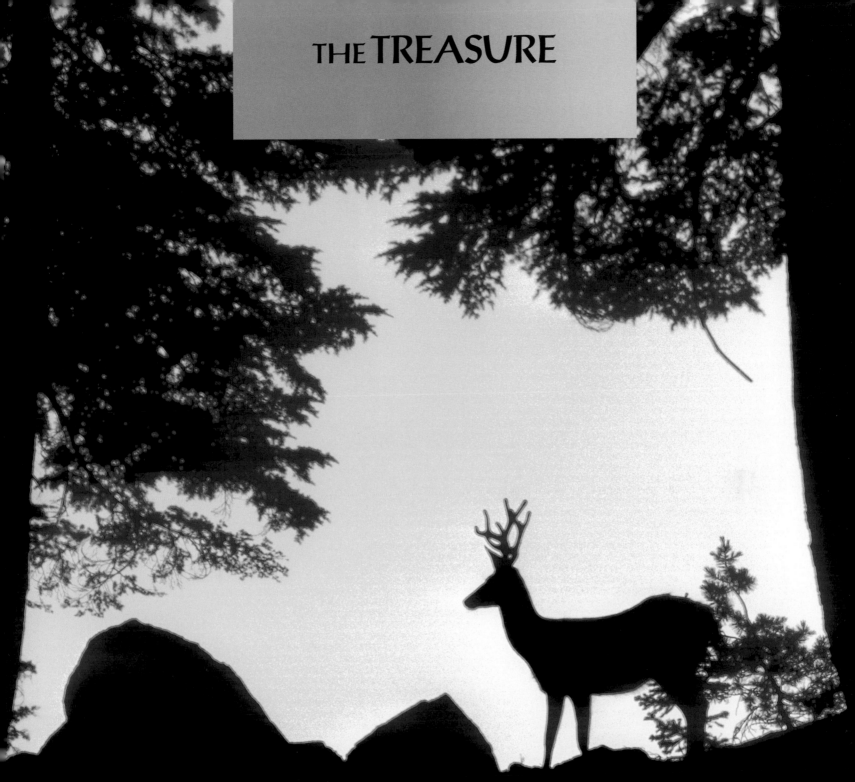

THE TREASURE

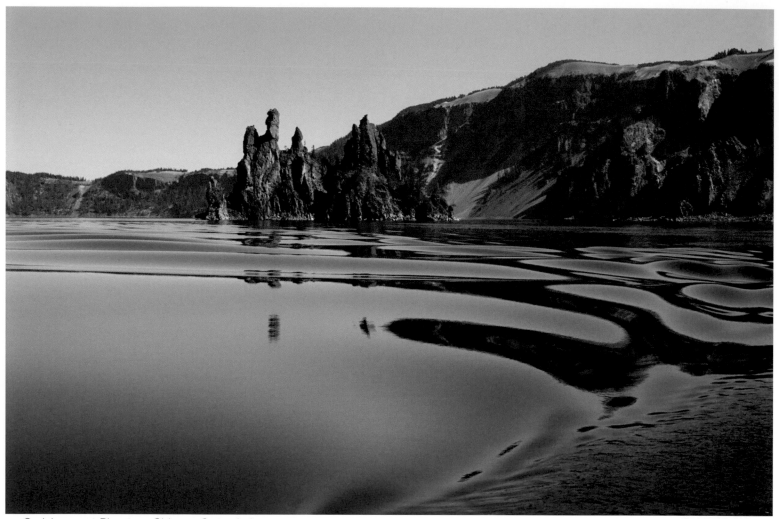

Cruising past Phantom Ship on Crater Lake.

Preston Mitchell

Morning sun streaming through lodgepole pine forest.

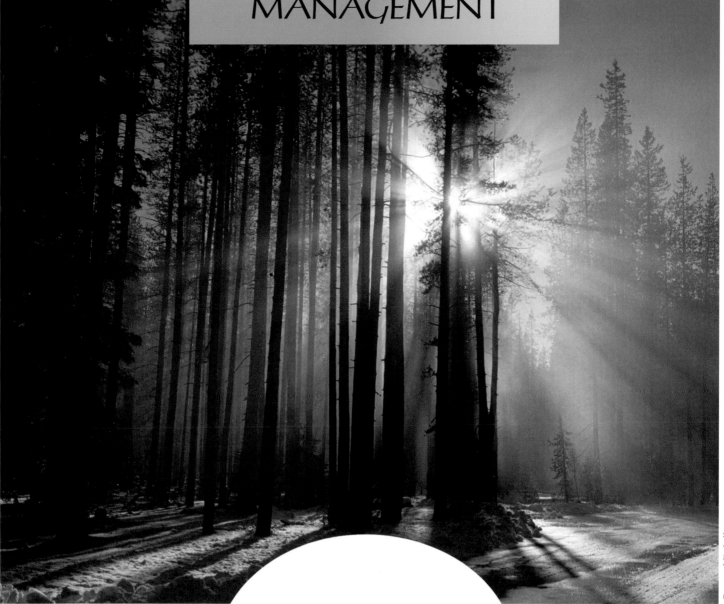

Preston Mitchell

Whatever is, is right.

Alexander Pope

I t might be easy to conclude that all the problems with which park staffs have to deal around Crater Lake are people-related. That the rest of the park— forests, meadows, and marshes— are so natural, so peaceful, so quiet, they don't need any tender loving care. True? False. Welcome to the world of natural resource management.

It used to be felt that nature could manage her own affairs, and that anyone who thought otherwise was pretty presumptuous. Today, the facts of life are that the National Park Service staff must stand like Horatio at the bridge to ward off invasions, intrusions, conflicts with neighbors, and threats from—of all places— nature herself.

If that is saying that human beings are better and wiser than the rest of the natural world, you are entering the never-never world of managing national parks. Workers pulled some pretty off-base stunts in the early years of Crater Lake National Park. But now, with accumulated wisdom and a vastly improved track record, human beings can correct past mistakes and encourage natural processes.

It is time for a reality check on how park staffs over the years have fought to keep this park in the natural state we enjoy today. A gardener can tell us how much work there is to keep domestic plants attractive for public display. To do so, the gardener must fight insect attacks, snails, slugs, and weeds.

In a national park, however, a tree need not be cleared away when it falls. No plant is a "weed" unless perhaps it is a foreign invader destroying native species. Likewise, no insect or mammal is unwanted—unless it has come from somewhere else and is competing with native species.

Even though conditions are sometimes trying to human guardians, the natural ecosystems at Crater Lake National Park are alive and well. When trees die, they fall, and that means logs being eaten by insects which are in turn preyed upon by birds and mammals. A bear, for example, finds delicious fare in the insects that inhabit old and decaying stumps.

All this enriches the soil, and you will readily notice new seedlings of pines which will someday grow up, fall over, and start the entire cycle again.

Some birds, like the Townsend's solitaire, nest on the ground among these trees. Larvae are food for mallard ducks in streams away from the lake. A listing of mutual relations could go on for a long time, because even though everything that lives in this park must be adapted to a very heavy winter, life flourishes. We can only admire the birds that remain alive here for those eight months during which the snow comes and goes.

However, in this centennial review of protecting Crater Lake in such manner and by such means that will keep it unimpaired for the enjoyment of future generations, let us focus on some of the trials and tribulations. If nothing else, we will debunk the notion that parks can take care of themselves.

Within this superbly operating ecological system, there is a principal irony in the care and keeping of any national park on earth: nature's not perfect. Adds the ecologist: man isn't either. Who are we to rule on whether nature is perfect or not?

The irony lies in the fact that lawmakers order national parks to be "maintained unimpaired." That's good wording, but there are different definitions of "unimpaired." Today we might say "maintained in as natural a condition as possible."

When fires raged over Yellowstone, the public and press shouted "catastrophe." But fire is nothing of the sort. If it results from lightning, it is a normal natural process. We do not go in and clean out all those burned trees. New growth will start as soon as the ashes cool. Instead of calling it catastrophe, call it change.

But what if we see an invasion of forest insects approaching? Congress and the public might plead: "Stop it! Don't let those insects spoil our national park!" All right, cut down all the trees so the insects can't get at them. You see how absurd this becomes? Think what Congress and the public would say if park officials cut down all the trees...

A student in a National Park Service training session was once asked in a similar situation: "If you were a Superintendent of the park, what would you do."

The student answered promptly: "Resign."

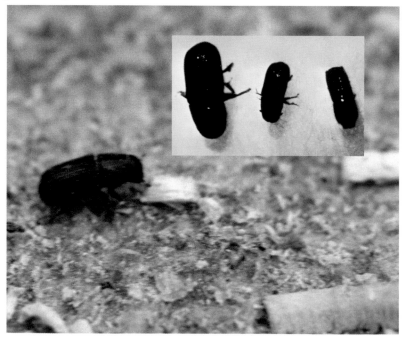

U.S. Forest Service

A Mountain Pine Beetle. The inset shows size comparisons, from l to r, of the Mountain Pine Beetle (approx. 1/8th in.), the Western Pine Beetle, and the Pine Engraver.

Twelve – Resource Management

Still, some things nature does just can't be tolerated. Call that treasonous talk if you want. Or join the school of Alexander Pope that "whatever is, is right." He referred to the Lisbon earthquake and meant that if God ordered something, however awful, that made it right. The statement outraged Voltaire, who issued a scathing indictment of it. And think of the indictment Congress would issue if park officials cut down all the trees to get rid of insect infestations.

We need not labor the point, but we must remember that life in natural ecosystems is difficult anyway. Birds and bats ram into trees and flutter to the ground. Deer break their legs. Ducks, asleep on freezing ponds, get trapped by ice.

Of course, the ultimate hope was to keep parks "pristine," but that is just about an impossibility these days, given human habitation, dust from Mongolia, and other effects from outside. Enough to keep a park natural. Natural processes do change, and parks are places where those changes can go on relatively undisturbed.

In fact, says Boyd Wickman, of the Pacific Northwest Research Station, referring to natural resources, "Park management today usually focuses on encouraging natural processes and mitigating human impacts. This is the real story of what park managers have learned over the past fifty years."

In Crater Lake National Park, the chief "enemy" of the forests is lightning. Yet forest fires are perfectly natural, and in fact, helpful to the growth of ecological communities. There has to be a little give and take, however, if a park is to remain beautiful the way visitors want it. For that reason, park staffs extinguish fires, even though the ecosystem may need fires to remain healthy. Firefighters do such a good job

of keeping fire out of the park, by the way, that no fire up here has ever burned more than an acre since the park was established. Prescribed fires were set in recent years and grew to several hundred acres in size as part of a forest management effort.

Another salient example of forest destruction is insect attacks. It is sometimes argued that because such attacks are natural, park managers should just sit back and watch. When insects destroy the forest and have nothing else to eat, they will go find another forest.

Which is a little like saying that when Uncle Joe dies his cancer will be gone.

The early managers at Crater Lake didn't buy the idea of leaving insects alone (any more than letting fires burn). The spread of dead snags would not be attractive to visitors. Said one: "When you get through looking at the lake, the forest is the next most important asset we have." People hike through it, camp in it, study it, and take away such memorable visions as a sunset or a full moon seen through the sagging branches of a hemlock tree.

If you let insects convert these living trees to the gaunt ghosts of dead snags, they said, you've eliminated a very big chunk of what the visitors come to see.

The first historic insect infestation started around Diamond Lake and moved south. By 1923 it had killed thirty square miles of lodgepole pines north of Crater Lake and entered the park. That may have been good news for grubs and woodpeckers, but the park staff became very concerned. With funding from Congress, and help from the U.S. Bureau of Entomology, they initiated a control project in 1925. Only dead trees infested with mountain pine beetles were felled and

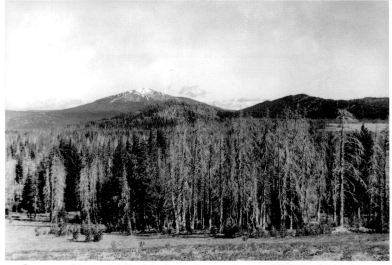

Groves of insect-killed lodgepole pine in Crater Lake National Park.

US Dept. of Agriculture,
Pacific NW Research Station

PINE BEETLES

Bark beetles have a fondness for the living cambium layer just beneath the bark. But that is the layer through which water and nutrients are supplied to the rest of the tree. If beetles eat up cambium in a ring around the tree, they cut off vital supplies, and the tree dies.

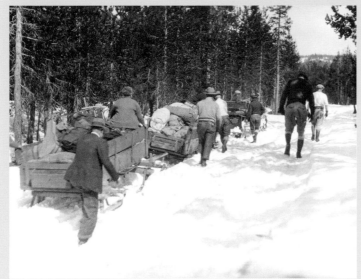

Crews carrying equipment to beetle control sites.

US Dept. of Agriculture, Pacific NW Research Station

Two species were initially targeted: the mountain pine beetle attacking lodgepole pines, and the western pine beetle attacking ponderosa pines.

One method was solar kill: fell the tree, lop off branches and let the sun's heat kill delicate larvae and pupae. The other method was to burn infested tree boles on the ground. Later, chemical sprays came into use.

treated. This slowed the advance of the insects and thus saved trees in the path of the devastation.

Says Boyd Wickman: "Bark beetles were and are usually impossible to control. They are a natural process and once the outbreak reaches a certain point, the combination of susceptible-aged trees and large bark beetle populations means death to many trees. Park managers are well aware of these cycles now and do not attempt to control outbreaks."

In 1929, however, the infestation expanded and the National Park Service went on the offensive again. To give you an idea of what they had to do, it was reported that between May and July, 1929, 23,239 trees were treated.

No sooner was this done, than here came the white pine blister rust. It happens that part of the life cycle of this pine-killer takes place on shrubs of the native wild currant (*Ribes*). So— eradicating shrubs was better than felling trees. But that put the federal government in the uncomfortable position of wiping out an endemic species of shrub. Before this scourge was eliminated, 133,600 currant bushes were removed.

That may sound like flagrant violation of park laws, but now you know that if park managers don't tinker with nature's excesses now and then, the national parks aren't going to be very pleasant places to visit. In many ways, of course, that's an artificial approach. There are no excesses in nature. Such events are benign or unwanted, depending on our values.

What to do about all this has come to constitute a continuous task for the National Park Service: resource management. The bubble that parks are pure and benign was burst a long time ago.

In fact, it sometimes takes a long time to clear up problems in parks, and only then can the intrinsic values be restored.

To wit: Crater Lake National Park came with sheep grazing, and history's first report on wild flowers in this park was that there weren't any. At these elevations and with such short growing seasons, flowering plants have a tough time of it anyway. Then, when they barely poked up through the melting snow and sent up buds, they were ripped out, roots and all, by flocks of grazing sheep.

When the National Park Service had to terminate grazing, once and for all, it opened itself to attack. Outlaw grazing and you come into conflict with regional wool growers. The

Twelve – Resource Management

Service never wants to come in conflict with anyone, least of all neighbors. Nevertheless, the dictum by the government on this issue was clear, forthright and easy to understand. When permission was sought in 1917 to graze 7,000 sheep in the park, the director of the newly formed National Park Service wrote:

"We cannot act…favorably upon applications for the grazing of sheep in the park. Sheep are not only very obnoxious to tourists, they absolutely destroy wild flowers and shrubs which we are particularly anxious to preserve in the parks."

Next came fish. By 1941, 1,656,000 fingerlings had been put into the lake so that fishing would be another attraction for people to visit the park. But in that year, when fishing was at its peak, only one in every 183 visitors fished anyway. John C. Merriam, a noted park official, wrote to the director of the National Park Service in 1943 that it was quite possible for fish to have a long-term detrimental effect on the lake. In 1946 a young graduate student named Orthello Wallis came to the park from Oregon State University. An aquatic biologist, Wallis pointed out that only .008 per cent of the fish stocked over the years had ever been caught.

Then he went on to a classic pronouncement that the National Park Service would be more consistent with its major conservation objectives if it did not attempt to expand an artificial fishery or to maintain the present inadequate one. (Wallis went on to become chief aquatic biologist of the National Park Service.)

Such statements may sound simple, but years of controversy are often necessary to develop guidelines for resource management. When that happens, such ideas go far and wide,

picked up by managers in other countries. Ideas fought for in Crater Lake and other American parks have been instrumental in worldwide conservation.

Eduardo Arango, a regional official in northern Colombia, where three national parks have been established on the shore of the Caribbean Sea, prohibited all *marine* fishing off the coast. For that unthinkable act, he got a great deal of flak. He was not fazed.

"That coral reef out there is a delicate ecosystem," he once told us, "and I'm not going to back down on this. We have too much to lose."

In the visitor center at Isla de Salamanca National Park, he put this sign at the entrance:

> **C**uando la tecnología no tenga nada nuevo que ofrecer al hombre, aún continuará la naturaleza mostrandole sus maravillas.
>
> *(When technology no longer has anything new to offer man, then Nature will go right on showing him her wonders.)*

Back at home, the idea of restoring a park's natural character always ran into the question of when. Its natural character yesterday? Last year? When the park was established? Or when human beings first arrived?

A great many biologists worked on this question, and many meetings were held to decide on which way to go. Eventually they settled on restoration to the time when the park was established. Easier said, however, than done. People were pouring in, which made it difficult to revert to the distant past. Visitors were welcome by law, and more and more facilities had to be constructed to serve them. Otherwise the place would become a scientific reserve with limited access.

Half way through Crater Lake's century, the idea of trying to attract more and more visitors to all the national parks was abandoned. The parks had become so popular and so inundated by visitors that fears arose about crowd damage to the very resources park staffs were trying to protect.

A new balance was struck. No more feeding bears for public entertainment, as was done in parks other than Crater Lake. No more feeding bears, period. A more sophisticated visitor wanted to look at the park as a museum in the wild, with guides to explain the processes of nature and history.

Hold the roads. Hold the elephant trains. In parks you got out of your car and walked. Today, buses are sometimes used to take visitors around. That helps reduce congestion.

Nevertheless, the time had come to restore the park to what it was.

An advisory board on Wildlife Management in the parks tried to put this in words: "that the biotic associations within each park be maintained or, where necessary, recreated as nearly as possible in the condition that prevailed when the area was first visited by white man."

That took the restoration goal back centuries—and biologists both applauded and wailed. "We can't do it! Too much has changed."

But it became a goal to work toward, even if it could never be reached. Natural integrity was the watch word, and so Crater Lake National Park's first century ended on a pretty large turnaround in policy: keeping wild animals back in their natural habitats where they can't injure, or be harmed by, tourists.

If this eventually became too much for a single government agency to handle, the problem was neatly solved by agreements with others, such as the Forest Service of the Department of Agriculture, U.S. Fish and Wildlife Service, the United States Geological Survey, and state universities.

Inviting independent researchers, especially those at universities, came to be a mutually favorable effort, and has been going on for a long time. Says Wickman: "The Pacific Northwest Research Station, a branch of the United States Forest Service, has had research responsibilities in Crater Lake National Park for over fifty years." Their reports put an imprint of academic value on the results, and save the National Park Service from having to hire many scientists. The park did hire some scientists, but a great deal of the research work was, and is, conducted by the United States Geological Survey and other scientific agencies, both public and private.

Park staffs draw up "wish lists" that prioritize the research they need most. These become the bases for funding. In some cases, independent scientists may see a neat fit with their own research.

Success is not necessarily automatic. A severe winter, such as that of 1998-99 when even in low-lying Medford, where it seldom snows, there were 16 snowstorms, the situation at Crater Lake became intolerable. The weather was so severe that winter that all research had to be canceled.

With sound scientific backing, policies for managing natural resources could be established. Human interference with nature would be kept at a minimum. Example: for years, bears were roadside pests in many parks, panhandling for cookies and cakes that did their nutritional balance no good. The National Park Service experimented for a long time before finding a bear-proof garbage can. With garbage no longer available, the bears slowly retreated into the wild where they belonged. Visitors would be taken to the natural habitat of the bears, rather than the other way around.

If you think this is hazardous, look at the Nepalese version of it. Go out at night in stocking feet looking for Bengal tigers in Royal Chitwan National Park in the lowlands of Nepal. Dangerous? All life is dangerous. Call it adventure, instead.

For many years efforts were made by world scientists and historians to tally up the earth's resources so that we would know where we stand (or stood) at any point in time. Many were given fancy names, but now those pie-in-the-sky ideas have morphed into satellite-in-the-sky triumphs.

Today, Crater Lake and other national parks are gathering detailed geographic information from research, field work, and satellite images—such things as lake data, vegetation maps, soil maps, and surface geology maps, even air quality readings.

With all these computerized and linked with other parks, you see what happens. As the century ended, a new, non-native species of blister rust was raising whitebark pine mortality throughout the Pacific Northwest. On hearing this, the staff at Crater Lake

Twelve – Resource Management

National Park becomes very concerned. After all, whitebark is the most common pine along the rim.

Such a warning system is quite an accomplishment against the outmoded theory that we can relax and let the parks take care of themselves.

So it was that Resource Management Plans came into being for American parks, including Crater Lake. Such plans are now sophisticated, based on experience and comprehensive studies. They need redoing now and then. So do policy statements. So do your own plans for managing the kids in the family as they mature.

But at any moment in time, whoever wants to know exactly what is going on inside a national park, and what is being done about it, can find out. It is heartwarming to see national parks held in such esteem by the people who own them, by the people who manage them, and by people far away in other countries on this planet looking for good advice.

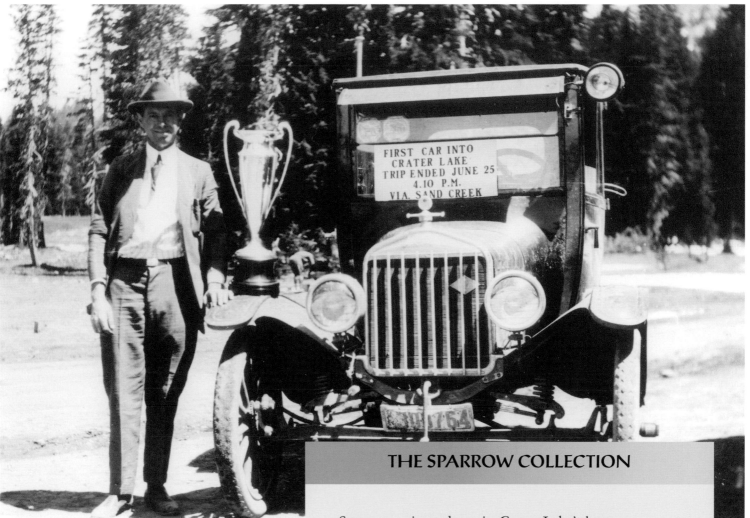

> FIRST CAR INTO
> CRATER LAKE
> TRIP ENDED JUNE 25
> 4.10 P.M.
> VIA SAND CREEK

Southern Oregon Historical Society

THE SPARROW COLLECTION

Some superintendents in Crater Lake's long history made a special effort to enhance the historical record. One, Alex Sparrow, came from the U.S. Army Corps of Engineers to oversee construction of the system of roads around the rim of the caldera. In 1917 he was appointed Superintendent. In 1918 he made the first trip around the completed rim road, "hazarding," as he said, "tight turns and deep ruts in a Park Service truck." (That old road has changed over the years to become the comfortable avenue of travel we enjoy today.)

Sparrow remained superintendent until 1922. He made a collection of about 1,500 photographs during his years as superintendent of the park. This collection is now in the Southern Oregon Historical Society in Medford. He died in 1932.

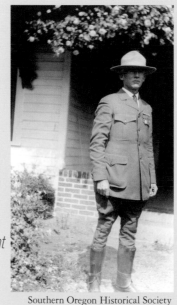

Superintendent Sparrow.

Southern Oregon Historical Society

Southern Oregon Historical Society

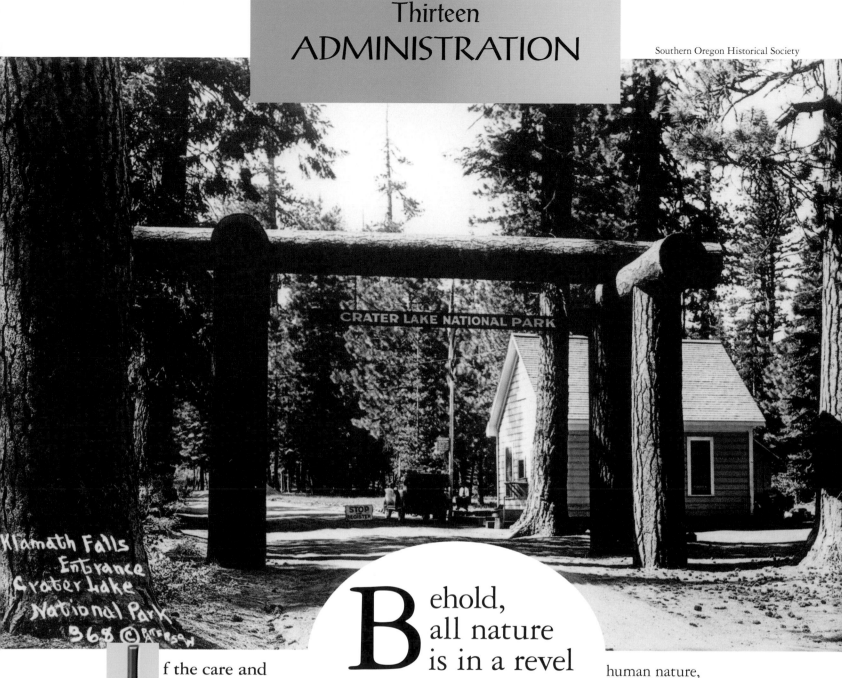

Klamath Falls Entrance Crater Lake National Park 365 © Patterson

I f the care and keeping of so precious a segment of the world landscape seems as though it ought to be a snap, that nature can do very well by itself, thank you, then you missed the previous chapter.

If you think that the Superintendent of a national park has only to sit back and issue orders to the members of his staff, then it is time to go back to the beginning.

The administrators of a national park usually have long experience in supervising the preservation of park lands. But like the CEOs of large corporations, they must understand

B ehold, all nature is in a revel of delight.

Washington Irving

human nature, work amiably with members of the staff, be considerate to all, and react to emergencies with grace and calm. The superintendent must be decisive when necessary, forthright when required, and gentle when the situation demands it. In short, a model of behavior and inspiration to the staff.

Down through the years, superintendents at Crater Lake National Park have had a formidable job in running the national park. The ranger force, said one superintendent, "continue to be filled with outstandingly able men." It was the job of the superintendent to maintain that standard. Ranger staffs in summer were often drawn from teachers, professors, coaches and other local people.

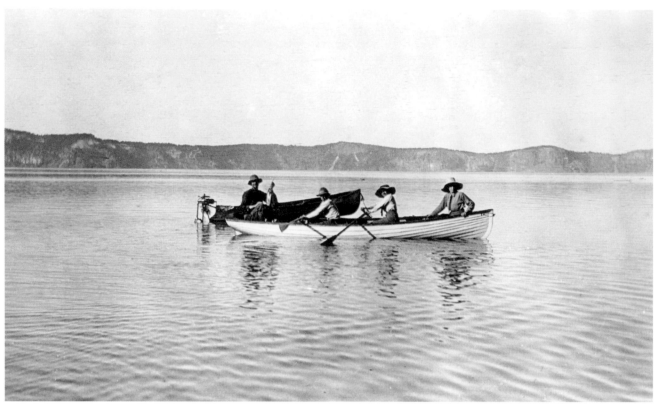

Early fishing party on Crater Lake.

Southern Oregon Historical Society

There were times, of course, when the top job wasn't exactly inspiring. Despite the great care with which superintendents and staffs fashioned laws to protect the public, visitors still violated regulations.

Example: In 1936, one tried to climb down into the lake, slipped, and fell to his death. The following year, a 17-year-old girl, daring to walk on snow inside the rim, slipped and slid down almost to the lake. To retrieve her body, rangers had to climb down a long snowy slide, then carry the body up until they could reach a hoist.

As we have seen in the ranger chapter, this kind of thing can chew on the souls of superintendents and staffs. For no matter how much the cause may have been visitor carelessness or disobedience of law, it was the top man who bore responsibility. He should have worked harder to prevent such events from happening.

He could blame it on lack of appropriations, or not enough staff to enforce regulations. But blame could go only so far. Register complaints, and then what? When the park opened to year round travel in 1936, more visitors could be served, and more venturesome, daring travelers admitted.

All right. Beef up the training. In July, 1938, the first ranger training school opened. Now the staff could be taught first aid, fire management, forest diseases, rescue and other

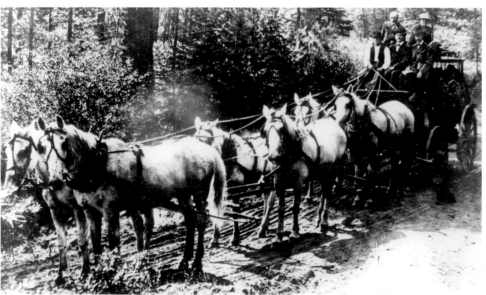

Party of Secretary of Interior James A. Garfield on visit to Crater Lake from Fort Klamath.

Southern Oregon Historical Society

skills. Thereafter, as soon as all the summer help arrived, the school became an annual event, followed up by the development of a ranger manual. In this way the rangers could learn to be the "eyes and ears" of the superintendent, able to observe and analyze "bewildering situations."

From all the analyses, the superintendent had to fashion and revise policies constantly, consistent with the never-ending flood of policies from higher echelons in the Department of the Interior.

The more complex park operations became down through the years, the more reports came from above and below. The more visitors, the greater need for Congressional appropriations to provide for them. It was the superintendent's job to write convincing pleas and send forth justifications for the establishment of new positions on the staff, and for the construction of new facilities.

Even today, changes in policy, administration and management still go on. For example, Crater Lake became the first national park to introduce concessioner-operated fee campgrounds, an experiment begun in 1957. In such ways, the complications of keeping a park unimpaired for the enjoyment of future generations is made perhaps a little easier.

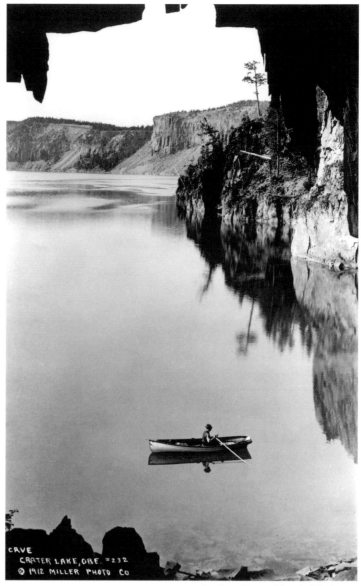

Southern Oregon Historical Society

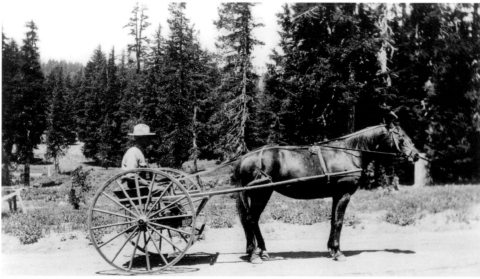

Superintendent Sparrow.

Southern Oregon Historical Society

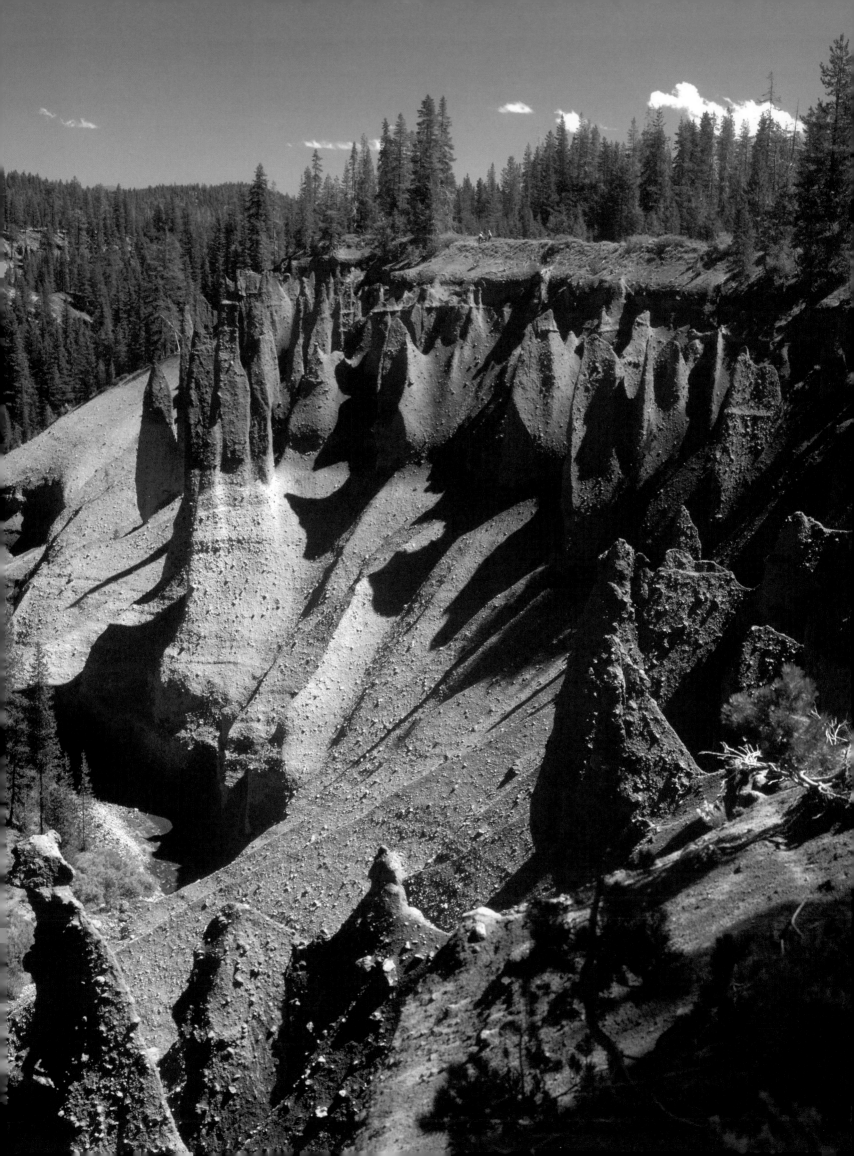

Patches of fog on Crater Lake.

John Erwin

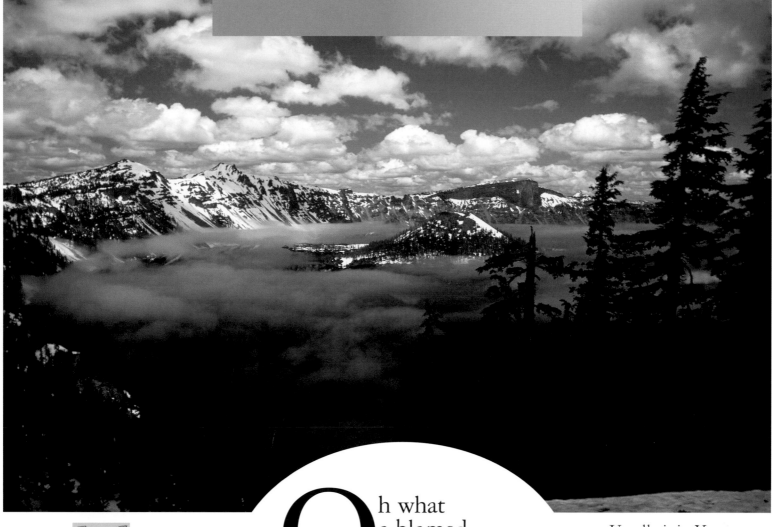

More snow falls in Crater Lake National Park than anywhere else in Oregon. The annual average is 495 inches, or more than forty feet. The record, as we have seen, is more than 900 inches, or 75 feet. No wonder climatologists call Crater Lake the "snow champion" of Oregon.

At first glance, such quantities don't seem possible. Crater Lake is in southern Oregon. Its elevation is less than other mountains in the Cascades. Why so much precipitation?

Outsiders often think of Oregon's climate as rainy but calm and relatively

Oh what a blamed uncertain thing,

This pesky weather is.
First it snew, and then it thew,
And now, by jing, it's friz!

Philander Johnson

warm. Usually it is. Yet, the temperatures in this state range from 54 degrees F. below zero to 119 degrees above. Only nine other states have a wider range. And winds can reach as high as 131 miles an hour. The temperature at Crater Lake once fell to 11 degrees in June, which is not exactly what you would call benign.

Yes, Oregon is wet. Some places along the Pacific Coast have had rain up to 204 inches a year. Other places have had three inches a year, and the State has extensive deserts.

Oregon's weather is dominated by patterns of air movement across the North Pacific Ocean. In summer, a high pressure becomes dominant over the region. Storms go north, and the state is bathed in sunshine and gentle breezes.

Opposite page:

The Pinnacles represent deposits of pumice and other material ejected from Mount Mazama.

John Erwin

In winter, storms move in from the west, which brings moisture for Crater Lake's heavy snowfalls. The extra ingredient in this mix comes from the southwest. Moist air from California and subtropical ocean regions grazes southern Oregon and lifts park totals to record levels.

A common memory taken away by visitors to Crater Lake is the beautiful weather of summer. "The air is so pure," wrote Heidi Lyn Ross and David Lee Fuller in *Crater Lake Nature Notes*, "that on the clearest day you can see at least 190 miles, and occasionally to the 240 mile limit. Actual day to day visibility at Crater Lake averages about 105 miles. The small amount of pollution we do have is not directly associated with an urban or industrial corridor. Weather patterns in those areas usually trap the pollutants to the ground. At Crater Lake, air movement is generally characterized by westerly winds associated with the presence of weather systems formed over the Pacific Ocean. Air pollution over the park is usually particulates from slash burning, wildfires, and agricultural burning.

"The National Park Service and the Oregon Department of Environmental Quality monitor the air at Crater Lake in four different ways. **Standard Visual Range (SVR)** data are collected by a 35mm camera which photographs a vista of known distance three times a day.

"The **Transmissometer** has a transmitting station at Rim Village that sends a light beam across the lake to a receiving station at Wineglass on the northeast side of the lake. By calculating how much light is sent and how much is received, the amount lost traveling from one site to another can be determined.

"The **Nephelometer** is an instrument that takes air into a vacuum tube and sends light through the sample. It then measures the intensity of light that is scattered by particles contained within the instrument's optical path. The park's Nephelometer is located at Rim Village.

"Finally, the **Improve** pulls air through many different filters. Each filter is a different degree or size, meaning each filter will catch a different sized particle. To see what particles are in the air, each filter is chemically analyzed. This device is located at Park Headquarters."

S now

It is all too well known that if half an inch of snow falls on a big city, traffic can be paralyzed. That is partly because a slick road surface, especially where there is a slight incline of the road bed, can cause a car to swerve, spin and stop sideways, blocking the lane. That backs up traffic for miles.

A snowfall of 18 inches one winter in Washington, D.C., so paralyzed the region that some people started chopping up furniture to use as firewood.

Now consider that a single storm at Crater Lake can leave behind more than three feet of snow, and the record annual snowfall, according to state climatologists, is more than 903 inches, set in 1950. (Ironically, the record for one day's snowfall was set not at Crater Lake but at Bonneville Dam: 39 inches in 1980.)

No city has to cope with such a crushing blanket, and you may think that no human beings could live where snowdrifts reach fifteen feet in the winter. But the workers at Crater Lake do, and if it seems as though they ought to hibernate like bears, that is a logical conclusion. On the contrary, they go right on working all winter, keeping the road plowed to the rim, and clearing pathways in residential, administrative, and public areas.

How do they do it? How does anyone cope with an annual snowfall of 75 feet?

To some degree, their milieu is designed for a heavy load of snow. Building roofs are steeply pitched, so that much of the snow slides off. Rare is the building that collapses these days.

Some buildings at headquarters are connected to others by roofed passageways. These turn into tunnels in winter, but they make it unnecessary for employees to plow through impossible snow drifts to get around. Some offices are on the second floor. Always there is the bizarre fascination of watching to see if the next snow fall will break old records.

If all this seems to lowlanders something of a never-never land, it may come as a shock to realize that a great many people actually like snow country. You'll remember the new ranger saying that when he got to Crater Lake he felt as though he had gone to Heaven.

It becomes something of an obsession to watch the records tumble. Witness these words by Chief Ranger Lou Hallock in 1952:

"The past winter, while not breaking any records for snowfall, did result in the greatest recorded depths of snow on the ground since park records have been kept. On March 1, 1952, there was 177 inches of snow on the ground which was only 31 inches from the record. A storm which began on the 3rd and ended on the 8th resulted in 39 inches of snowfall and increased the total depth to 200 inches. It was at this point we realized that if the normal cycle of storms continued, we would break a record. Thereafter, each storm, even though adding to our inconvenience of living and working in heavy snow, was watched with interest and anticipation. Another storm moved in from the southwest on the 9th and continued through the 15th and gave us another 38 inches of snowfall. The depth as recorded reached 201 inches, only 7 inches shy of the record we still hoped would be broken. There still remained 15 days of the month of heaviest snowfall. We should see the record broken.

"March 16 was clear and comparatively warm, maximum temperature 37 degrees. Still another storm crossed the Cascades on the 17th and continued through the 20th. This storm carried enough moisture to satisfy our anticipation. In four days 42 inches of snow fell. At the beginning of this four day period the measured depth on the ground was 198 inches. On the second day a total depth of 207 inches was recorded—only one inch shy of the record. Then on the 18th 6 inches of snow fell followed by 10 inches more on the 19th. This was it! At 4:00 P.M. on the 19th the measuring stake recorded 216 inches. The record had been smashed but it continued snowing, and we speculated on how much greater the depth would be. On the morning of March 20, 1952, the measurement reached 224 inches of snow [nearly 19 feet] on the ground. During the day, however, the storm moved on and the new snow gradually settled to 218 inches, still a record.

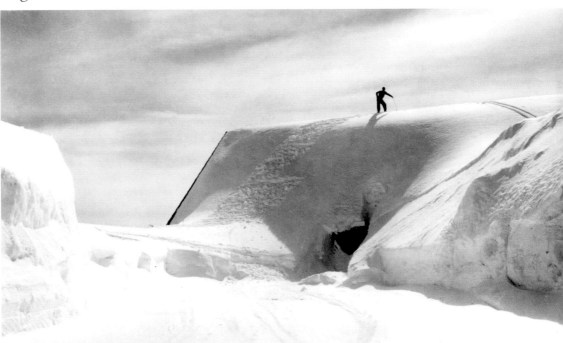

Record snows fell at Crater Lake in the years following WWII.   Southern Oregon Historical Society

"By the end of March there had been measured 798 inches of snowfall, and we now set our sights on the breaking of the record for total snowfall, but this was not to be. The last snowfall on June 14, brought the total to 835 inches, some 44 inches short of a record."

People have a wonderful way of adapting. There are perfectly natural reasons why Crater Lake is so well endowed with snow. One of them is its distance from the Equator.

Mountains to the south rise higher and have less snow. The upper limit of vegetation, the tree line, lowers as you progress northward, and the climate obviously

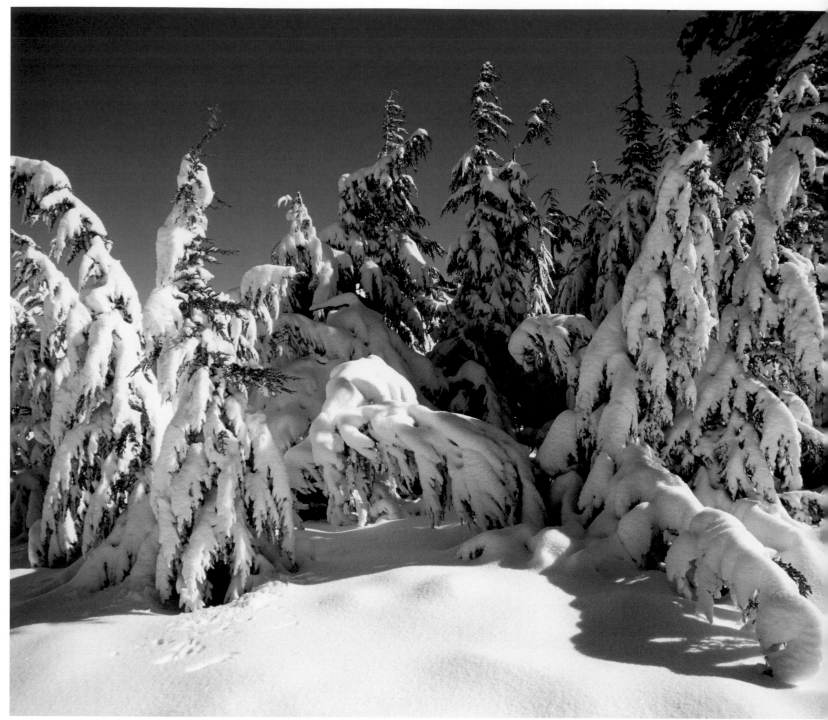

Heavy snows often deform young trees.

Preston Mitchell

grows colder the closer you get to the North Pole. Crater Lake's elevation of 8,000 feet is enough to guarantee accumulation of snow because the sun doesn't come up high enough in the sky each winter to bring about much melting.

Another reason, of course, is the abundance of water. The Pacific Ocean sends up great masses of moisture that move inland on prevailing winds. During the summer, those masses go north into Canada and a high pressure system sets in over the Pacific Northwest. That translates into relatively rain-free summers. An occasional electric storm, however, can wreak some havoc, and here and there you may find trees split down the middle by lightning.

The rest of the year, those moisture laden clouds move into Oregon, rise, turn to snow, and there you have it. When this moisture cools and freezes, the result is tons of snow.

Crater Lake is not alone, of course, in these endowments. Other high elevations in the Pacific Northwest (which means other volcanic peaks) are similarly covered with snow, some more than Crater Lake. Mount Rainier has 26 glaciers containing more than five times as much snow and ice as all the other Cascade volcanoes combined.

The mountains serve as natural water storage reservoirs. For example, Mount McLoughlin, a few miles south of Crater Lake, feeds Big Butte Springs, which yields pure drinking water to communities in the Rogue River basin at the rate of 33 million gallons a day. It is enough to make residents of drought-stricken regions envious.

The downside of heavy snow is that it closes roads. Every effort is made to keep Highway 62 between Medford and the park open to traffic in winter. The road into the park to the rim is also kept open, so that visitors can see Crater Lake when it is surrounded by snow. There may be times when four-wheel-drive vehicles are required. A quick call to the park is a good way to determine road conditions.

P lowing

Getting rid of all that snow so that at least a little traffic can move about is just what you think: a Herculean effort. Park Historian Steve Mark gives us a succinct summary in *Crater Lake Nature Notes*.

"There are still some people who are surprised to learn that Crater Lake can be seen at any time of the year. Much of this misperception is due to visitors focusing on the North Entrance and associating its closure each year with the park being shut for the winter.

"Since opening the North Entrance each year signifies the start of peak visitation, the casual observer might wonder why virtually all park facilities are situated on the south side of the caldera. One reason is that very little surface water exists on the north side of Crater Lake despite the prodigious snowfall. Efforts to develop a water supply were frustrated in the 1960s when contractors drilled wells at Cleetwood Cove and the North Entrance but netted nothing but air. A steep ascent from Pumice Desert to the North Junction, coupled with the difficulties of fighting prevailing wind

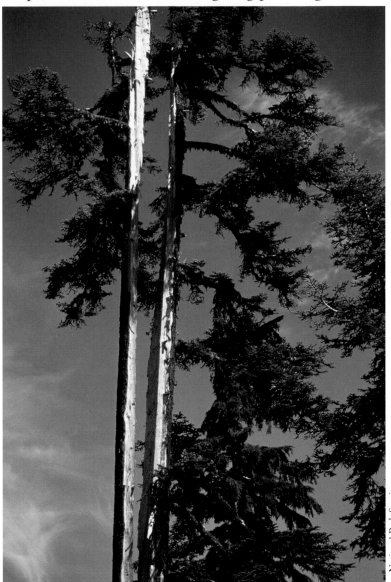

National Park Service

Lightning split this tree in half, but it lives on.

from the southwest, make consistent plowing of the north road exceedingly difficult. Clearing the route leading to Rim Village from Annie Spring and Highway 62 is, by comparison, much easier.

"Most visitors come to Crater Lake only during the summer months and are oblivious to the complexities

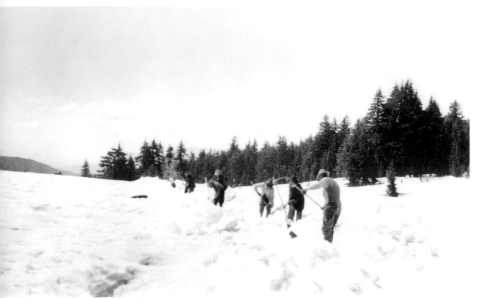

Crew clearing road in the early days. Southern Oregon Historical Society

associated with snow removal. Many of them see only a few outward manifestations of winter, such as snow tunnels attached to buildings at Park Headquarters. …Snow plows operated by park crews are usually out of sight by this time, along with the multitude of snow poles which line certain roads for most of the year.

"Prior to 1930, when the first rotary snow plow arrived at Crater Lake, opening any road to the rim each spring required a large crew armed with shovels. They began by chopping through most of the previous winter's snowpack to reach the road surface, which was often under many feet of snow even in June."

Warm weather and the high sun angle of late spring would help clear the road for cars to circle the caldera, but snow and ice still have to be removed by mechanical means in order to lengthen the visitors season. "With machines that could throw snow away from the road surface, and then above surrounding banks of ten feet or more, it became possible to keep a few roads open throughout the year.

"As might be expected, rotary snow plows gave winter use in the park a decided shot in the arm. Such use had amounted to virtually nil before that time except for the occasional venturesome skier coming from Fort Klamath, the closest permanent settlement. Improving economic conditions by the late 1930s gave rise to increased travel and an associated demand for winter sports. No permanent facilities for downhill skiing were ever constructed, but Crater Lake was listed as Oregon's second biggest winter sports area (behind Mount Hood) in 1940. That status has to be understood in the context that most leases for development of areas on

Forest Service land, such as on Mount Bachelor near Bend, were not issued until the explosion in leisure travel had occurred after World War II.

"Wartime restrictions on travel meant closure for Crater Lake National Park from 1942 to 1945. When the park reopened, there was uncertainty concerning whether to provide downhill skiing facilities. National Park Service planners studied several locations such as Applegate Peak, Arant Point, and the west side of Munson Ridge in 1948, but concluded that any new development aimed at downhill skiing carried far more long-term costs than benefits. They recognized, however, that existing use (visitors wanting to see the lake in winter, as well as cross country skiing and snowshoeing) was justification for keeping the park open all year round. This has occurred over the past 50 years by plowing snow as it accumulated on roughly 25 miles of park roads.

"Those visitors and employees who utilize the access provided by the snow plows have the opportunity to enjoy the beauty brought to the rim of Crater Lake by each seasonal change. During the long winter, the snow accentuates the glassy blue or steel grey of Crater Lake, depending on clear or cloudy conditions. Visitors often note the snowdrifts, especially where the wind puts vast deposits in some places (upwards of 60 feet at the Watchman) but scours bare spots in others."

Cloud Waterfalls

One striking phenomenon typical of volcanic calderas in other places as well as Crater Lake, is the rise of huge clouds up the outer slopes of the crater, and then their dramatic spill down into the caldera like a massive cloud waterfall.

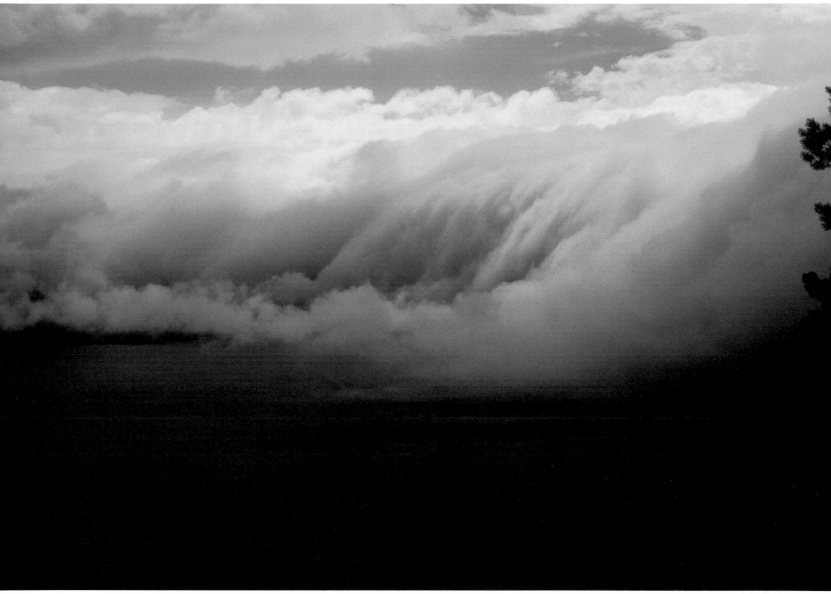

John Erwin

Rising clouds spill into the caldera at Crater Lake.

It is not surprising that so large and deep a body of water maintains its temperature most of the winter. To be sure, it is a cold lake, but when the surface is warmer than the air above it, clouds collect.

If the air above gets super cold the surface of the lake can freeze over.

But rarely.

And wouldn't it be wonderful to walk out on the lake when it is frozen?

Answer: No.

In the next chapter, two people who did it tell what happened.

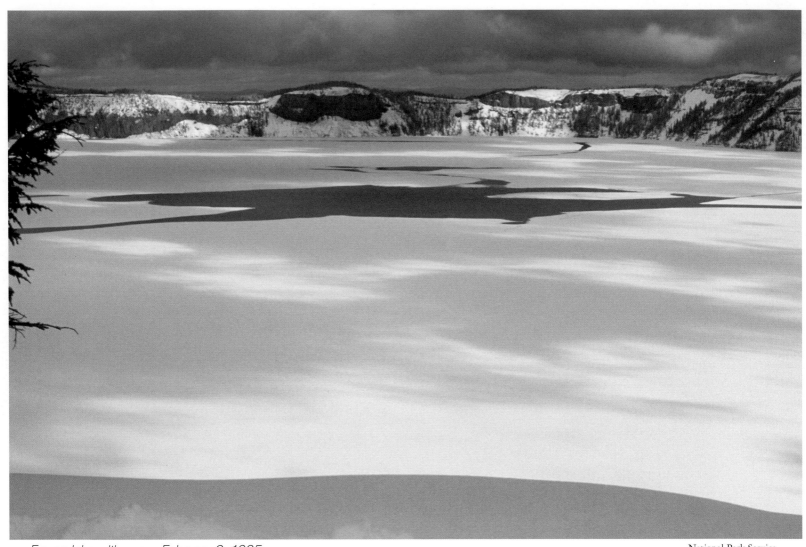

Frozen lake with snow, February 2, 1985.

National Park Service

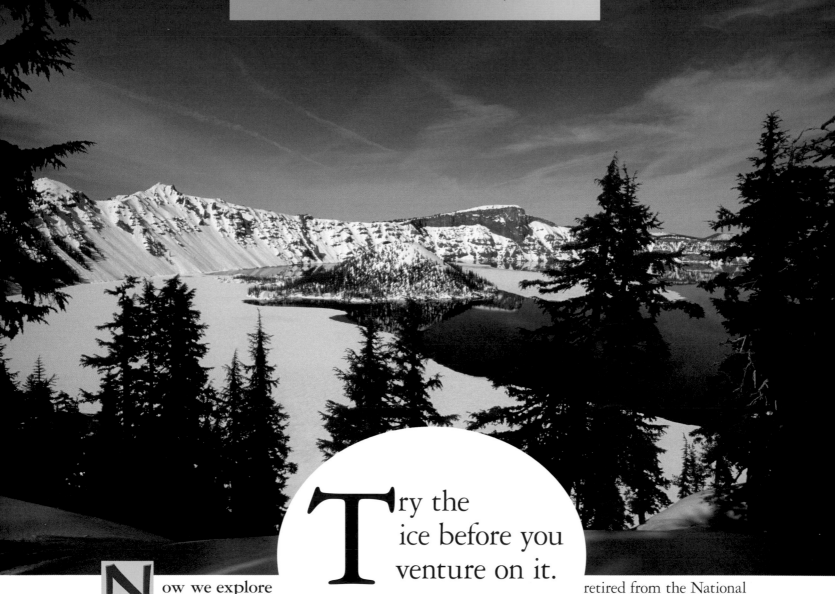

Lake partially frozen over, with snow on top of ice.

John Erwin

Fifteen
OUT ON A FROZEN LAKE

Try the **T**ice before you venture on it.

Proverb

Now we explore a little further the intriguing questions of whether Crater Lake freezes over and whether anyone has ever walked out on the ice.

Answer to both questions: yes.

George Cornelius Ruhle was one of those persons who never slowed to a walk. Short, stocky, dark eyes twinkling, he would lower his head, and whether walking down a corridor or up a trail, he seemed to charge like a military tank, defying anyone to keep up. He had accumulated so many experiences worldwide by the time he retired from the National Park Service in the 1970s that he could talk for hours upon just about any given travel or scientific subject. If there seemed a touch of braggadocio in his extraordinary presentations, it was probably in the eye of the beholder. Or his enthusiasm was so contagious that even if the stories were embellished a little here and there, you knew he had "been there and done that."

George was a Park Naturalist at Crater Lake National Park from 1940 to 1953, and his writings in issues of *Crater Lake Nature Notes* display his enthusiasm about everything in the park. To him, learning was everything.

He happened to be there on one of the rare times when the lake froze. 1949 was so unremittingly cold that heavy snow fell as far south as Arizona. No one, up to

Teams of horses moved people and supplies through heavy snows in the early days of the park.

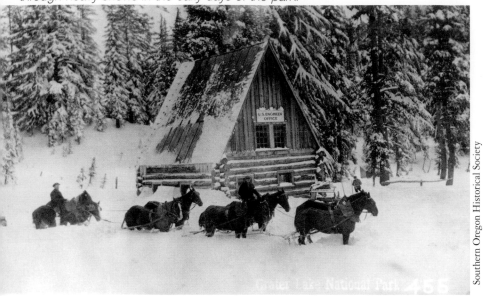

Southern Oregon Historical Society

that time, was certain what the lake surface was like when all or part of it froze. And did anyone dare to walk out on it?

Ruhle and others in the park knew that they would be inundated with requests from visitors to walk out on the ice. They had to know if it could be done, and head off efforts if such a venture proved unsafe. Should a daring visitor get down the icy cliffs, walk out on the ice and fall through, the rangers would have a devil of a time getting to him and pulling him out.

What follows is George Ruhle's description of that event, and his descent to the lake to go out and test the ice. It was just like him not to let the hazards of getting down and back deter him, much less walking on thin ice already burdened with heavy snow.

For the sake of brevity, we are going to edit this account slightly. George, wherever his spirit flies, would not mind old friends juggling a word here and there: the impact of what he did transcends all.

An Historical Passage by
Dr. George C. Ruhle, Park Naturalist

For a long time it had been contended that Crater lake never freezes, that what seemed to be ice was illusory, and that even in summer under certain optical and atmospheric conditions, the surface appears to be covered with skim ice. Nice explanations were given for the improbability of the Lake's ever freezing. New explanations are in order now, for this year, definitely, the lake not only was completely covered by a sheet of ice, but this ice was strong enough to support a significant blanket of snow. For over two months, from mid-February until May, park

visitors beheld a white expanse in place of the sapphire sea so justly famous. To obtain scientific data, to forestall stunt-loving publicity seekers, and to reconnoiter for information of importance in meeting situations of emergency, Superintendent E. P. Leavitt authorized Acting Chief Ranger Duane S. Fitzgerald and me to descend the caldera wall. Both of us had much experience with snow travel and operations in extreme cold; both had attended special schools of mountain climbing and are qualified as instructors. For two months we had watched the ice gradually sheeting the surface. Already early in the year, Grotto Cove and Skell Channel were completely encased and were receiving a deep blanket of snow. Ice formed elsewhere on the shore and the growing shelves encrusted more and more of the deep blue waters. By February 13th, only three patches of open water remained with a total area of a square mile. Late that week, these too were closed, and more and more snow collected on the surface. While intently watching the freezing, we commented on its significance, and finally determined to investigate the cover at close hand. The date picked for descent was March 14. Instead of a beautiful clear day, sullen skies disappointed us. We waited through the morning with no bolster to hopes. As the time was passing, it was decided to reconnoiter and prepare fuller plans for a more auspicious day. Our first attempt was to reach Discovery Point in the park snowcat, so that we could take advantage of the sloping caldera walls and the ice pack on Skell Channel. But hazardous snow stopped passage of our specialized vehicle. We returned to the rim-road to study critical slopes, slippage, depth, and sustaining loads of snow inside the wall. Equipped with snowshoes and ropes,

Fifteen – Out on a Frozen Lake

we gingerly experimented and tried out our aids. I personally investigated the feasibility of descent thru a forested strip, and discovered that while in some places I could sink to my neck if without snowshoes, the method proved perfectly possible. Attempts to climb back up were very arduous, being made only by use of brute strength. I tried my wings a little more thoroughly and the thought flashed thru my mind, "Do it now," and I was off with snowshoes strapped on my back. Ranger Fitzgerald above, seeing me make good headway down the strip followed in my trail but left his snowshoes near the rim. While twice the route had to zig-zag cautiously across an open col, no great avalanches of snow were precipitated. At the foot of the slopes, a twenty-foot andesite cliff had to be traversed by rappelling on an anchored rope. We reached the lakeshore at the boat landing. It was found that snow on the ice was eight to twelve inches deep, and that the ice readily supported our weight. I set out on snowshoes in a direct line for Wizard Island but Fitz discovered the snow too deep for good progress without his aid.

Several hundred feet from shore the ice began to crack and rumble ominously and numerous tests were made of its strength. Finally, about one thousand yards out, under a cover of only four inches of snow, I succeeded in chopping thru the ice, and with my thumb and index finger, estimated it to be two inches thick. The hole was enlarged to admit a snowshoe, which could be shoved three to four feet into the water beneath. This confirmed that the ice cover was on the lake water itself, and not over a pocket of surface ice. The lake is over 1000 feet deep at this place. With the disturbing information, I started a diagonal

retreat westward and shoreward, only to assay again and then again on a due course to the island. This maneuvering brought me several hundred yards west of the tip of the lava flow by the island boathouse, and a hurried finish was made to the trip.

I climbed ashore, visited the boathouses, and snowshoed to the base of the main cinder cone. Little of note was observed. There were no birds and no tracks nor sounds of wild folk. Utilizing knowledge gained, the return trip was considerably shortened.

Meanwhile Fitz had plodded a half mile or more thru sodden snow from the landing. Upon reaching him, I gave him my snowshoes so that he could continue on to the island. Traveling nearer the shore, at one place he discovered ice pushed shoreward that was a foot in thickness. Estimates of snow depth near the shore were of the nature of several feet. In my continuing on to the landing it was noteworthy that I found each of Fitzgerald's footprints to be completely filled with watery slush.

The real struggle lay ahead—the struggle up the rim. It took two hours of obstinate persistency and both of us were completely exhausted by it. A few hundred feet from the rim, the sun suddenly broke thru the clouds, and permitted taking a few photographs. Probably because of the limited number of years past that the road has been plowed, during which the lake never has frozen solid, and because of the handful of winter visitors before that arduously struggled to reach the lake in winter on snowshoes or skis, this is the first known crossing of Crater Lake on ice. Its justification as summarized for the press by Superintendent Leavitt, was in the interest of science, and as a result the park has gained valuable data.

In the year 2000 we talked with Duane Fitzgerald, who went down to the lake with Ruhle. Here are some comments by him:

"At the time of that walk, I was about 34 years old. We went out on the expedition largely to measure the thickness of the ice and of the snow covering the ice. We had one pair of skis which I wore, and one pair of snowshoes, which George wore. The ice along the lake shore was about a foot thick. Things went well as we walked along to Wizard Island, but then we noticed the ice started to move up and down like waves in water, so we decided we had had enough, and started back to the main shore. We didn't see any water collecting in our shoe prints until we started back."

WATERLOGGED EXPLORER

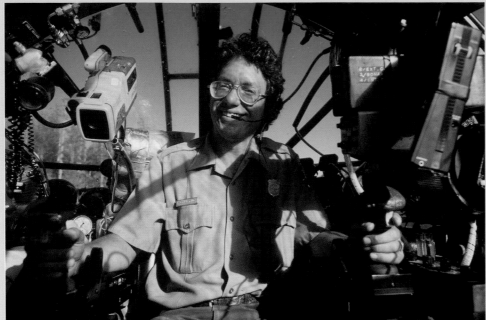

Mark Buktenica, at the controls of the submersible Deep Rover.

Photos by Mathias Van Hesemans.

"I was sitting alone in Crater Lake, 600 feet underwater in a small submarine called Deep Rover. I had just completed collecting rock samples along an underwater edge of Wizard Island, and I had 135 pounds of rocks in a basket attached to the front of the submarine. Unknown to me at the time, a couple of O-ring seals were leaking throughout the dive. Water seeping through the seals into the submarine, combined with condensation from my breathing, created an uncomfortable amount of water on the floor. My feet were near the front of the vessel, and as I prepared to start to the surface with the rocks, the submarine tilted forward. As the submarine tipped, the water level at my feet rose rapidly, giving the distinct impression that the submarine was filling with water. Garbled and intermittent communications with the surface crew aggravated the situation. Everyone operated expertly and efficiently; Deep Rover and the rock samples were recovered smoothly. Actual dangers and repairs turned out to be minimal, and the submarine dove again the next day. Nonetheless, I thoroughly reviewed emergency procedures at my first opportunity."

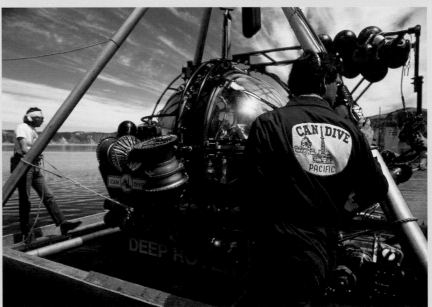

Preparations are underway for descent in the submersible Deep Rover.

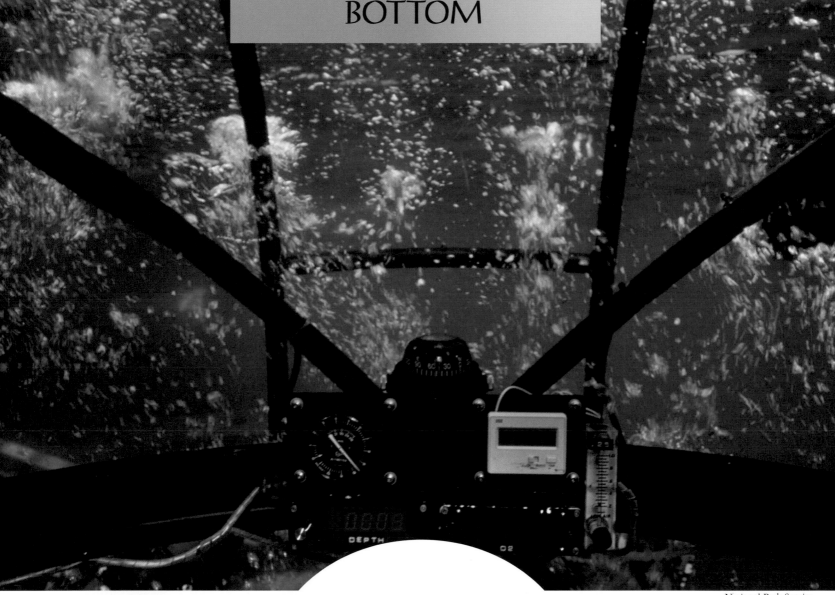

National Park Service

While other young people were seeking adventure by traveling the world, Mark Buktenica, the aquatic biologist at Crater Lake National Park, found great excitement by descending to the floor of North America's deepest lake. Exploring the lake's bottom was a goal made possible by the invention of *Deep Rover*, a bubble-like submarine made of five-inch thick acrylic.

On each side a window opened into this unexplored abyss.

Jules Verne

The Searchers

Scientific exploration of Crater Lake is not new, but the technology and apparatus used have certainly changed over time. Back in 1883, two U.S. Geological Survey employees, Joseph Diller and Everett Hayden, rolled logs down to the lake level, lashed them together, and rowed over to Wizard Island.

In 1886, Clarence Dutton and Mark Kerr of the USGS joined William Steel in a launch, called The Cleetwood, to sound the lake's depth with piano wire at some 168 locations. They recorded a maximum depth of 1,996 feet.

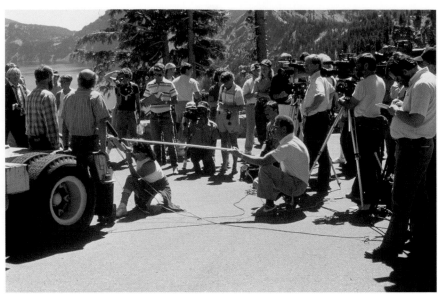

Press conference on the rim..   National Park Service

Many attempts were made to measure water level fluctuations, beginning in 1892. At first, measurements were made from a mark on a large rock projecting from the shore. Later, in 1896, a wooden gauge was installed along the shore, but it was broken off the following winter. Eventually, the USGS installed a water-stage recorder in Cleetwood Cove which records water-level changes hourly, transmitting its data by satellite to the world wide web.

Water temperatures were first measured at Crater Lake in 1896, when a deep-sea thermometer was used, showing 60 degrees F. at the surface and 46 degrees at a depth of 1,623 feet. Later, measurements using two thermometers failed to show any increase in water temperature from a constant 39 degrees F. between 300 feet and the bottom of the lake.

Beginning in 1912 and continuing sporadically after that, several scientists studied the chemical content and microscopic plant and animal life of the lake. One scientist found that sunlight actually penetrated to a depth of 400 feet because of the water's high transparency.

In 1940 a team of oceanographers came to study the lake with what was then state-of-the-art oceanographic equipment. Many aspects of the lake were studied, including measurements of light with a submarine photometer, studies of phytoplankton, and studies of water samples for dissolved chemicals.

During the 1940s and 1950s many scientists came to work as ranger-naturalists at Crater Lake, spending their free time following their own research interests and adding to the store of knowledge about the animals and plants found in the water.

A helicopter was also used to lower and raise the **Deep Rover** *submarine onto the lake.*

In 1959 several scientists from the U.S. Coast and Geodetic Survey sounded the lake bottom with some 4,000 echo soundings to map the topography of the lake bottom. From these soundings, a bathymetric map showing the significant geomorphic features of the lake bottom was developed.

From the late 1970s on, there have been numerous studies by professionals and graduate students from a number of universities.

Multiple Beams

As Crater Lake's first century came to a close, a 26-foot research vessel was lowered onto the lake by helicopter to begin a high resolution bathymetric survey using multi-beam technology. A device on the front of the boat sent out a wide band of 111 sound beams and received a "backscatter" of reflected beams. In all, more than seventeen million depth soundings were obtained. From all this came images of objects in the lake, and new information on the geology of the caldera floor.

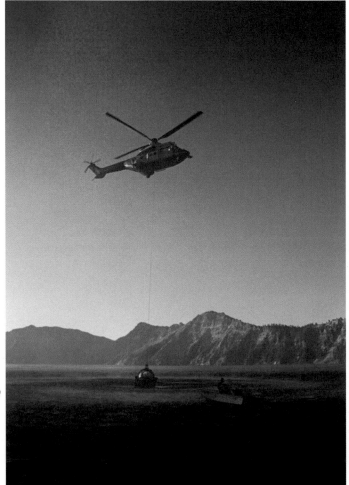

National Park Service

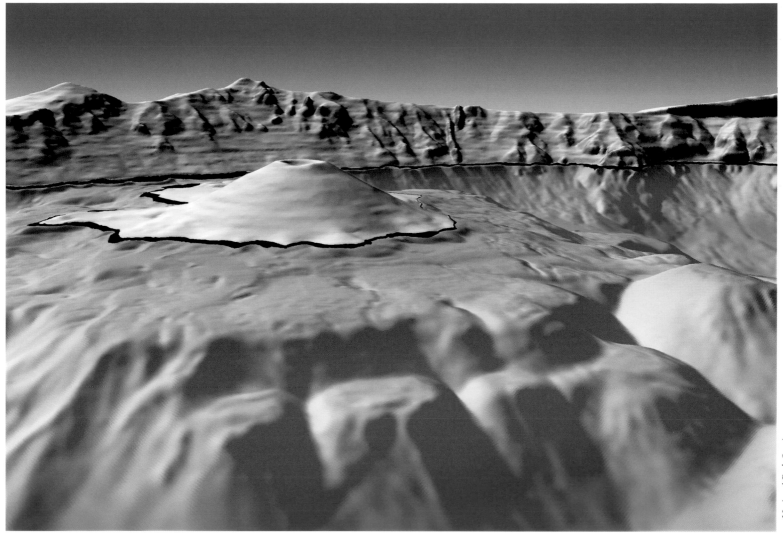

National Park Service

This oblique view of shaded-relief bathymetry, looking west, shows the underwater platform on which Wizard Island sits. Areas shaded in gray are above water. The distance across the bottom of the image is approximately 1.5 kilometers (0.9 miles)

Discoveries

The lake has been busy with boat trips, research projects, movie making, and air crashes during the first century as a national park, and a lot has fallen into it besides snow. In addition, forty nine little streamlets cascade from surrounding walls, pouring debris into the lake.

So much for what enters the lake from above. The ultimate question: what is coming into the lake from *below*?

With this question we also come to the most ominous inquiry: is the volcano dead or alive?

Did so massive an eruption thousands of years ago leave the ancient volcano completely devoid of fumaroles spouting bubbles of gas down there? Are there hot springs on the bottom? How big are they? How hot? How toxic?

We have seen that the lake has been under close surveillance since before the park was established. Not until the latter part of the century had technology developed the means of exploring the lake with multi-beam technology, and sending human beings to the bottom in small submarines.

A detailed investigation to find out if there is thermal (heat) attached to the hydro (water) down there. Hydrothermal activity, if any, could portend the beginning of some new eruptive cycle.

This investigation would also try to define the ecology of the aquatic environment: what plants and animals have come to live in the lake and how they relate to each

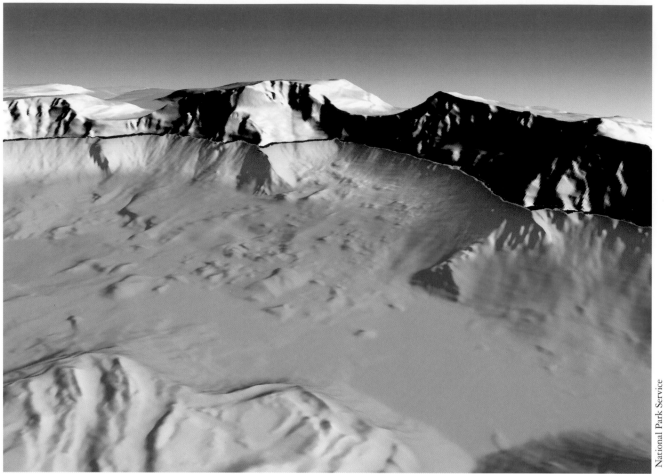

National Park Service

Landslides and avalanches that carry blocks of rock to the bottom are shown in this oblique view looking east toward Chaski Bay. Area shaded in gray is above water. The distance across the bottom of the image is approximately 2.6 kilometers (1.6 miles).

other. Were fish impacting the watery depths and what action should park managers take, if any?

The fish originally taken down to the lake were rainbow, brown, and cutthroat trout, plus steelhead, coho salmon, and kokanee (a landlocked form of sockeye salmon).

Only the kokanee and rainbow survive, but whether they were polluting the water remained unclear.

One of the most critical aspects of studying Crater Lake has been the clarity of water, which has been measured over the years by a number of devices. A **Secchi disk**, a 12-inch black-and-white plate, attached to a cable marked in meters, was lowered until it disappeared from sight. From that, researchers established what they call a "light extinction coefficient." From this point on it is the outsiders' minds that become murky when viewing the "extremely complex computations," as park biologist Mark Buktenica calls them, to determine how clear the

water. And how it compares with measurements years ago.

Transmissometers and **photometers** were also utilized to get a precise determination of water clarity. **Photo cells** have been lowered to

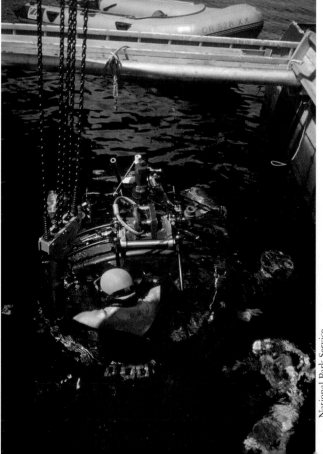

National Park Service

Sixteen – Descent to the Bottom

determine light intensity and reduction at different depths.

This might seem overkill in waters so obviously pure. But small changes over the years could upset the balance of life and lead to something ominous in the future.

It is true that there aren't as many nutrients in Crater Lake as in rich Arctic seas, but there are some. They include phosphorus, sodium, potassium, calcium, magnesium, and sulfates. In volcanic regions, dead or alive, waters could become clouded with toxic materials seeping up from below.

Nyos Lake, in the African Cameroons, filled with a huge amount of carbon dioxide, which stayed beneath the surface until land movements upset the equilibrium and released great amounts of it into the air. Human beings breathe carbon dioxide out, but they are not designed to take it in. The release of gas at Lake Nyos killed 1,700 people on the shores.

New Zealand's Ruapehu Volcano, in Tongariro National Park, simply erupts from time to time and throws out its crater lake water.

Fish captured from the surface to the bottom of Crater Lake yield data on weight, length, age, and food intake. Contents of fish stomachs show what they fed on: midge larvae, caddis flies, butterflies, Daphnia (tiny freshwater crustaceans), Odonata (aquatic insects related to damselflies and dragonflies), and tiny shrimp.

Underwater acoustical surveys were used to determine sizes and numbers of fish populations, and where each species lives. Echo soundings are converted to electrical impulses. Measurements of distance, intensity and time provide biologists with critical data that takes months to compute.

Mark Buktenica says, "There's a lot we don't know." But that seems like a wild understatement when we see what they have already learned.

For one thing, not much goes on near the surface. The water is so clear that a lot of activity begins quite far down. For example, the fish usually remain at 250 feet down during the day, and 180 feet down at night—a daily vertical migration. Fish have been detected as deep as about 450 feet.

Because Crater Lake water is cold and well oxygenated, fish don't need to migrate up streams to lay eggs. They simply dig nests along the shore and spawn.

Rainbows live six to eleven years and reproduce multiple times, reaching twenty inches in length.

Kokanees reproduce once, then die. Kokanee populations explode in numbers, then fall off precipitously. With them, life is a perpetual boom and bust.

Kokanees move in schools along the shoreline. In the mid-1990's, Mark Buktenica observed a school one June that "contained an estimated 200,000 individuals four to six inches in length, and took 42 minutes to swim past a boat dock at Cleetwood Cove."

If this seems like an astonishing amount of information about the depths of the lake, it still falls short of what is needed. For one reason, studying fish in this lake is virtually impossible from October to June because of the extreme danger of descending to the shore along icy cliffs. As a result, researchers lament the paucity of information on life habits in winter.

They do know, however, that the lake teems with food for the fish, especially abundant plankton, small bits and pieces of animal life that the fish scoop up with ease. Sometimes the fish have cycles of good health and bad, but the general view is that kokanee life styles here differ little from kokanees living elsewhere.

In general, the two types of fish occupy different habitats in the lake and consume different foods. Still, says Buktenica, the introduced fish, thriving as they are,

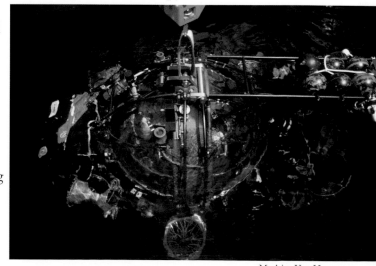

*Divers preparing the **Deep Rover** for submersion.*

Mathias Van Hesemans

have the potential to impact tiny residents in the lake. There just isn't enough known yet to say whether the fish are ruining the lake. They simply appear to be part of the aquatic habitat without much effect on water clarity. Since they have been there for so many years and afforded so much pleasure to anglers, there just doesn't seem any cause for concern. If fish begin to clog up the water, you might think that the introduction of sharks would solve the matter. But then we'd have a lake full of sharks. Better to stick with the kokanees.

The Descent

Inevitably, the next step would be descent to the bottom and observation of the lake floor through human eyes.

No one can swim very far down into America's deepest lake. Not even with scuba apparatus can you descend 1,932 feet. For that, a small pressurized $3\frac{1}{2}$-ton submersible craft was airlifted by helicopter to the surface of the lake.

With Congressional authorization and funding, descents were made in the summers of 1988 and 1989 by Buktenica and two other scientists. When Buktenica wrote up a description of his *Deep Rover* experiences, Park Historian Stephen Mark observed, "Rarely does a volume of *Nature Notes* have the opportunity to present stories as significant to resource management at Crater Lake." Indeed, rarely have the annals of publishing been enriched with such a remarkable article.

Why Enter a Sleeping Volcano in a Submarine?
by Mark Buktenica (Photos National Park Service)
Crater Lake Nature Notes

Operating a program that utilizes a submersible is a difficult undertaking in the best of settings, but especially challenging in remote areas at high altitude such as Crater Lake. The only access by land to the lake was the steep, one mile-long Cleetwood Cove Trail. Small four-wheel-drive tractors were the primary means of carrying supplies and materials from the top of the caldera to the lake shore on a daily basis. A base camp was established on Wizard Island and over 30,000 pounds of scientific and technical support equipment, including the 7,000-pound *Deep Rover*, were flown to the island by helicopter. The NPS insisted that no evidence of the operation remain on the island or in the lake after we were done. Researchers were meticulous in this regard and even transported dishwater out of the caldera.

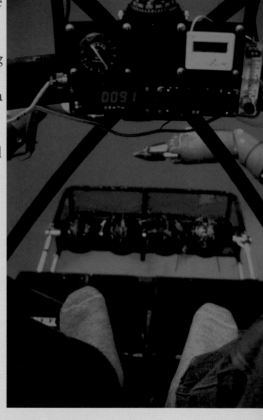

Deep Rover is a highly technical submarine that the NPS, National Geographic Society, and U.S. Geological Survey leased from Can-Dive, Inc., a company based in Vancouver, British Columbia. The vessel is engineered for intuitive operation by its single occupant, who must serve as pilot and scientist. The operator sits in a five inch thick sphere of clear acrylic measuring six feet in diameter. This sphere is attached to two battery pods, each containing ten 12-volt marine batteries. The acrylic sphere opens at the bottom, like a clam shell, allowing the scientist to enter and exit. Mechanical, electrical, hydraulic, and life-support systems are mounted inside and outside of the sphere. Two large manipulator arms are mounted on the front of the submarine and are operated by the pilot inside. A basket mounted below the manipulators is used to stow scientific samples. Cameras, sample bottles, suction samplers, and sophisticated thermometers are other examples of equipment attached to the submarine.

Learning how to operate *Deep Rover* required an intensive one-week training program that included classroom instruction and field work in operation, safety, and emergency response. This ensured that myself and two Oregon State University Oceanographers, Dr. Jack Dymond and Dr. Robert Collier, were ready by the time dives commenced in 1988.

Each dive day began with a trip to the dive site, which usually took one or two hours. *Deep Rover* was towed behind a research boat in a submersible "tender," designed specifically for use at Crater Lake. Once all systems were judged to be functional, the operator crawled through the narrow opening into *Deep Rover*, the submarine hull was sealed, and all outside noise was suddenly muted. Upon being sealed shut, *Deep Rover* heated up like a mini greenhouse, typically reaching 92 degrees F. before descending into the lake un-tethered. With permission to leave the surface, the pilot began the commute to the bottom of Crater Lake.

I had the distinct privilege of conducting 17 dives in *Deep Rover*. As I slowly sank into the depths of the lake, I was engulfed in blue which eventually turned to darkness. The only sounds in the submarine were the creaking and popping of the hull as it adjusted to the increasing water pressure and the persistent hum of the carbon dioxide scrubbers cleaning the air.

The journey to the bottom could take up to 30 minutes, during which time my personal fears were easily extinguished by the intrigue and demands of the work.

After reaching the bottom on my dive to the deepest part of Crater Lake, I shut off the scrubbers and instrument lights to better experience the solitude and quiet, and to briefly reflect on being the first person to visit the deepest part of the lake. After several moments, I looked up through the clear acrylic hull and noticed that the dive flag mounted on top of the submarine was visible, and silhouetted against a slightly lighter background. At 1,932 feet in depth my eyes could detect the vague light from the surface, a surprising testament to Crater Lake's incredible clarity.

Yet there was little time for introspection. With less than six hours allowed per dive, I was fully occupied with monitoring electrical and life-support systems, operating the submarine, collecting samples, recording observations on tape and film, and communicating with the surface boat via an underwater wireless telephone. Although the submersible was designed to operate instinctively, many of the tasks I had to perform required extreme concentration and were mentally challenging, physically demanding, and sometimes frustrating.

Most of the lake floor is covered by fine sand colored sediments, and operating the sub there was like flying at night over an uncharted desert.

One of the highlights of the research was discovery of bacteria colonies associated with hydrothermal fluids deep in the lake. These colonies form yellow-orange mats

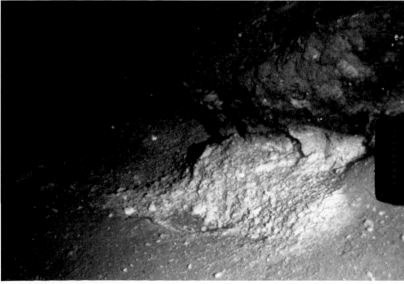

Bacteria colony.

which appeared to hang on to or cascade down sediment slopes and rock outcrops. The mats consist of thousands of *Gallionella* and *Leptothrix* bacteria, which live on chemicals (primarily reduced iron) in the hydrothermal fluids that slowly enter Crater Lake through the lake sediments. It is unusual that the chemical energy from the fluids allows the colonies to live in darkness on the floor of the lake, independent of photosynthesis, since that process energizes most biological communities on the planet.

Temperatures measured inside of the mats were as high as 68 degrees F., whereas ambient water temperature was 38 degrees. Chemical geothermometry models suggest that source temperatures of 104 to 329 degrees would account for observed water chemistry and temperatures at the lake-sediment interface.

Llao's Bath

Another interesting discovery was the presence of discrete pools of saline water on the lake floor that had a distinct blue color. The first "blue pool" discovered was named Llao's Bath by Jack Dymond, after the legendary spirit of the lake. The pool resembled an oblong bath, 10 to 13 feet long and 3 to 5 feet across. It appeared to be elevated on one side by precipitates, and was surrounded by golden-colored bacteria. This pool and others like it are composed of hydrothermal water with salt content as much as ten times higher than the surrounding lake water. The presence of

the salts makes the liquid in the pool heavier than lake water, and the pools appear blue because of the optical properties of the chemically enriched fluids. In general, many chemical indicators of hydrothermal origin were detected in fluids taken from the pools. In the most anomalous pool fluids, manganese was enriched by as much as a million times and Radon...was enriched 100,000 times over typical lake values. Helium-3, perhaps the most distinctive indicator of a magmatic heat source, was enriched 500 times more than values for water in equilibrium with the atmosphere.

We were surprised to find another area of hydrothermal activity below the Palisades along the northeast caldera wall during one of the dives. Small stream-like features originated from underneath boulders or rock outcrops along the base of the caldera wall. The stream-like channels were two to three inches in width and equally as deep. Although no flow was observed at the time, the channels formed networks which exhibited classic erosional flow patterns. The channels were lined with brilliant gold bacteria and often terminated down slope in a series of blue pools. Twenty or more pools with associated islands, embayments, and delta-like features were observed in an area approximately 160 feet wide and 320 feet long.

Along the base of the east wall below Skell Head, remnant spires served as a record of past hydrothermal activity. Over 30 feet high, the spires had a chemistry indicative of a hydrothermal origin and a morphology consistent with underwater formation. Similar spires have been observed around active, high-temperature, hydrothermal sources in oceans around the world.

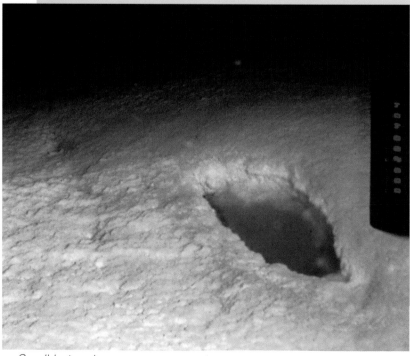

Small hot spring.

Sixteen – Descent to the Bottom

The spires form when chemically rich hydrothermal fluids come in contact with cold ambient water and the chemicals precipitate out of solution to form chimneys around the vents.

In addition to the hydrothermal studies, *Deep Rover* provided a unique opportunity to survey the lake floor for plants and animals.

Previous biological studies of Crater Lake were limited to sampling from a surface boat, collections along the shoreline, or shallow dives using SCUBA gear. During the submersible studies, several unusual and interesting biological discoveries were made. A thick band of moss, *Drepanocladus aduncus*, encircled the lake, and was observed growing at depths from 85 to 460 feet. It hung like icicles on vertical cliffs and formed thick lush fields on the gentler slopes around Wizard Island. The remarkable lower

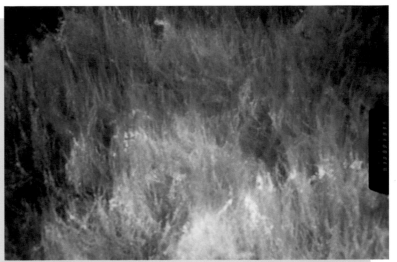

Beds of moss.

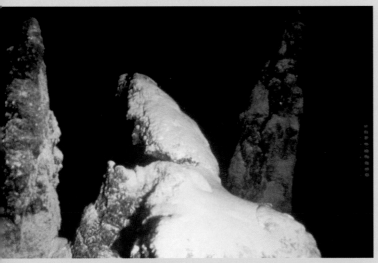

emnant spires.

depth limit of 460 feet was due to the ability of light to penetrate deep into Crater Lake's clear water.

Animals were found living in Crater Lake's deepest basin at 1,932 feet below the surface. This was particularly fascinating because of the extreme water pressure that these animals must sustain to live at this depth.

The deep-water animals were found at relatively low densities and included flatworms, nematodes, earthworms, copepods, ostracods, and the midge fly *Heterotrissocladius*. Many specimens survived the rapid pressure change during the retrieval from the lake floor and lived in the laboratory for several weeks after collection.

The geological studies conducted with *Deep Rover* expanded our knowledge of the eruptive history of Mount Mazama. Most of the rocks sampled from the caldera walls were lava flows which came from Mount Mazama, but a few samples collected from greater depth were rocks which predate Mount Mazama. These studies also provided new information on postcaldera volcanism by indicating which lava flows occurred beneath lake water and which erupted before the lake filled. Flows that formed the central platform, located east of Wizard Island, came about prior to the lake level reaching them. Merriam Cone and most of the submerged portion of Wizard Island formed beneath the water surface when the lake was approximately 250 feet below its present level. All of the postcaldera rocks sampled were andesite, with the exception of those from a small rhyodacite dome on the east flank of Wizard Island. The rhyodacite dome rises to approximately 100 feet of the lake surface and may have formed when the lake was close to its present level. The dome is the youngest volcanic feature known, with an age of approximately 5,000 years.

The dives were not without an element of mystery. I observed craters with a diameter of two to three inches in the deepest part of the lake. The origin of these

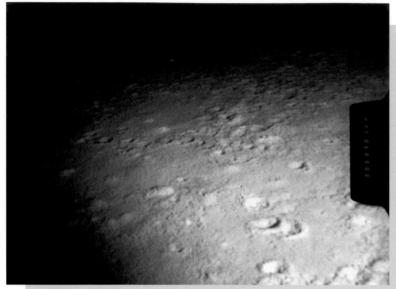

Small craters of unknown origin.

craters is still unknown, though they may have formed from biological activity or from processes associated with gas and/or fluid release from the lake sediments.

With so much to explore, it was hard to accept that the voltage remaining in the submarine's main batteries dictated the length of each dive. At the end of a typical six-hour dive, the temperature of the submarine was a comfortable 68 degrees. Tired but still operating on adrenalin, I stretched the length of the dives out as long as possible. When the dive was over, air was added to the submarine's ballast tank allowing *Deep Rover* to slowly leave the lake floor. This was the first opportunity to relax during a dive. The ascent into natural light was peaceful. As *Deep Rover* rose and the water pressure decreased, air in the ballast tank would expand and spill out the base of the submarine, rising around the sphere in a silvery blue veil of bubbles. Once on the surface, a crew of scientists and technicians quickly descended upon the submersible to secure and preserve the invaluable samples.

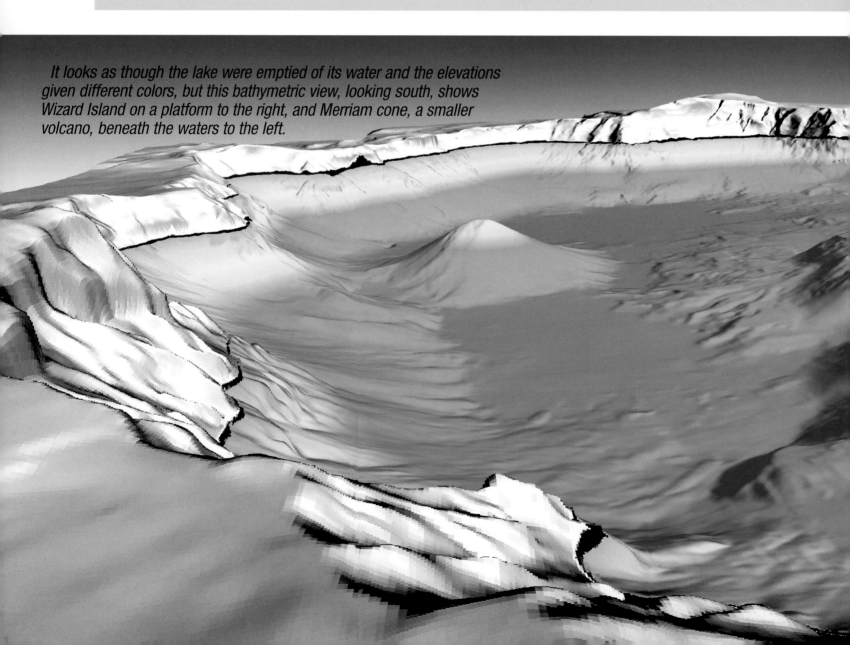

It looks as though the lake were emptied of its water and the elevations given different colors, but this bathymetric view, looking south, shows Wizard Island on a platform to the right, and Merriam cone, a smaller volcano, beneath the waters to the left.

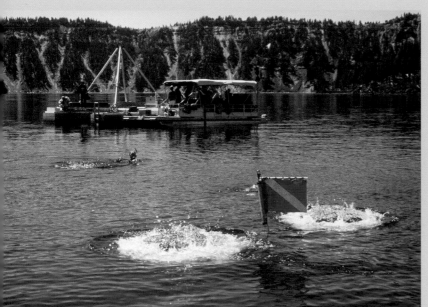

Deep Rover near the surface of the lake.

Deep Rover opened a brief and rare window of opportunity to view and explore secrets hidden at the depths of Crater Lake, yet less than two percent of the lake floor was explored. Discoveries from the submersible program not only provided valuable information on lake ecology and evolution important to understanding and protecting the lake. The program also documented previously unrecorded lush fields of moss, animals living at the bottom of the lake, and hydrothermal streams and vivid blue pools that supported exotic gardens of yellow-gold bacteria. The unusual scenes on the lake floor are consistent with the aerial view that visitors experience today; a sight only slightly altered from that which inspired people a century ago to dedicate themselves toward the establishment of Crater Lake National Park.

National Park Service

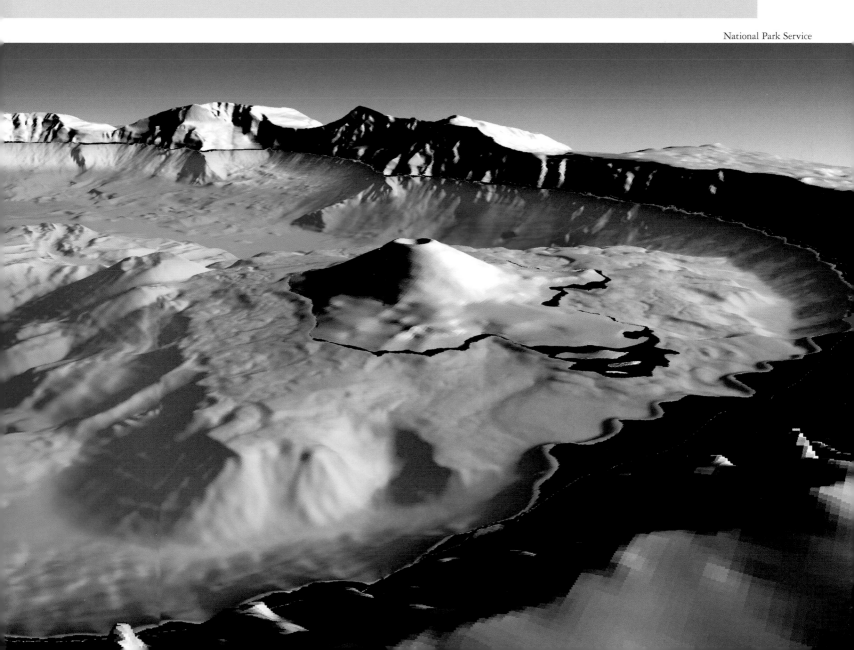

WHY THE LAKE IS BLUE

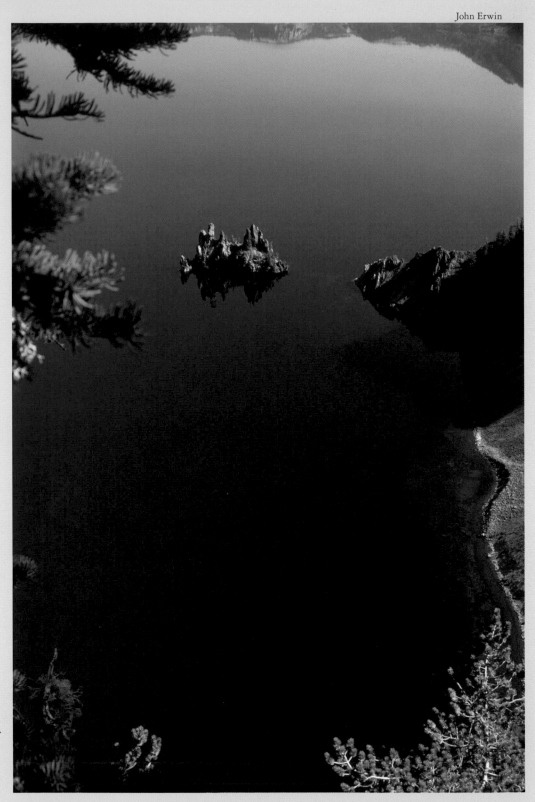

John Erwin

To many observers, the breathtaking beauty of Crater Lake lies largely in its color—as they perceive it. "What an intense blue!" they say. "Celestial hues, terrestrial blues" write the poets. Problem is: it's all in the eye of the beholder. What comes as a surprise is that the waters of this lake are not blue and never have been. For Crater Lake is no more composed of blue water than the sky is composed of blue air. So where does the blue come from? In a word: the sun. That light is intensely white, of course, but every school child knows that when sunlight passes through a prism it breaks up into many colors. As light goes through space, it is seldom impeded by anything other than sparse space dust. Once it strikes earth's atmosphere, however, it begins to encounter a greater concentration of dust particles. What happens to the light then depends on the sizes of the particles encountered. If they are too big, the light can be absorbed, as in sooty smoke, or scattered in various directions with little regard to color, as in white clouds. If the medium is composed of particles or clumps of particles smaller than the wavelength of the light, in this case, as small as a molecule of water or air, then a different kind of scattering takes place, called Rayleigh scattering after British physicist Lord Rayleigh, who first explained it quantitatively in 1871. In Rayleigh scattering the light sets up vibrations in the individual molecules or clusters of molecules. The vibrations give rise to scattering. But the effect is exquisitely sensitive to color. Blue and ultraviolet light are scattered much more strongly than light in the red end of the spectrum. Result: a lake emitting scattered rays of blue.

In other volcanic areas some lakes are green because their content of plant organisms overwhelms the blue. Some are brown because they are loaded with silt. Some are yellow because of a high sulfur content. Or black from mud. Others have hollow black balls of elemental sulfur floating on them.

Few lakes have a color as intense as this one; in Crater Lake are some of the most richly scattered blues on earth.

Art on opposite page based on photo by John Erwin.

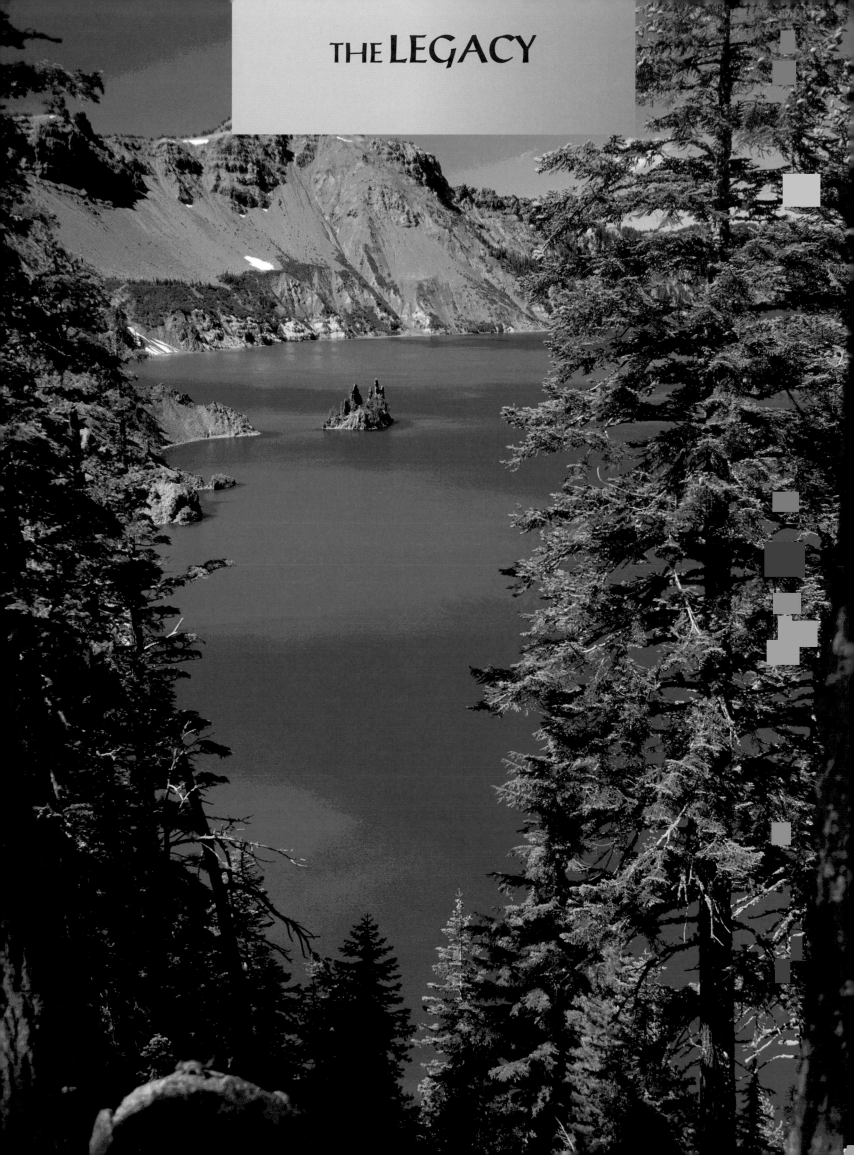

THE LEGACY

THE LEGACY OF CRATER LAKE

Araucaria pines frame Lake Huechulaufquen and Lanín Volcano, Lanín National Park, Argentina.

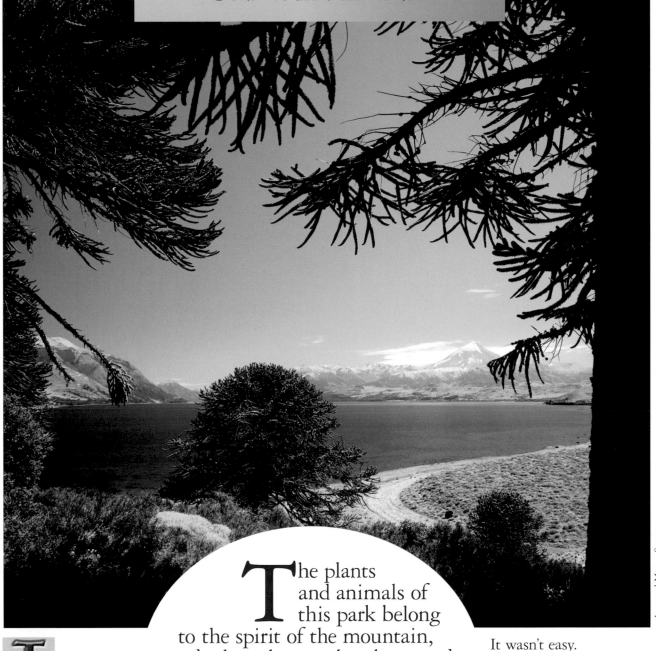

Ann and Myron Sutton

The plants and animals of this park belong to the spirit of the mountain, and whoso harms the plants and animals harms also the spirit and brings misfortune unto himself.

Shrine at the entrance to Khao Yai National Park, Thailand

This book started with the natural and human history of Crater Lake, including the fight to protect it, then a larger fight to keep it natural and manage it trial by trial, error by error, with increasing sophistication—as one of the world's premier national parks.

It wasn't easy.

The first hundred years of managing a national park is sometimes a microcosm of adventures and misadventures in wild land conservation. Crater Lake was an early entry in a massive global experiment with a new idea.

That idea started in the Yellowstone country of Wyoming, and the region was set aside as a "public park and pleasuring ground" in 1872. (Australia's Royal National Park, in 1879, was the first actual use of the term "national park" in the body of legislation.)

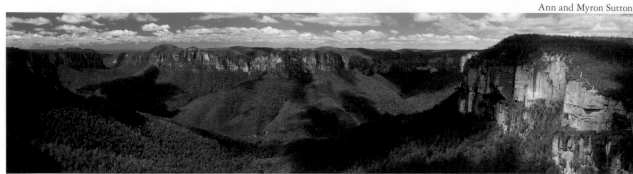

View from Govetts Leap, Blue Mountains National Park, New South Wales, Australia.

That term was first used in Yellowstone legislation in 1883.}

The experiment: could human beings, intent on colonizing, farming, grazing, and mining untamed lands, set aside a remarkable piece of real estate and manage it for public enjoyment? Just, heaven forbid, leave it *alone*? To a great many people, the idea was patently unthinkable. Hundreds of square miles? What if gold lay underneath? The idea must have seemed like a form of madness. In an era of land rushes and mineral discoveries, explorers were trying to examine every square inch of everywhere. Dig up anything of value. Cut down forests. Plow up landscapes.

Would congresses and parliaments agree to *restrict* nearly every commercial access to potential riches just because the place was scenically and scientifically outstanding?

The answer was a rousing shout heard round the world: Yes, they would. And yes, they did.

More than any other factor behind the rise of national parks worldwide was one simple concept that anyone could understand, and four words that anyone could fight for: "Protect our national heritage!" Trite it may seem now, but on the farthest frontiers, from the highest mountains to deep inside tropical forests, that phrase had a universal ring of patriotism and sovereignty more powerful, and permanent, than gold, lumber or sheep.

And what an experiment it has been!

In a single century, the number of national parks and other protected areas around the world has risen from dozens to more than thirty thousand.

Private citizens joined the crusade early. In 1887, a Maori chieftain, King Teheuheu Tukino, donated land to form the nucleus of Tongariro National Park in New Zealand. A year after Crater Lake National Park was established, a soldier of fortune in Argentina, Perito Moreno, donated land to set up Nahuél Huapí National Park, in the Andes Mountains.

By 1900, nearly a dozen such parks had been set aside, including Banff and Waterton Lakes in Canada, Ku Ring Gai Chase in Australia, and Egmont in New Zealand, plus Yellowstone, Yosemite, Sequoia, and Mount Rainier in the USA.

In Crater Lake's century, this experiment of planetary dimensions

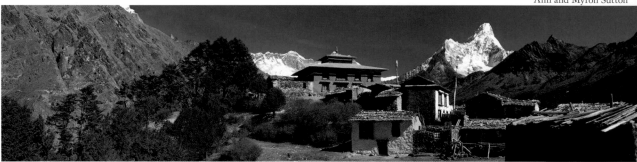

Tengboche Monastery, 14,000 feet, with Mount Everest in background. Sagarmatha National Park, Nepal.

made parks of the highest peak, Sagarmatha (Mount Everest) National Park, Nepal; the highest waterfall, Angel Falls, in Canaima National Park, Venezuela, and the most spectacular scenic gorge, Grand Canyon in Arizona, plus biological treasures like the Galápagos Islands of Ecuador, and historic masterpieces such as Ephesus National Park in Turkey.

Once set aside and properly managed, these places began to take in more perpetual, renewable income than could have been earned by any extractive industry. Hundreds of millions of tourists visit these gems of the earth every year. Crater Lake alone receives half a million visitors annually,

Seventeen –
The Legacy of Crater Lake

a low figure because of the short summer. The money spent by tourists is spread throughout the region. And then, of course, there are always the intellectual and psyche-restoring resources.

No wonder the parks surged in number. It was a new and profitable road to riches.

Ann and Myron Sutton

From the top of the well-preserved amphitheater in the historic city of Ephesus, in western Turkey, visitors get a view of what once was a port city on the now-silted Meander River.

So, after a hundred years at Crater Lake, what is left?

What is the legacy of all that work, research, experience, trials and tribulations?

That is easy to answer.

The most obvious legacy is that Crater Lake is still there, as magnificent as ever.

The forest and flowers around it are thriving, despite grazing, insect attacks, poaching.

Ann and Myron Sutton

Machu Picchu Historical National Park, Peru. These dizzying ramparts above the Urubamba River contain the remains of an Inca village, not discovered by Europeans until 1911.

The men and women who oversee it have grown more sophisticated with the tools of management, computers, submarines and multiple-beam radar.

The result is a compilation of technical and management information that has became one of America's greatest exports.

As late as the 1960s, the U.S. Department of State was insisting that "there isn't much interest in national parks around the world."

But then, largely through the Agency for International Development, Americans began to assist in funding park development projects, largely in Jordan and Turkey. U.S. National Park Service experts were sent abroad to live there and help the local experts fashion a complete park system. Then experts from scores of countries came to the USA to attend field courses in park management and development.

In the planetary progress of conservation, this became a godsend. No longer did other countries have to go through decades of experimentation. Techniques for preservation of historic ruins and priceless artifacts, for example, had been tried out. Now the same guidelines could be reviewed for possible use in preserving Ancient Troy and Ephesus in Turkey, the ruins of Tihuanaco in Bolivia, the spectacular fortress of Machu Picchu in Peru, the birthplace of famed àuthor William Henry Hudson in Argentina.

Based on the American experience in preparing master plans to guide the development and management of every national park, New Zealand authorities launched the master planning of their parks in 1964.

To say that Crater Lake National Park was a part of this effort may seem like a long shot. But the fact that Crater Lake and other American parks were making money, and stimulating the economy of surrounding areas was like a shot heard round the world. Any foreign expert seeing the operation at Crater Lake, a park with modest visitor statistics, and watching the cash registers ring in and around the park, took back home a very powerful stimulus. This was one of the strongest reasons for setting up protected areas, although saving the national heritage was more important to most nations. Indeed, by the 1970s parks were beginning to overtake petroleum in importance because they were earning money through non-extractive methods. You can run out of petroleum, but not inspiration.

The worldwide exchange of experts stimulated an immense effort to save not just bits and pieces of the local heritage here and there, but to protect the world heritage on a massive scale while there was still time.

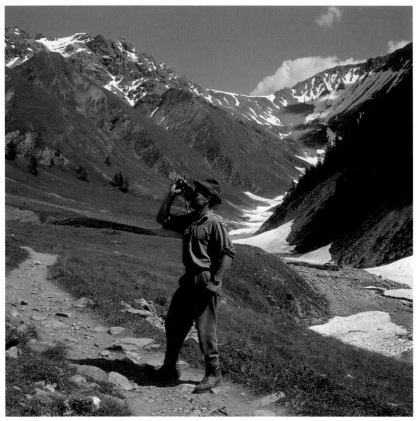

Swiss National Park Ranger.

The U.S. Department of State fell in line, though at first they wanted only to include historic places in UNESCO's list of World Heritage Sites. But parks cost money, and who would pay for it? Better to drill more oil wells for immediate profit? "Selling oil," came the outcry, "means milk for our babies' mouths."

In a sense, it was Crater Lake all over again: opponents fighting with arguments that mining and grazing were more important in the building of America.

That was the crux of it. And a powerful counterargument it was. Parks cost money. Poor countries could get oil companies to drill for oil and pay for the operation, but who would help to set up parks?

In delineating an international plan for protecting places of outstanding significance, experts of numerous countries gathered together and offered help to poor countries with scant resources to save endangered places.

When Crater Lake National Park was established, there existed scarcely a dozen officially protected areas around the world. Today there are 30,000. And some are very significant, indeed. They include the greatest concentrations of wildlife, and some of the most cherished historic sites. America helped the international community to restore the largest Buddhist stupa (Borobudur in Indonesia). Nor was this massive help limited to government experts, either. The University of Wyoming pioneered a great deal of research in Rapa Nui National Park, on Easter Island, Chile.

One of the most notable examples of inter-governmental cooperation was experienced in the setting up of Sagarmatha (Mount Everest) National Park, in Nepal. You may ask how anyone could take seriously the notion of establishing a national park at elevations where visitors come down with altitude sickness the day after arrival. And visitors die from it, especially hardy young people who want to pit their strength against the rigors of climbing with a heavy pack among these high mountains and valleys.

The American experience, Crater Lake included, is that visitor protection is of paramount importance. Lessons learned elsewhere taught that hospitals are needed in remote areas,

Seventeen –
The Legacy of Crater Lake

or else quick access to them by such transportation as helicopters.

Gordon Nicholls, long time New Zealand park official, visited U.S. parks, especially those in the Cascades and Alaska, asking questions practically every step of the way. He was then seconded by his government to set up a national park at Mount Everest. In doing so, he invited us to come look over his shoulder and advise from our experience in nearly 200 parks around the world.

The first trouble he met was the existence of villages in a national park. Sherpa villages were a part of the park.

Gordon had learned from the American experience that it is almost mandatory to have good relations with local populations. So he set up a management committee consisting of representatives of each of the villages, and they made decisions under his guidance.

Perhaps the most important American lesson he passed on was that of forest management. Not that the Khumbu Valley beneath Mount Everest was suffering from pine beetle attacks such as those that had devastated Crater Lake National Park.

The problem was that dense forests in Sagarmatha National Park, consisting of pine, fir, spruce, beech and giant rhododendrons, flourish at 14,000 feet, and dead limbs were harvested by the Sherpas for cooking fuel. Now came visitors heading for the summit of Everest, accompanied by retinues of up to 800 Sherpas. Green wood began to appear for sale. With this, Nicholls instituted a forest management program that would conserve that resource for the local inhabitants above all. "We've learned a lot from you chaps," he often told us, referring to the American experience. When we reviewed the efforts made by national

park people in the Yosemite and Crater Lake National Parks against bark beetles and other infestations, we said simply: forest resources are priceless. Take good care of them. Watch for insects. Watch for blights. Watch for illegal cutting. Watch for fire.

He started a master plan for the park, attempting to set up a procedure for handling problems. One of his most severe was, of all things, drinking water.

Ann and Myron Sutton

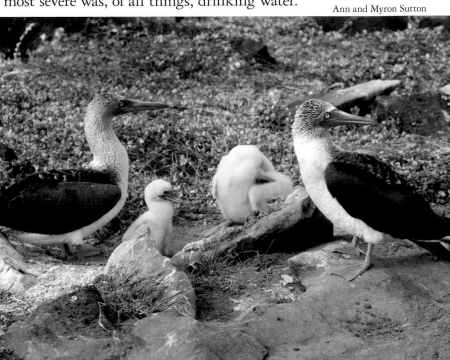

Family of blue-footed boobies, Galápagos National Park, Ecuador.

American parks had to deal with contamination in wild streams, but nothing like the slopes of Everest, where mountain cattle called yaks had for years carved thousands of trails on the slopes. The water in those glacial streams, so lovely and crystal clear, contained, as stated in the master plan, concentrations of 42,000 coliform organisms in each gallon.

Call it attention to detail. Americans were good at that. And their master plans told how to watch for problems. How to recognize them. And how to solve them. Said the final Sagarmatha Master Plan: "The degradation of the forest through human use, particularly firewood collection and grazing, is the most important and critical park management problem."

During Crater Lake's first century, park management has become a global effort. Theodore Roosevelt and Will Steel would be very proud.

Without a shadow of a doubt, the greatest story in Crater Lake National Park's first century is the spread of similar protected areas worldwide. It is a story little known, and its proponents are less well known in the USA than Roosevelt and Steel and John Muir. But a great many of them worked just as hard as the pioneers at Crater Lake to save what was left of their tattered heritage

As to those 30,000 protected areas today, not all are national parks. Some are strict nature reserves in which only scientists may enter. Some have no trails, no maps, no signs, deliberately. What better challenge for a cross-country hiker than that?

Some allow limited hunting. But the goal of all is to stop wholesale destruction of ecosystems on this planet and manage the natural resources on a sustainable basis.

Today, with all the interchange between countries going on, it may seem grandstanding to give much credit to the American experience. But that's where it started, and no one disputes the importance of the American effort to save vast portions of the earth. The Japanese, for example, unabashedly patterned their park systems in the American mold in the 1930s. In the 1960s the US National Park Service, in association with the University of Michigan and the Canadian National Parks Service organized field traveling courses for world park officials, then carried the effort on to Latin America with the involvement of Puerto Rican, Dominican Republican, and Argentine park and tourism authorities.

Each of these officials went back home to train others, even to organize their own training systems. To wit: a College of Wildlife Management in Tanzania, Africa, and a park ranger school in Chile. Poaching began to come under control, park-based education proliferated. No longer were Magellanic penguins slaughtered for sport. They now thrive by the millions in Punta Tombo and other refuges in eastern Argentina.

On the negative side, some experts come to the USA to "see how *not* to do it." "You have too many roads and too many hotels in your national parks," they said.

Well, that's a sign of success. The world is coming of age, on a scale unimagined by the pioneers at Crater Lake. The largest national park on earth today was set up on the northeast corner of Greenland by the government of Denmark: 97 million hectares, 1,312 times the size of Crater Lake National Park

Anyone who thinks that's too frigid to contain many resources worth saving would do well to visit the Greenland National Park web site for a short slide

program. Or write the Danish government for more information.

Another huge national park is in Arabia, the Rub'-al-Kāli Desert, perhaps one of the last refuges of the Arabian oryx. The more populous the world becomes, the more valuable are these protected areas. Even in heavily populated China, there are more than 300 protected areas, some crucial to the survival of the panda.

The flip side is that disasters still occur.

As part of a United Nations team, we helped the Ecuadorian government set up Galápagos National Park in 1970. Our recommendations to build trails to limit visitor access among bird nesting sites, and charge visitors fees to gain income for park management were adopted with vigor. The President of Ecuador approved the plan. Later a marine reserve was set up, all with guidance by fishermen and others.

The result was a national park composed of 23,000 square miles of land and water.

Restrictions were imposed on taking sea cucumbers and sharks. Alas, in late 2000, restrictions imposed on the taking of lobsters infuriated fishermen so much that they destroyed the Darwin Research Station, park staff homes, automobiles, and files, and removed tortoises from research pens. They also bumped tourism boats in menacing gestures. No one was hurt, but the damage to tourism, by then very lucrative, could be imagined.

Americans have suffered, too, especially when the economy turns down disastrously. There has been poaching not only in Crater Lake but in such places as Florida's Everglades National Park. The price offered by Asian nations for shark fin and cartilage is a very powerful stimulus

Seventeen –
The Legacy of Crater Lake

to enter waters such as those in the Galápagos Islands.

If nothing else, all these experiences, parallel to Crater Lake's first century, show that the world is rapidly becoming one vast ecosystem where natural regions and human populations are dependent on each other. Especially with new discoveries of medical benefits from plant and animal life.

Thus has Crater Lake, on a comparatively small scale, helped to influence the progress of thousands of other reserves and the saving of millions of wild animals. It may not seem like there could be many more areas protected, but the effort goes on, with new national parks established even in the USA.

We can't feel entirely secure yet, as the Galápagos experience demonstrates, and with frequent calls for oil-drilling in the national monuments and wildlife reserves. But when you consider what has happened to the pioneering ideas of Will Steel, John Muir, José Rafael Garcia, and all the others, we can take immense pride in what a great many human beings have already accomplished to protect this fragile planet and its priceless forms of life.

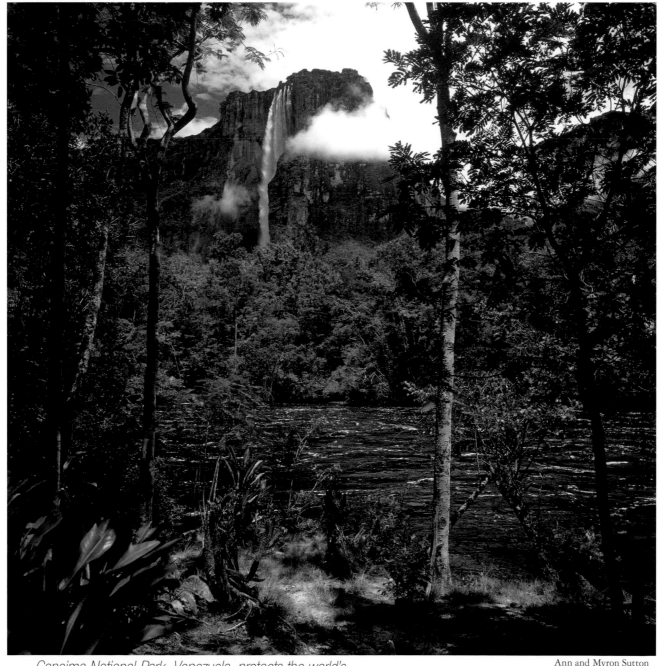

Canaima National Park, Venezuela, protects the world's highest waterfall, Angel Falls, 3,000 feet.

Ann and Myron Sutton

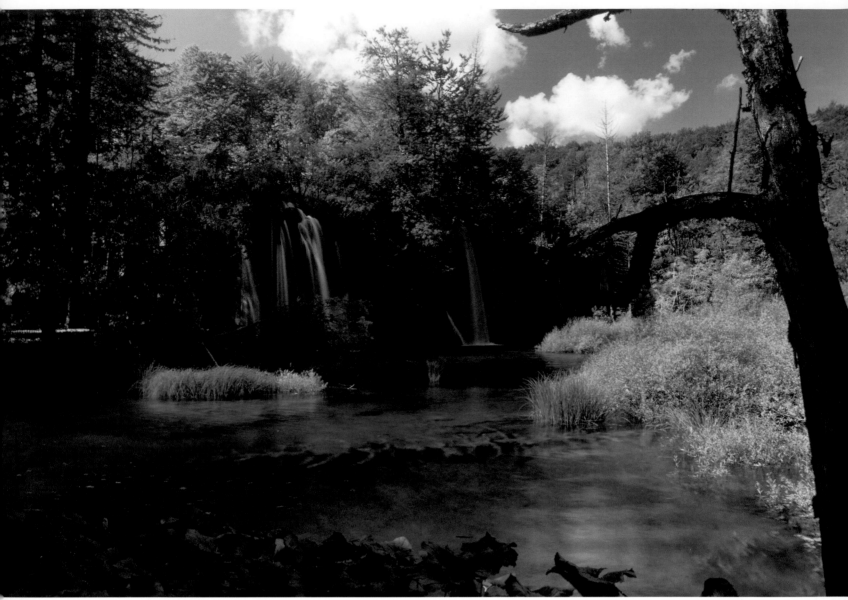

Plitvice Lakes National Park, Croatia.

Ann and Myron Sutton

ACKNOWLEDGMENTS

This book is the work of many minds. National parks are remarkable repositories of historical and biological data because the staffs through the years have taken great care to record events for posterity. They have written monthly reports, composed articles, written about their discoveries and adventures, and otherwise assured a continuous archive linking one era to another.

Such resources are of great value when a summary is produced, as are the advice and counsel of the existing staff. We are particularly indebted to John Miele, Administrative Assistant at Crater Lake National Park, and to Steve Mark, Park Historian. Mark Buktenica, aquatic biologist, wrote eloquently about his descent to the bottom of the lake. Superintendent Charles Lundy and others on the staff helped to smooth out obscure phrases and to correct errors.

Charles Bacon, of the U. S. Geological Survey, advised on our interpretation of the geologic history of Crater Lake. Willard Scott, of the Cascades Volcano Observatory, helped with accuracy and review of diagrams.

Boyd Wickman, of the Pacific Northwest Research Station of the U.S. Forest Service, guided us through the complexities of fighting insect infestations in the park and other aspects of resource management. The staff of the Gifford Pinchot National Forest and Dr. Carleton DeTar, of the Physics Department at the University of Utah also provided helpful information.

George W. Buckingham, retired chief ranger at Crater Lake, added insights from his long experience in the park. W. Drew Chick shared his memories of early days in the park, as did Denny Fitzgerald, who walked out on the frozen surface of the lake. Larry Smith talked with us about his experiences as a summer seasonal ranger. Many voices came to us from the *Crater Lake Nature Notes*, which go back more than 75 years describing the park in great detail.

Lee Webb, Frank Lang, and Paula Fong of the Crater Lake Natural History Association, helped by reviewing the manuscript at various stages. John Dellenback described what it was like to represent this district in the U.S. Congress.

Photographers Jim Phelan, John Erwin, and Preston Mitchell provided their images for illustrating this book, as did Ian Smith, University of Aukland, New Zealand. Other photographs were provided by the Cascades Volcano Observatory and by Dr. James Gardner of the U.S. Geological Survey, Menlo Park, CA. The staff of the Southern Oregon Historical Society provided valuable assistance in locating historical photographs of early days at Crater Lake. We also thank individual photographers as credited throughout the text.

We are especially indebted to Dan Schiffer, our art director, for skillfully converting the text and images in this book into its present form, and to Bob Smith for seeing the book through the printing process.

Any errors that remain are ours. The above mentioned people and many more helped us to produce this tribute to a wonderful national park.

Ann and Myron Sutton

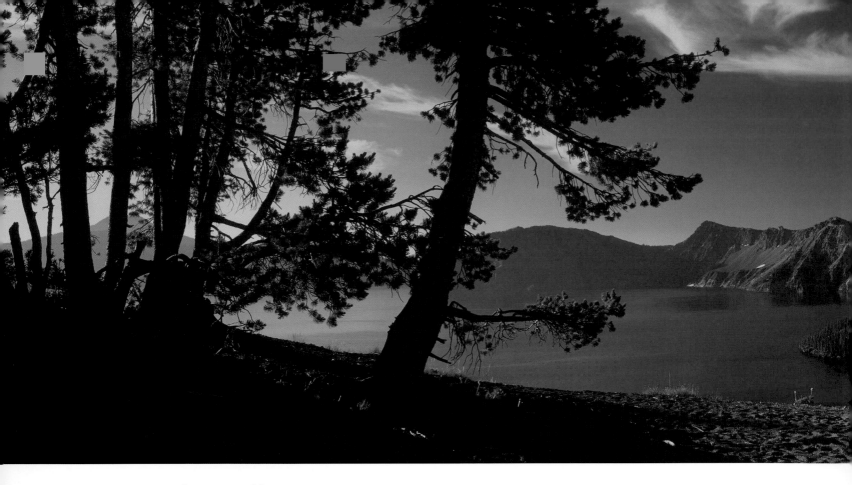

For Further Reading

Bacon, Charles R., 1983, *Eruptive History of Mount Mazama and Crater Lake Caldera, Cascade Range, USA*, Journal of Volcanology and Geothermal Research, v. 90, p. 11, 243-11, 252.

Bacon, Charles R., et al, *Volcano and Earthquake Hazards in the Crater Lake Region, Oregon*, United States Geological Survey Open File Report 97-487, Vancouver, Washington, 1997.

Diller, Joseph and Patton, Horace, 1902, *The Geology and Petrography of Crater Lake National Park*, United States Geological Survey, Professional Paper 3, Washington, D.C.

Drake, Ellen T., et al, 1990, *Crater Lake: An Ecosystem Study*, American Association for the Advancement of Science, San Francisco.

Harris, Stephen L., 1998, *Fire Mountains of the West*, Mountain Press Publishing Co., Missoula, MT.

IUCN, 1997, *United Nations List of Protected Areas*, International Union for the Conservation of Nature and Natural Resources, Gland, Switzerland and Cambridge, UK.

Klepadlo, S. and Campbell, W., eds., 1998, *A Checklist of Vascular Plants of Crater Lake National Park, Oregon*, Crater Lake Natural History Association, Crater Lake, OR.

Sigurdsson, Haraldur, 2000, *Encyclopedia of Volcanoes*, Academic Press, New York.

Taylor, George H. and Hatton, Raymond R., 1999, *The Oregon Weather Book: A State of Extremes*, University of Oregon Press, Corvallis.

Unrau, Harlan D., 1988, *Administrative History of Crater Lake National Park, Oregon*. 2 vol., U. S. Government Printing Office, Washington, D. C.

U.S. Department of the Interior, 1999, *Visitor Service Plan, Crater Lake National Park, Oregon*. National Park Service.

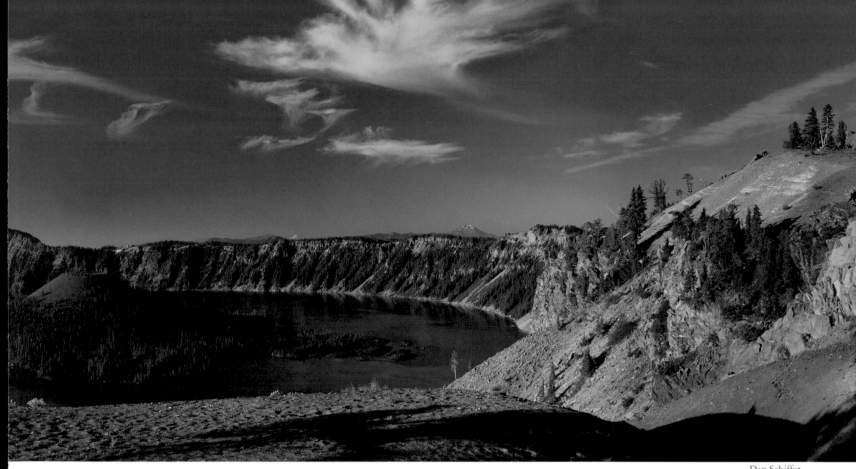

Dan Schiffer

Wickman, Boyd, 1990, *The Battle Against Bark Beetles in Crater Lake National Park, 1925-1934*. Gen. Tech. Report PNW-GTR-259, Portland, OR. U.S. Dept. of Agriculture, Forest Service, Pacific Northwest Research Station.

Winthrop Associates Cultural Research, Ashland, OR, 1994, *Archeological and Ethnological Studies in Southeastern Oregon and Crater Lake National Park, An Overview and Assessment*. National Park Service, Cultural Resources, Seattle, WA.

Williams, Howel, 1941, *Crater Lake National Park: The Story of its Origin*, University of California Press, Berkeley, CA.

Williams, Howel, 1942, *Geology of Crater Lake National Park, Oregon: With a Reconnaissance of the Cascade Range Southward to Mount Shasta*, Carnegie Institution of Washington, Washington, D.C.

INDEX